CONTRACTING FOR COMPUTERS

CONTRACTING FOR COMPUTERS

A PRACTICAL
GUIDE 133172346
TO NEGOTIATING EFFECTIVE
CONTRACTS
FOR THE ACQUISITION OF
COMPUTER SYSTEMS
AND RELATED SERVICES

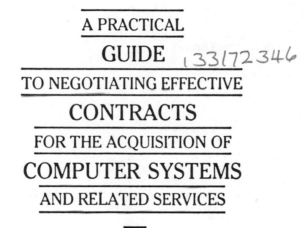

SECOND EDITION

George S. Takach

McGraw-Hill Ryerson
Toronto   Montreal   New York   Auckland   Bogotá   Caracas
Lisbon   London   Madrid   Mexico   Milan   New Delhi   Paris
San Juan   Singapore   Sydney   Tokyo

Contracting for Computers
Second Edition

First published in 1989 by
McGraw-Hill Ryerson Limited
300 Water Street
Whitby, Ontario
L1N 9B6

ISBN: 0-07-551387-0

1 2 3 4 5 6 7 8 9 0   A G   1 0 9 8 7 6 5 4 3 2

This book is sold with the understanding that neither the author nor the publisher is hereby rendering legal, accounting, or other professional advice. If
such advice or other assistance is required, the personal services of competent
professional legal counsel should be sought.

Care has been taken to trace the ownership of any copyright material contained
in this text. The publishers welcome any information that will enable them to
rectify, in subsequent editions, any incorrect or omitted reference or credit.

Canadian Cataloguing in Publication Data
Takach, George S. (George Steven)
Contracting for computers

2d ed.
Includes bibliographical references and index.
ISBN 0-07-551387-0

1. Computer contracts - Canada. I. Title.

KE936.C6T3 1992   346.71'024   C92-093934-1
KF905.C6T3 1992

Printed and bound in the United States

To my family.

CONTENTS

PREFACE TO THE
SECOND EDITION

A good reference book is not unlike a successful software product in that both need to be updated from time to time. That is why, barely two years after the initial publication of *Contracting for Computers*, a second edition makes a lot of sense. Also like good software, however, the essential format and the bulk of the narrative of the first edition remain intact. What has been added is a discussion of a number of new issues and topics, including electronic data interchange, document image processing, outsourcing, the Goods and Services Tax as it relates to computer equipment and software purchases, and the use of information technology consultants. Readers will also find an expanded discussion of responsible computing—a subject of great importance to everyone inside (and beyond) the computer field—which includes a proprietary rights protection policy that every organization using computers should consider implementing.

I am very happy with the reception given *Contracting for Computers* over the past 24 months. Numerous readers have mentioned to me that they have found it useful for a lot of different reasons. Some readers have added that the book is the first piece of writing authored by a lawyer that they can understand. While this may seem a dubious distinction, in fact it pleases me greatly because I very much intended the book to serve as, among other things, a bridge between the legal profession and those who work with computers. I hope the second edition continues to bring together these two groups, which have a great deal to teach one another.

In preparing this work I have incurred a large debt to my partners at McCarthy Tétrault, particularly those in the firm's Technology Law Group, who have provided me with an environment extremely conducive to the preparation of this book. The people at McGraw-Hill Ryerson have also been, as always, helpful, professional, and fun to work with.

Most importantly, thank you Janis and Natalie, for continuing to support wholeheartedly my literary endeavours.

This edition of *Contracting for Computers* likely will not be the last. The updating process for a text, like the upgrading exercise for superior software, should strive to reflect the particular concerns and issues relevant to its users, namely, the readers of the book. Accordingly, I would be obliged if those of you with thoughts for new topics or other comments or suggestions would jot these down and mail them to me at the following address:

McCarthy Tétrault
Suite 4700
Toronto-Dominion Bank Tower
Toronto Dominion Centre
Toronto, Ontario
M5K 1E6
Tel: (416) 601-7662/362-1812
Fax: (416) 868-1891/868-0673

I look forward to hearing from you.

George S. Takach
Toronto, March 1992

INTRODUCTION

The person responsible for the acquisition and operation of a computer system for his or her company or other organization is confronted with a challenging task. This individual, referred to in this introduction as the data manager even though he or she may be the company controller, vice-president of finance or administration, or perhaps the owner of a smaller business, must thoroughly understand the computing needs of the organization, select a cost-effective computer system that satisfies the needs of the organization and, once a system is acquired, ensure that it operates with a minimum of malfunction or error. Achieving these goals is not easy, particularly when the financial and personnel resources at the disposal of the data manager are limited.

This book is intended to help data managers perform their demanding task. The method proposed in the following pages may be termed "effective contracting." Effective contracting requires data managers to become actively involved in two essential activities: first, understanding what problems tend to occur with the implementation and operation of computer systems, and second, addressing these problems in a written contract between the buyer organization (the data manager's employer) and the supplier of the computer system. The first requires data managers to become familiar with the technology of computing, to assess how specific computing resources may or may not fulfil the needs of the buyer, and to ascertain what risks are posed to the business by the acquisition and use of computers. The second activity involves discussing these risks with the computer supplier and negotiating a contract in which the supplier assumes a reasonable share of such risks. The aim of this book is to help data managers with both of these activities.

The book is also intended to assist the representatives of suppliers of computers who are involved with marketing, sales, contract negotiation, and related activities. Suppliers are increasingly confronted by customers that want to shift all the risks inherent in computers onto the supplier. Interestingly, some large user organizations are drafting standard form computer contracts that are as unreasonably one-sided in the user's favour as many suppliers' contracts are in the supplier's favour. The book attempts to illuminate the sensible, responsible middle ground on contracting issues, where most users and suppliers should feel comfortable. In short, effective computer contracts that reflect the reasonable expectations of both parties take less time to negotiate than those weighted heavily in favour of one party and help build better long-term relationships between users and suppliers.

A few words are in order about the applicability of this book. There is a tendency in the business world to seek professional assistance with the acquisition of only very large, complex, and expensive computer systems. This book, however, is equally relevant to the smaller business for the simple reason that effective contracting pays handsome dividends whether the computer system costs $30,000, $300,000, or $3 million. In a similar vein, many business people seem to think that if professional advice is needed at all, it is relevant only when acquiring the company's first computer system and unnecessary for second and subsequent systems. This is not always the case. Indeed, just as the initial conversion from manual to automated procedures raises important technical, negotiating, and contracting issues, so do both the conversion from one computer system to another and the stringing together of two or more different systems, an activity happening with increasing frequency as companies endeavour to interconnect several, and perhaps incompatible, computer systems. In short, it is usually the case that the more extensive a company's computer facilities, the greater the need for effective computer contracting for each additional system.

The usefulness of effective contracting extends beyond computers to many related and even unrelated technologies. Word processors, large photocopiers, and telephone systems known as PBXs or private branch exchanges are not always looked upon as computers, but they are based on computer technology; the discussion contained in this book is very relevant to their acquisition. Many other types of equipment found in the office and on the factory floor, such as automated production and control technology, computer-aided manufacturing and design processes (CAD/CAM), and industrial robotics, to name a few, contain elements of computer or other advanced technologies. The corporate executives responsible for the purchase and operation of these types of systems — including production managers and engineers — would do well to consider the substantive and procedural issues involved in effective contracting.

The applicability of this book is by no means confined to the business world. Throughout the following pages reference is made to corporate users of computers, but computer systems are now in widespread use in government, in the fields of education and the professions (medicine, engineering, accounting, law, architecture, etc.), by all kinds of non-profit organizations and, increasingly, in the home. This book is intended to assist virtually anyone involved with the acquisition or supply of computer systems and services.

Although certain passages of this book discuss various legal issues that arise when contracting for computers, and although the author is a lawyer, this book is not intended to convey legal advice and does not contain precedent contract clauses. Readers who have particular legal questions, or who require appropriate contract language, should consult a lawyer, preferably one experienced in computer law, as it is only through such personal contact with a professional adviser that specific situations can be addressed. The law itself is continually evolving, and many of the legal rules discussed in this book will change over time. It is therefore only through live legal advice from a lawyer that the reader can be sure of being informed of the most current legal rules affecting his or her particular case. Accordingly, this book makes no attempt to substitute for live professional assistance; rather, it aims at providing a general education which can then be applied to particular circumstances with the help of competent legal counsel.

A final word ought to be said about the scope of this book. The impact on the legal system of computers and the so-called information revolution, engendered largely because of the developments in computer technology, has been profound and wide ranging, and has been the subject of several books published in Canada and abroad. The following pages discuss only a small portion of this much wider subject area. For example, in addition to computer contracts — the focus of this volume — business people and their advisers ought to be generally aware of the practical concerns raised by such matters as access to information legislation (in large measure the product of the development of vast computer banks of information kept by governments); computer-generated documents and whether they are admissible in court under the law of evidence; the various forms of legal protection, such as copyright, trade secrets, patents, the law of confidentiality, and semi-conductor chip protection legislation, for computer-related intellectual property; the commercial and legal aspects of distributing computer resources (i.e., the relationship between manufacturers and software developers and their distributors, dealers, and retailers); and the law's response to computer crime. While some of these topics are mentioned in passing in the following pages inasmuch as they relate to computer contracts, a proper treatment of them is beyond the scope of this book.

HOW TO USE THIS BOOK

This book is divided into five parts. Part A discusses why effective computer contracts are necessary from a buyer's point of view and why many responsible suppliers appreciate them as well. Part A also includes a short overview of computer technology because the other parts of the book, while written in a nontechnical style, will assume a certain familiarity on the reader's part with some of the buzzwords and jargon prevalent in the computer industry. Part A ends with a brief description of the major types of computer contracts. Parts B and C canvass the key contract provisions that prudent buyers should consider including in their contracts with suppliers. Part D provides a discussion of how a computer purchaser may best go about negotiating with a supplier in order to get the desired provisions included in the contract. Contracting points that are discussed throughout the book are gathered into handy checklists in Part E, organized under the various types of computer contracts. Books, articles, and other materials referred to in the text are listed for further reference in the "Notes" section.

Part B contains a discussion of the contracting issues that are relevant to agreements for the purchase of hardware and the licence of software, the two most common forms of computer contracts. Many of these issues are also relevant to the other computer contracts that users of computing resources tend to encounter, including those agreements discussed in Part C. In Part C, however, there is a discussion of issues related only to these other types of agreements. For example, in section C.3, "Maintenance," there is an analysis of some important questions relevant only to hardware and software maintenance agreements. In order to determine which issues in Part B are also relevant to hardware and software maintenance agreements, the reader would turn to the maintenance contract checklist in Part E, which would list the issues covered in both Part B and Part C.

The usual point of entry for most regular users of this book after the initial reading will likely be the Part E checklists. The best way to use this volume is first to read it from cover to cover to attain a general understanding of the key issues in various computer contracting situations; readers can then use the relevant checklist as a yardstick against which to gauge their own form of computer agreement or, more likely, those of suppliers of particular computing resources. This latter process is illustrated by the following example.

Suppose a user is interested in having some custom software developed. The user's data manager has contacted two potential software developers and, in response to the user's proposed software development agreement, each software developer has sent the user a copy of its standard software development contract. Based on the software development agreement checklist in Part E (p. 262), the data manager notices that neither of the standard form contracts contain provisions regarding ownership of the custom software or its acceptance testing after delivery. In order to review why these two issues are important in software development agreements, the data manager would turn to section 4 of Part C for a discussion of the ownership issue and section 9 of Part B for a discussion of acceptance testing. (This latter issue is in Part B because it also relates to hardware acquisitions as well as to the licensing of standard, as distinct from custom-developed, software.) These particular cross references to Parts B and C are noted in the Part E checklist. By following this one exercise through it will become obvious to the reader that anyone who wishes to negotiate an effective contract for computers or related technology will find this book not only useful, but essential.

PART

The Need for Effective Computer Contracts

1. THE BENEFITS AND COSTS OF COMPUTERS

Computers are a pervasive presence in business, government, education, and the professions and are found increasingly in the home. Not only are more and more organizations utilizing computers, the tasks assigned to them are continually increasing in number and complexity. Computerized accounting, payroll, and inventory control procedures are now widespread in business, and even the small business has access to a variety of accounts payable, accounts receivable, general ledger, and similar computer programs, with the increasingly widespread use of the microcomputer, popularly known as the personal computer or PC.

The computer, however, is no longer the exclusive preserve of the company controller or auditor but has been put to use in the critical day-to-day front office operating areas of the business. Banks and other financial institutions now use on-line computer systems to effect numerous transactions such as electronic funds transfers. Insurance companies could not offer certain complex life insurance policies without the support of computer systems in the administration of these products. Property managers now keep tenant records on computers. In the hotel and restaurant industry computers are used in all aspects of servicing customers, from the moment a guest enters an establishment to presentation of the final bill. Engineers and architects have access to sophisticated computer work stations that not only assist with mathematical calculations but also provide impressive modelling and graphics capabilities. Hospitals are storing patient records in computer banks, and doctors are increasingly using "expert systems" which help them to diagnose patient conditions and prescribe appropriate treatment. Many of Canada's traditional resource-based industries, such as mining, are looking towards new computer technology to permit them to increase productivity and reduce costs. It became apparent during the 1991 Gulf War that a great deal of modern military hardware is dependent on computer technology; indeed, a recent press report indicated that a software error was responsible for the failure of a Patriot missile launcher to fire at the Iraqi Scud missile that killed 28 U.S. soldiers in Dharan, Saudi Arabia, one of the deadliest Iraqi attacks of the Gulf War. Computers are also permeating the world of the average consumer. A recent press article described how the use of microchips and on-board computers in automobiles have transformed the traditional car mechanic into a computer maintenance technician.

The widespread use of computers in today's society would seem to indicate that users generally view computers as a blessing, an electronic dream come true. A computer system that has been carefully selected to meet the needs of the user and that runs without interruption and free of errors certainly is an extremely valuable asset to any organization. It can automate manual procedures for collecting, storing, processing, and communicating data, resulting in more efficient and less expensive records management procedures. It can streamline office and other corporate operations and help the company become more competitive in the marketplace. Such a system is indeed a blessing and the data manager responsible for its acquisition and operation will earn the respect and admiration of his colleagues.

For some companies, however, the computer experience has been a curse, an electronic nightmare of awesome proportions. For example, there have been cases of established businesses forced into bankruptcy after the acquisition of an inappropriate or malfunctioning computer system. Even the generally satisfied business computer user probably has occasional doubts about the value of the company's computer (and of the people within the organization responsible for its acquisition and operation), because not all computer systems perform faithfully and unfailingly every task assigned them.

Many, many things can go wrong with computers. They can be delivered by the supplier weeks, months, or even years after the estimated delivery date (and sometimes not at all), thereby throwing a wrench into the company's carefully scheduled business operations development plan. Quite often what is delivered, even though it is exactly what the business ordered out of the supplier's catalogue, or is exactly what was displayed at the supplier's booth at the most recent computer show, simply does not meet the needs of the business because it is not fast enough, big enough, accurate enough, or easy enough to operate. Even if it does meet all these requirements, the computer system may break down with infuriating regularity. It may have a habit of losing valuable data, or, perhaps worse, it may manipulate data inaccurately in a context where the error goes undetected until a supplier or customer, or worst of all, Revenue Canada, informs the business of the error. Or, and this is every computer user's supreme fear, the system may "crash" — the jargon term meaning the computer is completely inoperable because of some failure — at a most inopportune time. For instance, a public company's automated financial accounting system might be out of order during the week that the company must complete its financial year-end documentation for the purpose of meeting a stock exchange or securities commission deadline for the delivery of year-end financial statements.

It is not difficult to see why a poorly functioning or nonfunctioning computer is a curse (and why the people associated with such a computer problem within the organization would become very unpopular). All the wonderful advantages of the properly functioning computer become massive liabilities when things go wrong with the system. In a fully computerized organization the computer has centralized corporate data collection, processing, and distribution. In essence, it is the information spinal cord of the business, and has usually replaced several previously manual (and probably poorly integrated) functions in the accounting, controller's accounts payable/receivable, manufacturing, marketing, customer service, and other offices of the company. Accordingly, when the computer malfunctions for any period of time, all the operations of the organization may well grind to a halt. Moreover, as the purpose of acquiring the computer was to replace dreary, inefficient, and expensive manual procedures, chances are that when the computer's lights go out there probably is no back-up clerical system to serve as an interim candle until the end of the painful computer black-out. Of course computer problems can usually be overcome, but solutions usually take money (sometimes lots of it) and, equally important, time (almost always lots of it). In effect, it is quite common for a business to conclude, often after a very short period of time trying to make a "lemon" or inappropriate computer system work, that the costs far outweigh the benefits.

Computer Acquisition Disasters

Then there are the numerous misfortunes that can befall a buyer of computers during the procurement of the equipment or software. Computer acquisition disasters do happen — more often than many business people care to admit. Usually such disasters are kept secret for fear of the damage they might cause to a company's reputation generally, and particularly in respect of clients or customers who rely on the company's computer system to function properly and reliably. Every now and then, however, a major computer acquisition disaster is reported in the press, confirming publicly that computers indeed can be a curse.

One such press report appeared in *Computerworld* a few years ago, an American publication. The report chronicled the sad experience of a major American bank. Essentially, the bank wanted a software developer to implement a computer system that would process the bank's trust business (at the time the bank was trustee or agent for assets of about $40 billion). To make a long, sorry story very short, the system was never able to work properly, its cost went from $20 million to $80 million, its failure caused the bank to lose customers, and the bank's top trust and information systems executives left the bank (whether voluntarily or otherwise was not stated).

Disasters such as this happen in Canada as well, with equally dire consequences. Consider one such tale of woe that involved a Vancouver-based company a number of years ago. The facts of this acquisition disaster, taken from the judgment of the court that finally had to decide where the blame for the fiasco should lay, are recounted at length because this story illustrates very well some of the things that can go wrong with computer acquisitions, especially those involving the development of custom software.

The company in this case was a well-established and successful family-owned business involved in the manufacture and sale of plastic products. The success of the business was largely due to the efficiency of its production control system which monitored the costs of materials, labour, and overhead; scheduled production on the various machines; controlled the inventory of raw materials and finished goods; and generally enabled the company to accurately forecast costs and to profitably produce normally large-volume items in small quantities. In 1977 the company decided to expand, which meant that both the production control system and the accounting system would be computerized.

The plastics manufacturer, in this case the buyer, contacted several computer companies, and in June 1978 the job was awarded to the Canadian arm of a large multinational firm engaged in the supply of computer hardware and software. The supplier informed the buyer that the supplier's P430 computer would suffice, and that its standard software programs would be adequate for the buyer's accounting needs. The production control system software, however, was to be custom designed and programmed. The buyer agreed to all this, but insisted that the designing of the custom software be done solely by the supplier and not be contracted out by the supplier to another company. The buyer was also concerned as to the amount of time that its senior staff would devote to the implementation of the system, but the supplier assured the buyer that only some time of the buyer's accountant and a secretary familiar with the buyer's operations would be required. The supplier also agreed that the whole system would be in place by the end of 1978 and that payment would not be required until the buyer had accepted the entire system. Finally, the prices agreed upon were about $50,000 for the hardware, $10,000 for the accounting package, and $22,000 for the custom-designed production control software. When everything appeared in order, the supplier produced a contract. This was signed on the spot by the buyer without so much as a glance at the terms on the back of the agreement, which attempted to limit the supplier's liability and responsibility.

In the early fall of 1978 the supplier suggested that the buyer accept delivery of the hardware and the accounting package to familiarize the buyer's staff with the computer and to facilitate operator training. The buyer agreed; these items were delivered and paid for, notwithstanding the original agreement that payment be made only when the total system was accepted. The supplier also introduced to the buyer a software developer unrelated to the supplier as the third party responsible for the design and programming of the custom software. The buyer objected — the original agreement was that the supplier would do all the work — but the buyer was assured that the supplier would continue to be solely responsible, so the buyer went along. The software developer assigned a designer and a programmer to develop the production control software system. As became clear later in evidence brought out at the trial, the designer had no previous experience with a production control system similar to the one to be designed for the buyer, the programmer had no experience with the supplier's P430 machine recommended for the project, and the designer and programmer had never before worked together.

As so often happens in custom software acquisitions, the original delivery date for the production control software for the end of 1978 proved entirely unrealistic, given the complexity of the system, and the programmer's inexperience with the P430 computer. In March 1979, a new delivery date was set for 30 April 1980. The programmer plugged along during 1979, dealing with the many facets of the production control system on a piecemeal basis, with no real appreciation of how they were to interact in the overall system. A key problem here was that although the buyer set out in great detail the various functions of the production control system, the designer grossly underestimated its requirements and overestimated the capabilities of the programmer. The buyer started to spend time directly with the programmer to explain the production control system. The buyer eventually tried to have the programmer replaced but was unsuccessful. In the meantime, in July 1979 the supplier attempted to charge the buyer $12,300 for modifications to the standard accounting package which did not after all meet the buyer's needs. The buyer objected, but finally agreed to pay $6,300, with the supplier absorbing the remainder.

In December 1979 the programmer gave a demonstration of the production control software — it was a complete failure. The judge, in his decision, concluded that the main problem associated with this and the other failures that were subsequently to plague this development effort was that the supplier lost interest in the project after being paid for the hardware and the accounting software and had farmed out the custom software portion of the contract; as far as the supplier was concerned, it was up to the third party software developer's designer and programmer to satisfy the buyer.

To make matters worse, the designer left the project in May 1980. The buyer then hired an operations manager whose first priority was the completion of the production control system. He had to learn the system and this took time. Meanwhile, the programmer, after the departure of the designer, was contracted directly by the supplier to complete the system design, programming, and implementation. It was agreed that the programmer would complete the project by 1 August 1980. This date was not met —

it was extended to 1 September 1980. That date was not met. Demonstrations were conducted in December 1980 and February 1981, and again the system was found to be unsatisfactory. The judge, rather generously, concluded that "obviously the work was beyond" the programmer.

As if all this weren't bad enough, the supplier decided around the middle of 1980 that a second disk pack of memory was needed on the P430 to handle the required data capacity. A dispute arose between the supplier and the programmer as to responsibility for the extra work needed to reorganize files by reason of the second disk pack. Also at this time a "source pack" kept by the programmer was wiped out, something akin to burning the only copy of a manuscript, or the only set of blueprints for a building. The programmer had failed to keep a back-up source pack to safeguard against such an event. These matters caused further delay. It did not help that around this time the buyer's operations manager, who had worked closely with the programmer, suffered a breakdown (the court decision does not say whether it was caused by the computer acquisition saga!) and had to be hospitalized. Also, by October 1980 the supplier had paid out most of the funds in the programmer's contract and no further funds were forthcoming. The programmer then had to find other work to support himself, after which he only worked part time on the buyer's production control software. Finally, at the end of March 1981 the programmer ceased working on the project. In the following months the buyer tried to get the supplier to face up to the problem, but to no avail. The buyer called in its lawyers, who also tried to prod the supplier into action. Letters were written and meetings were held throughout the remainder of 1981, with the buyer demanding completion of the project and the supplier being noncommittal. In January 1982 the buyer commenced a lawsuit against the supplier.

In July 1982 the supplier approached the buyer with a view to resolving the matter. The supplier assigned a systems analyst to test the production control software for a full week. She advised the supplier that it would take five months to complete a review to determine the full extent of the problems and to correct the minor ones. On the basis of this preliminary review, the supplier informed the buyer that completion of the project would cost the buyer an additional amount of money anywhere between $30,000 and $60,000. After this bombshell numerous alternatives were explored, including using a third party's standard system, which the buyer concluded would not meet its needs. If all this were not enough, during the latter part of 1982 all the key people at the supplier who had been dealing with the buyer over the life of the project resigned. The reason for their departure became apparent in January 1983 when the supplier announced that it was closing down its whole business computer systems division.

To illustrate how bad the relationship had become by this time, in early 1983 the supplier appointed a consulting firm to review the system. The buyer's lawyers requested a copy of the consultants' report. The supplier's lawyers refused this request, so the buyer asked the consultants to leave the buyer's premises. The supplier's lawyers applied for a court order compelling access to the buyer's premises. The judge ordered they have access, provided the buyer receive a copy of the consultants' report. The consultants did not return to the buyer's premises. The buyer also engaged a senior data processing consultant to review the state of the production control system software. He found serious deficiencies, as well as problems in the accounting system that could not be described as minor.

One month short of five years after the date that the total system was to have been in full operation according to the initial agreement, the judge delivered a decision that concluded, not surprisingly, that the supplier had committed a fundamental breach of its contract with the buyer. The judge did not even take into account that the buyer had a functioning piece of hardware that had been running the accounting package since the fall of 1978. He found that the main object of the contract was the implementation of the production control software, that this had not been achieved, and that no one could even estimate when it would be completed or at what cost. Indeed, rather than the buyer receiving any benefit from the supplier, the judge found that the supplier, in its protracted and unsuccessful efforts to deliver the bargained-for systems, in effect dismantled the buyer's adequate manual systems that had been in place before the supplier entered the picture.

Accordingly, the judge allowed the buyer to return the hardware and software to the supplier, and ordered the supplier to pay to the buyer just under $175,000 in damages together with interest from April 1979. These damages included hardware and software costs, the expense of hiring the operations manager, consulting fees, and additional salary expenses. In turn, the supplier successfully claimed as damages this amount from the third party software developer contracted to develop the production control software. Of course, regardless of who actually ended up paying this amount to the buyer, in all likelihood this money did not adequately compensate the buyer for all the aggravation and expense of this extremely unfortunate computer acquisition disaster.

This painful story is by no means unique. All too many histories like this one litter the Canadian computer landscape. As with this one, many, but by no means all, are chronicled in the court decisions of judges who are finally called upon to ferret out the party responsible for each unhappy mess. And it is not always the supplier that gets stuck with liability. There are plenty of examples in which buyers have lost in court because of some shortcoming on their part, or because the supplier's contract was so weighted against the buyer that, although the buyer was innocent, recovery from the supplier might be only partial or might be precluded altogether.

With respect to the lengthy example given above, it might reasonably be asked what actions the buyer could have taken to better protect its interests. Here are a few suggestions. All of these points are expanded upon later, but it is useful to list them briefly here as an introduction to the remainder of the book.

1. The buyer should have read, and requested that changes be made to, the supplier's standard form agreement.

2. The buyer should not have accepted delivery of and paid for the computer hardware and accounting system separately from the production control system software.

3. The buyer should not have paid the extra amount for the supplier's standard accounting package.

4. The buyer should not have allowed the supplier to subcontract the custom software to a third party.

5. The buyer should have exercised much sooner its legal rights regarding breach of contract for late delivery (indeed, initially, nondelivery) and nonperformance generally. In particular, the buyer probably should have put an end to the agreement

immediately after the demonstration in December 1979 proved a complete failure.

All of these suggestions are discussed in detail in the following pages in the hope that through effective contracting buyers and suppliers of computer systems can avoid such disasters.

While the case discussed at length above happened several years ago, there is evidence to suggest that developments in computer technology since this case have not brought an end to the computer acquisition disaster. Rather, as computers are asked to do more and more, it may well be that the likelihood of problems increases. To illustrate the point that computers are far from being risk free, consider the following random sample of headlines that have appeared in the press over the past three years:

- "Disasters Get Bigger As Tech Goes Higher"

- "Fundamental Breach In Computer Contract"

- "Recall Issued for Smoking Printers"

- "Busy Airline Systems Blank Out Screens"

- "TSE Paralyzed at Critical Time"

- "With Complexity, a Threat of Chaos"

- "Flaw Found in 486 Chip"

Another indicator of the risky nature of computers is the increasing availability of products and services that are intended to keep computers up and running. Following is an excerpt from an advertisement by a software company specializing in such a product:

A Few Minutes of Downtime Can Have a Devastating Effect On A Vital System.

[The picture accompanying the ad shows a model of a human heart.]

A company's computer is the very heart of its operations. But let it respond slowly to its users, and you'll hear complaints up and down the halls. Let it go down for any length of time, and you'll find cases of cardiac arrest, right there in the data centre.

This book is intended to lessen the likelihood that readers will become the subject of headlines like those listed above, and to help data managers avoid the heart attacks (or at least the palpitations) that accompany such stories.

2. REDUCING THE COSTS OF COMPUTERS THROUGH EFFECTIVE CONTRACTING

It is because computers are like no other business asset that effective contracting is extremely useful to computer users and suppliers. Compare computers to other equipment used by large organizations. Computers are expensive. A typical medium-sized company could easily spend several million dollars a year on computer equipment, software, and services. Most large companies would have annual information systems budgets in the $10 million to $25 million range, and many companies spend much more each year on information and technology. Equally significant are the indirect costs associated with computers, particularly when something goes wrong with them. Computers are extremely fallible; design mistakes and manufacturing shortcomings are part and parcel of computer technology, as discussed later. And even though computers are prone to break down, they are becoming increasingly vital to the daily functioning of virtually all large, medium-sized, and even smaller organizations. Finally, in almost all aspects of the computer acquisition process the buyer and supplier are expected to deal in "futures," the terribly risky activity of taking decisions today that require another person to perform certain obligations at some time in the future. For example, a buyer may order a product that has not yet been developed, or tested, thoroughly. Then there is the unique dimension to computing resources — as opposed to most other corporate assets — that a buyer invariably enters into an on-going relationship with the supplier rather than merely buying a machine, given the need of the buyer to return to the supplier again and again for various follow-up services and additional products.

Effective contracting is a mechanism that can help a buyer reduce risks and costs associated with computers by helping to ensure that an appropriate computer system is acquired and that it operates properly (or that if it does not, the problem is promptly corrected at the least possible expense). The quality of the buyer-supplier relationship can be vastly improved by an effective contract that anticipates potential problems and irritants and either lessens the likelihood of their occurrence or at least addresses what is to happen if they arise. Unfortunately, *ineffective* contracting for computers by users is quite widespread: the user or buyer contacts only a single supplier of computer equipment, permits this supplier to dictate the kind of computer equipment to be purchased, and then signs, with little or no question, the supplier's standard form agreement. This type of contracting seems efficient because it takes up relatively little of the buyer's time, but it can lead to great additional expense and heartache in the long run, as the plastics manufacturer in the case study noted at page 5 discovered. The comfort and security provided by effective contracting is well worth the initial time and expense.

Responsible suppliers also appreciate the benefits of effective contracting. They do not like surprises cropping up in the acquisition process — problems and lawsuits, or any type of unhappy buyer — any more than buyers do. Computer acquisition disasters, while devastating to buyers, can be ruinous to suppliers as well. Intelligent suppliers understand this and will therefore approach the contracting process in an even-handed manner, particularly when the buyer is equally reasonable. Unfortunately, there are still many unreasonable suppliers (just as there are unreasonable buyers), and even generally reasonable suppliers can sometimes succumb to the temptation of certain unreasonable contracting practices. Effective contracting will likely be required for some time to counteract the worst habits of unreasonable suppliers (and unreasonable buyers).

A primary cause of ineffective contracting is the deference paid by buyers to the standard form contracts of unreasonable suppliers. All computer equipment and services are invariably supplied pursuant to the supplier's standard form purchase or other agreement. Usually a one- or two-page document of small, even eye-strainingly miniscule, print, the standard form contract's main purpose, not surprisingly, is to protect the interests of the supplier. Indeed, such contracts are often weighted lopsidedly in favour of the supplier. More important from the buyer's point of view is that very often the standard form contract does not address certain key issues of concern to the buyer. In short, as far as the buyer is concerned the problem with most standard form contracts is twofold: there is usually much that is missing from it, and what appears in it can be grossly preferential towards the supplier. It should be noted, however, that certain suppliers — the reasonable ones — are drafting standard form contracts that are quite even handed. This is not to say they do not require some modification from the perspective of the buyer, but they do require much less of it. Some suppliers go so far as to trumpet their reasonable standard form agreements to buyers as a genuine advantage of dealing with the particular supplier. Such a marketing pitch does not fall on deaf ears, particularly when the prospective buyer has recently experienced an unnecessarily painful set of contract negotiations that used as its starting point a grossly unreasonable, supplier-oriented standard form contract.

When confronted with an unreasonable standard form contract, the first step towards effective contracting is insisting that the supplier's standard form contract will not constitute the whole agreement between the buyer and the supplier. As discussed in more detail in Part D, certain sections of the standard form contract may be amended or deleted altogether, and clauses necessary to protect the buyer may be added by means of an addendum attached at the end of the supplier's standard form contract. Or, if the standard form contract is clearly unsuitable even as a starting point, particularly in respect of a larger, more complex computer acquisition, the buyer should suggest that a new contract be drafted, which, while it might incorporate parts of the supplier's standard form contract, goes well beyond it in terms of completeness, clarity, and even-handedness.

Assuming that the buyer has surmounted the psychological barrier presented by the unreasonable supplier's standard form contract and has convinced the unreasonable supplier that the standard form requires alteration, it is useful to consider the major goals of effective contracting. These are (1) putting the whole deal into writing, (2) uncovering the supplier's weaknesses, (3) establishing project control checkpoints, and (4) achieving equality with the supplier. Each of these points is discussed in turn.

Putting the Whole Deal in Writing

Perhaps the most obvious purpose of an effective computer contract is to set out clearly and comprehensively all the obligations and rights of the supplier and the buyer. The installation of an especially large computer system, or a major telecommunications system, or any other item of computerized or similar technology of any size, is a complex transaction with many different aspects, of which the financial and technical are only two of the most important. From both the buyer's and the supplier's point of view it is extremely useful to put down on paper all the responsibilities of the parties. This is particularly important from the buyer's perspective where the supplier has made oral promises to the buyer over the telephone or at numerous meetings concerning the equipment being purchased. These promises may relate to the technical capabilities of the system, or may have to do with how easily the buyer can convert from its existing manual or computer system to the system proposed by the supplier, or may entail a certain amount of training for free. If the buyer has agreed to acquire the supplier's system partly on the strength of these promises, or if the buyer wishes to rely on them at some point in the future, it is imperative that they be committed to writing so that there is no misunderstanding between the parties as to what they agreed upon.

There are several other good reasons for putting the whole deal in writing. Doing so provides certainty, both in respect of what the buyer is getting and what it will cost. Responsible suppliers of computer systems value certainty as much as buyers do. In order to accurately price the sale, the computer system supplier must know exactly what the buyer requires. Accordingly, responsible suppliers are not hesitant, and indeed are quite happy to have all the elements of the agreement reflected in a written contract.

Reducing the agreement to writing also serves the useful purpose of imposing discipline on both the buyer and supplier. It forces the buyer to think through its computing requirements and to determine whether the solution suggested by the supplier meets these requirements. In this sense the contract acts as a blueprint for the project. Just as a building contractor would never commence to construct an office tower before seeing the architect's plan for the structure, equally no buyer should agree to purchase a computer system before seeing in writing the complete scope of the acquisition process. The scope of the project should be considered not only from the point of view of particular implementation activities, but also from the perspective of the probably long-term relationship between the user and the supplier. As opposed to many other commercial arrangements of the buyer, its contract with its computer supplier should address probable and even merely possible events occurring many years after the system is installed and accepted by the user, such as how and by whom maintenance will be provided over the useful life of the system, or how the system might be traded in when some superior system comes along. In brief, the "whole deal" that should be reflected in the contract has certain components that will be relevant at some point in the future but which should be contemplated and expressly addressed when the agreement is signed.

One important aspect of putting the whole deal in writing entails having the supplier disclose the complete cost of the computer system to the buyer. The price that appears on the supplier's marketing literature or equipment price list is rarely what the system finally costs the buyer. Leaving aside the system itself (and the numerous — and usually expensive — modifications that may be required to be made to the system's software, especially if it is a major system), there are often a number of ancillary costs for the buyer to consider: shipping charges from the supplier's factory or warehouse to the premises of the buyer; installation charges and expenses, which for a large system might include laying cable, even constructing cable conduits, and outfitting or renovating the room that will house the computer with expensive air conditioning and similar facilities; additional insurance premiums; data conversion charges; and education and training costs (which some experts estimate can cost up to 50% of the price of certain computer systems). The supplier is often best placed to reasonably estimate these costs, and possibly even to perform the services for a fixed cost. In any event, a data manager practising effective contracting will use the contract negotiations to ascertain the full extent of the various costs associated with the acquisition. By doing this, the data manager will not be found in the embarrassing position of having to present an upset superior with a budget overrun several months after the computer contract is signed.

In a similar vein, by capturing the whole transaction on paper the buyer can often effectively avoid being subject to "low-balling" by unreasonable suppliers. This term refers to the practice of certain suppliers of computer systems to offer on occasion cheaper but inadequate systems in order to win the tender. Once chosen, the supplier quickly reveals that its larger, and more expensive, model is really the one suitable for the buyer. This more expensive model also costs more than the competition's equivalent system, but by this point "supplier lock-in" may have occurred — the buyer ends up buying the low-balling supplier's bigger model and paying more than it initially budgeted. This unfortunate situation might be avoided if a clause were included in the contract for the cheaper system to the effect that the cheaper system could handle twice the buyer's current transaction volumes without any degradation in performance or any additions of new hardware or software, or, if such were required, they would be supplied at no additional cost to the buyer. Such a provision, which is discussed in detail in Part B, likely would flush out any unreasonable supplier engaging in low-balling and hence allow the buyer to make a more reasoned procurement decision.

Of course it may be equally reasonable, and useful to both the supplier and the buyer, that the exercise of putting the whole deal in writing includes setting out in some detail the obligations of the buyer. Depending on the nature of the computer acquisition, there may not be much for the user to do; it is more likely, however, that the project's success hinges, in part, on the user's committing certain resources to it, hiring some highly qualified staff, and having key people attend critical meetings at which the specifications for the system are discussed and finalized, to name just a few common activities. These requirements should be recorded in the contract in the interests of having the agreement set out the respective commitments that the supplier and the buyer are making to the project.

Uncovering the Supplier's Weaknesses

Effective contracting is intended to have the extremely useful result of bringing to light any problems with the supplier's proposed computer solution before the buyer is committed to the purchase. It is often not until a supplier sees its marketing promises, made during sales pitches to the buyer or in the supplier's advertising literature, on paper in a contract that requires the supplier to live up to these promises, that the supplier concedes that some of these promises are unrealistic, overly ambitious, or even completely untrue and not at all feasible.

It is commonplace in the extremely competitive computer industry for sales representatives to overstate the virtues of their companies' products. In order to win the contract a sales person may exaggerate, or perhaps even knowingly misrepresent, when orally describing, for example, the ability of a computer to interact with other computers already in place at the buyer's premises. If these misstatements are taken at face value, the buyer may be sorely disappointed when, once installed, the supplier's system does not have all the compatibility characteristics promised by the sales representative. If the buyer presents the supplier with a reasonable contract clause that clearly sets out the compatibility features of the system and that requires any compatibility deficiencies to be paid for solely by the supplier, the buyer likely will learn early on whether the supplier's sales representative is really honest about the system's compatibility features (again, such a provision is explained in detail in Part B).

Sometimes the supplier weakness uncovered by effective contracting is that the supplier in fact does not have a product to deliver to the buyer. Suppliers often greatly underestimate the date by which a new item of equipment will be available for shipment to customers. Competitive pressures may induce a supplier to state to a potential buyer that the supplier's proposed new machine or system will be ready for installation in a few months. When the buyer, however, presents the supplier with a contract clause providing for a firm delivery date, together with effective remedies in the event that the supplier fails to meet the date, it often comes to light that the particular product cannot be shipped to the buyer for a year or more, a date much further into the future than the buyer initially was led to understand. Effective contracting will make the buyer aware of any supplier "bad news" before the procurement process advances to the point where the same bad news would have far more serious adverse consequences for the buyer.

Establishing Project Control Checkpoints

When an unreasonable supplier succeeds in having the buyer sign the supplier's standard form contract without any amendments or additions, the supplier is virtually assured of establishing and maintaining control over the acquisition project. While this might be opportune for the supplier, it can have serious negative repercussions for the buyer. But through effective contracting a buyer is much more likely to take charge of the buyer-supplier relationship, or at least achieve a balance where both parties participate jointly in all those aspects and phases of the procurement process where it is sensible, or indeed necessary, to have the buyer's imput.

A buyer can exercise effective control over the acquisition process by providing for project control checkpoints in its contract with the supplier. There are at least two such checkpoints in a standard computer system purchase situation: (1) delivery of the system and (2) the system's successful passing of an acceptance test which allows the buyer to learn whether the system performs according to certain predetermined standards prior to having to call the system its own. Additional checkpoints may be relevant in other types of contracts, such as most software development agreements where the principle of periodic formal evaluations of the various stages of work performed by the supplier is usually absolutely critical from the buyer's perspective.

Not surprisingly, standard form contracts used by unreasonable suppliers tend not to provide the buyer with adequate project evaluation checkpoints. Rather, the supplier is permitted to carry out its obligations according to its unilaterally determined schedule and performance criteria. This can result in an acquisition process full of unforeseen and unfortunate twists and turns which quite often extends for a much longer period of time than anticipated by the buyer. To counteract this defect in the unreasonable supplier's standard form contract, the prudent buyer will endeavour to have several of the project evaluation provisions discussed in Parts B and C included in its contract with the supplier.

Particularly in the case of larger, more complex acquisitions, smart suppliers also appreciate the need for contract control checkpoints, in that they want to have the buyer expressly sign-off on the blueprint for the next phase of the project before commencing work on it. While such a process protects the buyer, as noted above, it also protects the supplier because it prevents backsliding, or a total reneging on commitments, on the part of the buyer. Contract control checkpoints, therefore, are a key part of a "win-win" approach to computer contracting.

Equality and Fairness

A further rationale for effective contracting is to provide the buyer with certain rights and remedies which allow the buyer to stand on a far more equal footing with the unreasonable supplier than is permitted by their standard form contracts. The average standard form contract is careful to exclude certain supplier warranties and to severely limit a buyer's remedies in the event of poor performance by the supplier or the computer system. Usually, such contracts do not address many of the reasonable and essential requirements of the buyer.

One purpose of a well-drafted computer contract is to deal with the consequences of nonperformance by one or other party to the contract. No buyer should enter into such an agreement knowing for certain that it will have to rely on its contractual remedies, but neither should it be so cavalier as to imagine that it could never need such remedies. Accordingly, a key element of an effective contract is the inclusion of certain buyer remedies which stipulate clearly what corrective action may be taken by a buyer if the supplier fails to satisfy one or more of the contract provisions.

The reasons for effective contracting are compelling, yet too many buyers are content simply to sign the supplier's standard form agreement as it is presented to them. True, effective contracting requires an investment of time on the part of the representatives of the buyer and the supplier responsible for the computer acquisition. It is, however, time well spent, an investment that will pay the buyer and the supplier dividends of both time and money saved as the acquisition project proceeds.

3. A BRIEF SURVEY OF COMPUTER TECHNOLOGY

A primary requisite to effective contracting for computers is a thorough understanding of computing technology. The following short description of computer technology is by no means an attempt to give such technical knowledge. Parts B to E, however, do use certain basic computer terms and thus it is useful to describe, even if briefly, these terms. It is also useful to discuss in very general terms the methods used to market computers, and this is done at the end of this section.

Computer

A *computer* is a device that can be programmed to perform certain predetermined information processing functions. Understood at a very high level of generalization, the computer is a machine into which information is entered in a predefined format, this information, or *data*, is then processed or manipulated in accordance with certain instructions; the results of this processing are made available to the computer user, usually in the form of printed reports or, increasingly, immediately, in an "on-line, real-time" context, for example, a bank's automated teller machines.

Computers are generally said to consist of *hardware* and *software*. Hardware comprises the computer's *central processing unit* (CPU) and peripheral devices. Software is subdivided into *application software* and *operating system software*. Software also comes in largely two formats, *source code* and *object code*, each accompanied by *documentation*. It is worth expanding a little upon each of these terms.

Hardware

The physical, tangible elements of a computer are called, appropriately enough, *hardware*. Hardware is the machine segment of the computer, its equipment. Or, as someone in a lighter moment once put it, hardware is that part of the computer that, when dropped, causes a dent in the floor.

The essential component of hardware, and the heart of any computer, is the CPU or *central processing unit*. The CPU is made up of a *processor* where the basic arithmetic functions and calculations of the computer are carried out, and *memory*, where, as its name suggests, data is stored before and after it is processed by the CPU.

Processors and memory devices comprise various *semi-conductor chips*, which are the building blocks of most computer equipment. It is largely a result of huge advances in chip technology, including the ever-increasing miniaturization of computing power, over the past decade that has permitted computerized technology to find its way into virtually every nook and cranny of human endeavour.

The smallest unit of data storage in a computer's memory is a *bit* (*b*inary dig*it*); bits are the currency of information in the computer world. A bit is equivalent to an electrical switch with two settings, "on" (corresponding to "1") and "off" (corresponding to "0"). Larger units of data are made up of several consecutive bits. Eight such bits strung together have 256 variations of 1 and 0, and each such group of eight bits, known as a *byte*, can represent a separate data item such as a different number or letter of the alphabet.

Bytes, in turn, combine to form *words*, which might be human language words or telephone numbers, and words are further organized into *fields*, such as the names or addresses of the customers of a business. Fields are then collected into *records*, which are sets of related fields, such as a particular customer's name, address, and telephone number. Finally, records are aggregated into *files*; a file in our example could comprise a collection of names, addresses, and telephone numbers arranged perhaps alphabetically, or by city.

Computers are generally categorized by the processing speed and the size of the main memory of the computer's CPU. A *mainframe* computer is the fastest and largest (and most expensive) type of computer in general business use, while *minicomputers* are slower and smaller (and less expensive) than mainframes. *Microcomputers* or *personal computers* are in turn smaller than minicomputers, though in some cases advances in chip technology have produced microcomputers with virtually the same performance features as certain minicomputers. In addition to these three standard categories of computers, there are now a host of other model ranges, such as *super computers*, which are more powerful than mainframes, and *workstations*, which generally fit in somewhere between minicomputers and personal computers and are very popular for engineering and scientific applications. At the low end are the *laptop* and the *notebook* computers, which, as their names suggest, are rather small in size but can be remarkably powerful. Future advances in chip technology will likely continue the accelerating trend to squeeze even more computer power into a smaller space.

Connected to a computer's CPU are various peripheral devices. A *keyboard* is required to enter data into the computer. A sophisticated electronic cash register, called a *point-of-sale* terminal, can serve the same purpose in a retail business where information about sales and inventory is entered directly into the computer's memory. A *terminal* is connected to the CPU if the user wishes to see in a visual format the data that is being entered, stored, or communicated by the computer. In order to retrieve the data that has been processed in a format easily accessible to the human user, a *printer* will often be attached to the CPU. Printers come in many shapes and sizes, and in several technologies: an *impact printer* prints characters on a page one line at a time, while a *laser printer* operates more quickly (and, of course, more expensively) by printing the page as an image, in a manner akin to a photocopier. There are numerous other peripherals, ranging from extra data storage devices, such as *disk drives* which retain digitized information on aluminum platters coated with a magnetic medium and which may be accessed by the CPU, to *optical character readers* which can read data directly from printed text into a computer or decode the universal product bar code (UPC symbol) on the labels of merchandise in a grocery store point-of-sale terminal for stock control purposes.

Given the extremely dynamic nature of computer technology, new peripheral and related devices are constantly being developed. Over the next few years we will likely see, for example, technologies that facilitate data entry by voice recognition and by traditional handwriting. Change is the only constant in the computer industry, and change makes effective computer contracting an imperative.

Software

The programs that operate a computer are called *software*. Software consists of a set of instructions that direct the hardware to perform certain functions. Software can be stored in a number of media, on *diskettes* in the case of many personal computer programs, or on *magnetic tapes,* or directly in a *hard disk drive,* or increasingly on *chips* built into the hardware and often known as *firmware.* There are generally two types of software: application software and operating system software.

Application software are those computer instructions designed to perform a particular task for the user, such as payroll, general ledger, accounts payable, or word processing. Application software is available from hardware manufacturers, although today a great deal is produced by third-party software developers who have no corporate affiliation with any hardware producer. Some software suppliers have created a large number of standard application programs which have been mass marketed to many thousands of users through software licensing agreements. Other software developers specialize in producing custom application software which is intended for a single computer user or a small number of users.

Operating system software, often called system software, does not perform specific tasks for the user; rather, it takes care of the functions essential for the operation of the computer. It controls the operation of the hardware, directs data flows from the various components of hardware, dictates access procedures to the disk drive, keyboard, printer, and other peripherals, and supervises the interplay of the application software with the hardware. The operating system software is also responsible for a computer's security access mechanisms, such as the user password system. System software is generally made available and maintained by the supplier of the CPU and, as with application software, is nearly always licensed and almost never sold outright, for reasons which will be discussed later. An important recent trend in the computer industry, however, is a move towards nonproprietary or "open" system software, generally based on one of several versions of the UNIX operating system. While this development is welcomed by many because it offers, among other things, the opportunity to link together computer products of different suppliers, effective contracting is very much required to understand precisely what each supplier means by its particular "open system."

It is worth mentioning that no software, be it of the application or operating system variety, is error free. Regardless of how well software is designed or written, virtually all of it contains defects or errors — *bugs* in computer jargon. Even the most carefully tested and debugged software program will not have had every one of its logic flows checked for consistency and operability, given the innumerable combination of calculations that any software program is capable of performing. There will therefore always be parts in any program that could (and invariably do) malfunction. It is simply a fact of computer life that software is not perfect. While this imperfection should not discourage potential users from acquiring computer technology (and it clearly has not), it should lead users to shift a reasonable portion of the resulting risk to the software suppliers. This shifting, or more precisely, sharing of risk, can be greatly facilitated through effective contracting.

Software in general is written in one of several English-like, high-level *computer languages*, such as BASIC (Beginner's All Purpose Symbolic Instruction Code), COBOL (Common-Business-Oriented Language), FORTRAN (Formula Translation), or a more recently developed fourth generation language. When written in such a language, the software is said to be in its *source code* format. The source code sets out the logic flow of a software program and often includes a programmer's *narrative* explanation of the various steps of the program. Accordingly, a user usually must have source code in order to make modifications or corrections to the program. Software suppliers, however, rarely provide users with the source code version of a program. Suppliers have the not unreasonable fear that the source code might fall into the hands of an unscrupulous user or user's employee, who would use the confidential concepts embedded in the source code to create similar programs which could compete in the marketplace with the supplier's own product. Although the supplier who provides a user with source code can attempt to protect its source code by treating it as a trade secret and licensing it only under the strictest conditions, the danger of exposing the source code to theft or exploitation has led most suppliers to license software in another format, its *object code* version.

Source code cannot be used directly on a computer. The high-level computer language in which it is written (e.g., BASIC) must first be translated into a machine-readable language through the use of programs called *compilers* or *interpreters*. These programs translate the computer language into electronic *binary* instructions ("1's" and "0's"), which can be directly executed on the hardware. The resulting binary translation of the source code, generally termed the *object code* version of the software program, may be supplied on magnetic tape, cassette, diskette, or hard disk, or may be etched directly into chips which are then embedded into the body of the hardware. It is far more difficult, though usually not impossible, to glean from the object code the internal structure of a software program.

Hardware and software are usually supplied together with *documentation,* a set of written instructions which explain the functions of the computer and how to operate the hardware and software. Depending on the level of sophistication of the documentation, it might also provide instruction on the correction of programming errors. The quality of documentation, particularly in respect of custom-made software, is of great importance in that poor documentation may cause the user endless difficulties.

The Marketing of Computers

The means used to market computers are constantly changing. Traditional distribution mechanisms are always being supplemented, and sometimes supplanted, as new computer technologies and suppliers appear and older or inefficient ones disappear. When acquiring a mainframe computer system the user will generally contract directly with the manufacturer or, in Canada, with the manufacturer's Canadian subsidiary, for the hardware and the systems software. Minicomputer manufacturers employ several routes to get their equipment to market. They sell directly, but they also rely heavily on OEMs, original equipment manufacturers. The term OEM is a misnomer, however, because so-called OEMs seldom manufacture original equipment. Rather, they usually produce application software for certain industries which operate on a computer hardware manufacturer's equipment. Microcomputers can be purchased from OEMs, or other "value-added resellers" (VARs), or directly from the hardware manufacturers, or, along with laptop and other smaller computers, through retail outlets.

While most hardware manufacturers tend to be large companies, given the large amounts of capital and human resources necessary to produce computer equipment, software developers generally are much smaller entities, often consisting of no more than a handful of key employees (there is a joke in the computer industry that any two unemployed software designers need do no more than rent office space to call themselves a software development company). Many buyers of computer systems are often bigger than the software developers they contract with for the production of custom application programs. Finally, hardware maintenance services are generally available from the equipment manufacturer, but there are growing numbers of third-party suppliers who provide maintenance and service for all kinds of computer systems.

4. THE VARIOUS TYPES OF COMPUTER CONTRACTS

An organization may acquire computing resources in several different ways. It may purchase outright some computer hardware and licence application programs to operate on the purchased hardware, or the user may prefer to lease or rent hardware rather than buy it. In both cases the user would be wise to contract for hardware and software maintenance services so that computer malfunctions have a minimal impact on the user. Or instead of purchasing or leasing hardware and licensing software, a user may choose to purchase computing services from a service bureau. Regardless of how an organization obtains the use of hardware, it may retain a software developer to produce customized software for a particular or unique requirement that cannot be met by standard programs. In this case a software development contract will be called for. If the user receives only the object code version of the customized software program it may wish to ensure that, upon any disruption of the software developer's business, the user will be able to have access to the source code version. This kind of provision can be dealt with in a source code escrow agreement entered into by the user, the software developer, and a suitable neutral party.

These types of computer contracts, and a few others, are briefly described immediately below; in Part B contractual provisions pertaining to all these types of agreements are discussed in the context of hardware purchase and software licence agreements, while Part C takes up certain issues relating to master supply, lease/rental, maintenance, software development, consulting, proprietary rights protection, source code escrow, service bureau/outsourcing, disaster recovery, document imaging system, and electronic data interchange trading partner agreements.

Hardware Purchase Contract

The contract addressing the purchase of hardware is perhaps the most common form of computer agreement. It is used when a buyer wishes to acquire absolute ownership of the hardware from the supplier. A hardware manufacturer will not sell to a buyer unless the buyer first enters into the supplier's standard form contract or some negotiated equivalent. The substantive contracting issues relevant to a purchase contract are discussed in Part B.

Software Licence Contract

An equally common form of computer contract is the software licence agreement. In order to protect the proprietary rights of the software developer, as outlined earlier and discussed more fully later, software suppliers rarely if ever sell their products. Software is usually provided through licences. Whenever a business intends to use someone else's software it invariably will have to enter into a licence agreement. Under a licence agreement the user does not obtain ownership of the software; the user acquires only a licence to use the software. In many other respects the issues in Part B that are relevant to the hardware purchase agreement are equally germane to the software licence agreement.

Master Supply Contract

Over time, many organizations tend to acquire more than one computer system and a collection of ancillary equipment and software from the same supplier, but this does not necessarily mean that a new contract is needed for each acquisition. A whole sheaf of contracts can be very cumbersome and inefficient, particularly if the supplier changes its standard form agreements during the buyer-supplier relationship. A simple alternative is to enter into a long-term master supply agreement, essentially a hardware purchase and software licence agreement, but with extra provisions relating both to the process of ordering additional equipment and software under the same contract, and to the calculation of volume discounts for multiple purchases.

Lease/Rental Contract

When an organization leases or rents hardware it obtains the right to possess and use, rather than to own, the equipment (although many leases provide for a purchase option exercisable after a period of time). The owner may be the manufacturer or a third-party financing company. The user makes periodic, usually monthly, rental payments. There are at least three reasons why some companies prefer to lease or rent, the difference being one of duration — a rental rarely exceeds two years, while leases can run for many years.

By leasing, a company can avoid incurring up-front capital costs, which, especially for larger computer systems, can amount to a significant outlay. As well, leasing does not tie a company to a particular make or model of a computer the way a purchase does. Particularly in respect of those computer product lines where quick obsolescence is the rule (traditionally just about every area in the computer industry), some companies prefer to have the flexibility of regularly trading in their leased equipment for a newer product offering. Finally, if the lease is correctly structured the rental payments are deductible as a business expense for the company leasing the equipment. Many companies find this tax advantage particularly attractive, and it is often the case that the decision to lease is ultimately made for tax reasons.

Maintenance Contract

Software by its very nature is prone to contain design or programming errors. Nor can hardware be built to perfection. Hardware malfunction and software errors are facts of computing life. It is therefore imperative that computer users be able to call upon maintenance services that can repair any problem promptly, all the more so if the computer resource in question is of great importance to the successful day-to-day operation of a business.

Maintenance services are generally made available pursuant to agreements that enumerate the types of services to be provided and the charges to be paid by the user. These agreements are invariably standard form documents of suppliers. Rarely do they contain provisions respecting performance guarantees on the part of the maintenance supplier. A user who signs such an agreement without first considering all the ramifications of poor or inadequate service is committing a grave error, particularly where it is essential that a computer system run virtually continuously.

Software Development Contract

Perhaps the riskiest computer contracting relationship arises when a user retains a software developer to create and implement a custom application software program. There is so much that can go wrong with a software development project. The user can improperly define its own computing needs and requirements, the so-called functional requirements for the program. The software developer can plan a program that, although it is workable, contains many design and structural errors. In coding the software the developer can make serious programming errors which can take months of testing to iron out. In cases where the user has contracted to receive source code, the source code delivered may be of such poor quality — the programmer's narrative may be inadequate or not there at all — that no third party can decipher it, let alone work with it. In such a case the user may become perpetually wedded to the software developer for maintenance and future modifications and additions to the program. The instruction manuals or documentation may also be of poor quality in terms of accuracy, clarity, and organization.

In order to minimize such problems, the user and the software developer must enter into a software development contract that clearly and comprehensively maps out the several stages through which any successful software program must pass. Moreover, for the user to meaningfully monitor the project, each development stage must be accompanied by an evaluation mechanism, together with suitable remedies that may be exercised by the user if the software developer's performance is not satisfactory. Any buyer foolhardy enough to attempt to acquire a custom program without entering into a well-thought-out software development agreement may well pay dearly for such an omission in the long run.

Consulting Contract

A user may have occasion from time to time to hire a consultant to work on some aspect of the user's computer system, for instance, training of the user's personnel or a review of the user's future requirements. The consultant may be the developer of the user's custom software, but could just as well be a company, firm, or individual previously unconnected with the user's system. Particularly in the latter case, the user should enter into an agreement with the consultant that ensures, among other things, that the consultant will keep confidential all the software materials owned by or licensed to the user. As well, if the consultant's role extends to developing any modifications to the user's software, then the consulting agreement should clearly spell out who owns such modifications.

Proprietary Rights Protection

The same kind of protection ensured in a consulting contract should be obtained from any other party hired by the user, typically by means of a proprietary rights protection agreement. In particular, the user should have its employees sign proprietary rights protection agreements in order that the user can discharge its duty of confidentiality to the software developer whose software the user is licensing. The employee proprietary rights protection agreement should also address who owns the software developed by employees in the course of their duties.

Source Code Escrow Contract

Mention has already been made of the reluctance of software developers to provide users with source code for computer programs. On the other hand, if the particular program is of great importance to a user, the user might be satisfied with initially obtaining the object code version only if it is secure in the knowledge that if it needs to obtain the source code for purposes of on-going software maintenance or to develop modifications and additions to the program, it could do so readily. Such a need may arise, for example, if the software developer ceases to perform these services for the user or goes out of business either voluntarily or because of bankruptcy (a not uncommon occurrence with smaller, less stable, and often extremely undercapitalized software developers).

A user can help assure access to the source code by having the software developer deposit a copy of the source code with a third party escrow agent, in Canada usually one of the large trust companies, pursuant to a source code escrow agreement between the software developer, the user, and the escrow agent. This agreement typically provides that upon certain events of default, such as the software developer's ceasing to maintain the user's object code program, the escrow agent must release the source code in its possession to the user. The source code is only released upon an event of default; the software developer is guaranteed that its source code will not be made available to the user unless and until the software developer is unable to satisfy the user's requirements. In this way, the source code escrow agreement attempts to protect both the software developer and the user.

Service Bureau/Outsourcing Contract

In a service bureau relationship a user is essentially buying computer time on someone else's (the service bureau's) machine. The user delivers or transmits data to the service bureau, often by means of terminals installed at the user's site. The service bureau's computers process this data and return it to the user in the desired format, either on-line via the user's terminals or in a printed report. There can be several advantages to a business in using a service bureau. As with leasing there are no large up-front capital costs. An advantage over leasing, however, is that a user might be able to have its data processed on larger, more powerful machines than it would be likely to lease. A smaller business may not have enough computing demands to justify leasing a mainframe, but a service bureau can permit several smaller users to share time on the service bureau's mainframe, thereby allowing these users access to computing resources otherwise unavailable to them.

There are, however, distinct dangers to using a service bureau. The most obvious is the potential disclosure by the service bureau of the user's confidential data. The user's data is sent outside the confines of the company and is exposed to non-company personnel. Therefore, a key issue that must be dealt with in a service bureau agreement, from the user's perspective, is the measures to be implemented by the service bureau to protect the confidentiality of the user's data. This is particularly true where the user's data contains the sensitive information of its customers and such data is being processed by the service bureau.

Disaster Recovery Contract

Consider for a moment a large computer facility of a major corporation. Housed in a whole floor of a downtown office building, it contains several mainframe computers on which all of the financial, inventory, and other data of the company is processed. It is no exaggeration to say that this computer centre is the information spinal cord of the company. One day a fire breaks out in the floor above the computer centre. The water used to fight the fire virtually floods the computer room, knocking out all the computers and the facility for about two weeks until repairs can be made.

This presents a real problem for the company. The week's-end employee payroll has to be run. The month-end financial statements have to be processed. The hundred and one other computing functions have to be carried on, but how? Luckily, the senior information management officer of the company had previously convinced the company to enter into a disaster recovery contract with a so-called disaster recovery facility that has a mainframe computer and related equipment set aside in special premises for just such an emergency. Within hours the company's key back-up tapes are loaded on the computer at the disaster recovery facility, providing the company with a life-support system until the company's own computer room is back in working order.

EDI Trading Partner Contract

Many companies and other organizations are replacing their paper-based forms of conveying commercial information (such as printed purchase orders) with electronic data interchange (EDI), which is the direct computer-to-computer transmission of information in a structured electronic messaging format. While EDI is a compelling technology for many reasons, it also raises some legal challenges, given that the law has not yet had time to accommodate expressly certain aspects of EDI. Accordingly, organizations contemplating implementing EDI should enter into EDI trading partner agreements which, among other things, attempt to reduce the legal uncertainties currently inherent in EDI.

Having reviewed briefly the various types of computer contracts, there now follows in Parts B and C a discussion of the key contracting issues raised by these agreements.

PART

B

General Contract Provisions

Part B deals with some two and a half dozen *general* contract issues that users should give some thought to when acquiring hardware and software, whereas Part C discusses *additional* contract provisions with respect to master supply, lease/rental, maintenance, software development, consulting, proprietary rights protection, source code escrow, service bureau, disaster recovery, and electronic data interchange trading partner contracts. It should be noted, however, that many of the provisions addressed here in Part B are also relevant to the agreements analysed in Part C.

No actual precedents of contract clauses are presented in either Part B or Part C. Rather, issues such as delivery, acceptance testing, supplier warranties, and user or buyer remedies are discussed in a narrative manner. The goal of the analysis is to focus attention on areas of the computer contracting process which involve the most risk and are the most likely to lead to a situation where either the buyer's or supplier's expectations are not met if not properly dealt with in a contract.

Whether in any particular acquisition situation all or only some of the provisions in Part B are covered usually depends on the dollar value of the system in question. There is generally a direct relationship between the size of the computer system being acquired and the amount of time spent on contract negotiations. This is unfortunate in the sense that smaller systems can often be as crucial to an organization as large systems. All of the provisions in Part B should be considered whether what is at stake is a large mainframe acquisition or a much less expensive small network of microcomputer terminals. Contract issues checklists are provided in Part E to assist in this task.

Many general contract issues are addressed in the standard form agreements of most suppliers, albeit almost invariably in a manner highly favourable to the supplier when dealing with unreasonable suppliers. More and more suppliers, however, are beginning to use more reasonable standard form agreements in order to cut down on the long negotiating time typically spent on unreasonable ones. Data managers will want to consider the following discussion with a view to negotiating amendments to and deletions from the supplier's standard form. In addition, several of the following contract provisions appear in the standard form contracts of only the most reasonable suppliers.

Many standard form contracts do not address four of the most important issues discussed in Part B: delivery, acceptance testing, supplier's warranties, and user's remedies. Data managers will want to read Part B with the goal in mind of having clauses that address these four issues added to the supplier's standard form agreement.

The contract provisions discussed here and the contract issues in the checklists (Part E) are presented in "chronological" order, that is, as the issues raised by these provisions would likely be encountered during the course of a computer acquisition. The reader is taken through the various steps involved in a computer system implementation project, from defining the hardware and software to be acquired, to preparation of the installation site, through delivery of the equipment and its testing, to provisions that deal with the consequences of a supplier's failure to live up to its obligations. While this chronological format is useful in highlighting various aspects of the computer acquisition process, it is equally valuable in actual contract drafting and negotiating situations — it helps the buyer to think through its relationship with the supplier from the beginning to the end of the acquisition project. It also makes the resulting computer contract an eminently more readable and understandable document. This is particularly important to the buyer. The supplier may not be overly concerned if the clauses in its standard form contract are in no particular order, thereby making it difficult for the buyer to see how various clauses affect one another, because the supplier is invariably familiar with its own contractual handiwork. From the buyer's perspective there is much to be said for a computer contract whose clauses appear in an organized, common-sensical order.

1. DESCRIPTION OF HARDWARE AND SOFTWARE

Specifying the Hardware

Virtually every contract for the acquisition of hardware will include a clause that sets out what the purchaser is buying. The major danger here is that the actual hardware might be enumerated inadequately. Many computer systems are known by

generic names, for example, the "System 2000." Such a designation usually denotes a certain hardware configuration, a collection of items of equipment which are generally sold together
and comprise the system. Accordingly, when a user approaches
a computer hardware manufacturer in order, say, to automate
the business's inventory control procedures, the supplier might
advise that the System 2000 is just what the user needs, and a
price is quoted for the System 2000.

The contract should break down the System 2000 into its constituent parts, with model references noted as well. The most
effective way to do this is to attach to the contract an appendix or
schedule that lists the individual items of hardware to be purchased, such as one "ABC CPU Model STU," two "XYZ disc
drives," three "HIJ video display terminals," three "DEF key-
boards," three "LMN data multiplexing devices," and so on.
Other items to be provided by the supplier such as cabling,
wiring, and mounting brackets or stands for the hardware should
also be listed. If there is any doubt as to what any item is — for
example, there might be confusion between the supplier's "XYZ
disc drives" and its "TUV disc drives," perhaps one having more
storage capacity than the other — then a brief functional description to accompany the "XYZ disc drive" entry would be in order.

There are several good reasons for insisting on such exact-
ness. First, with so many buzzwords and jargon in the computer vocabulary it is very easy for a buyer and a supplier to misunderstand one another as to what is to be delivered under the
contract if only general, acronym-filled references are made to
the hardware to be supplied to the buyer. For example, the
System 2000 might have several models, each different in price
and performance. Of course, all industries and professions —
including the legal one — have their own vocabulary and
nomenclature to a certain extent, but the degree to which the
terminology in the computer sector can be misleading or confusing is attested in the following passage from an American
judge's court decision in 1970 in a case dealing with a computer
contract that gave rise to a lawsuit:

> *Lawyers and courts need no longer feel ashamed or even sensitive*
> *about the charge, often made, that they confuse the issue by resort*
> *to legal "jargon," Law Latin or Norman French. By comparison,*

*the misnomers and industrial shorthand of the computer world
make the most esoteric legal writing seem as clear and lucid as
the Ten Commandments or the Gettysburg Address; and to add
to this Babel, the experts in the computer field, while using
exactly the same words, uniformly disagree as to precisely what
they mean.*

While this statement is more than 20 years old, things have
not improved much on the computer lingo front. For this reason, if there is ever any doubt in a computer contract about the
meaning of a technical term, then the term should be defined,
preferably in relation to its function rather than by resorting to
further buzzwords. For example, if the hardware list on the
equipment schedule to the contract includes the item *IBM PC
clone,* it would be a start to change this at least to *a personal computer fully compatible with an IBM personal computer (of a certain
model),* but even better would be a detailed technical description
of the degree of compatibility intended for this non-IBM
machine inasmuch as there are several different views in the
industry as to what "compatible" means. Clarity of meaning
should be an objective of every computer contract.

Another reason for a buyer's insisting on a precise enumera-
tion of deliverables has to do with several warranties that the
buyer may want to obtain from the supplier relating to the performance capabilities of the system. These are discussed in
Section B.13 under the heading "Warranties," but suffice it to
say at this point that a buyer that wants the supplier to promise
that the hardware will operate in accordance with certain specifications, or that certain software (perhaps obtained from another supplier) will operate on the hardware, or that the hardware
can be expanded to be able to process twice the user's current
volume of data or transactions, cannot secure a meaningful
promise on the part of the supplier unless a detailed breakdown
of the components of the hardware is given and agreed to by
both the buyer and the supplier.

Specifying the Software

Just as the various components of hardware being acquired
should be specified in detail, so too should the software being
licensed be set out with precision in the contract. All the various

software programs being supplied should be listed, again probably in an appendix or schedule to the contract. This list should be comprehensive. It should include the various operating systems software programs that run the hardware, as well as the applications software programs that will carry out the particular data processing functions required by the user.

Most mass-marketed software is continually in a state of evolution. Some period after the initial appearance of a particular software program it will likely be updated and modified in a "new release." New releases correct errors found in the original program, add functions and features, and generally give improved performance. It should be stated in the contract which release or version of the program is to be delivered to the buyer. As discussed under "Warranties" (B.13), it is sometimes useful to state that the software (and hardware) being delivered to the buyer are at the time of delivery the most current versions or the most advanced technology available from the supplier. Similarly, the agreement should specify whether the buyer is obtaining all the ancillary software necessary to operate the system according to the buyer's requirements. A buyer may have seen a demonstration of, say, the System 2000 performing a function that is only possible with an extra item of software or hardware, which is not included with the System 2000. Such software would include programs generally called "utilities" or "tools."

If the supplier, either in the normal course of marketing its software (which is not likely) or in unusual circumstances (somewhat more likely) agrees to make the source code to the computer software available to the user, then this should be recognized by a clear statement that source code is in fact what is to be delivered to and licensed for the buyer's use. Without such a specific acknowledgement, it could be argued that the words "software program" referred merely to the object code version of the program. The distinction between source and object code was discussed in section A.3 under "Software."

Another deliverable often referred to under the heading of software is documentation. These written materials are typically the manuals prepared by the supplier which describe the operation and other functions of the software and hardware. Documentation is important, and the contract should specify the actual type and quantity of the documentation to be delivered.

If the user is to receive source code, then a further matter is the quality of the written material to be delivered along with the source code. Source code is most useful when it is accompanied by a detailed narrative commentary describing the various logic flows and other elements of the program. Source code that lacks this critical component is far more difficult, and sometimes impossible, for a user to work with in terms of maintaining the software or making additions or modifications to it. Accordingly, a user expecting to receive source code would be wise to review the state of the source code before entering into a contract with the supplier. If this is not possible — in software development situations the source code is often to be developed in the future —the buyer may wish to stipulate that all source code must pass an objective qualitative test. For example, the source code ultimately delivered has to be of such quality as to permit an applications software programmer with average skills and experience to understand the operation of the program, or even better, the narrative that accompanies the source code must be similar in quality to the narrative for some other specified software program already in existence. Benchmarks such as "the source code will be developed according to industry standards" should be avoided, because it is likely unclear what the relevant industry standard is. Having a specific referent point, such as the source code of another product of the developer, is the best approach when articulating a quality standard for the new source code.

Specifying the Price

The supplier, of course, will invariably ensure that the aggregate price to be paid by the buyer for the purchase of the hardware and the licence of the software is clearly enumerated, inasmuch as the supplier will be keen to collect these amounts with a minimum of fuss or dispute. What sometimes is lacking, however, is a breakdown of such total price into its constituent components. This would entail, at a minimum, the unit price per item of hardware or software, as well as any applicable taxes as a separate-line item, in the schedule or appendix containing the list of deliverables. As well, if the licence fee to be paid by the user for the software is not a lump sum amount, then the formula used to calculate the periodic licence fees must be clearly set out so that no question arises later as to what amounts are to be paid to the supplier. For example, it is not uncommon for insurance companies that use computer software to pay licence fees based on the number of policies supported by the relevant software, with discounts applicable if the user attains certain volumes of customer premiums. This form of payment can require complicated pricing algorithms, and these should be reviewed carefully by the user to ensure that they reflect accurately any particular discounts or other benefits negotiated by the user.

Breaking down the total price into constituent elements serves several purposes from the buyer's perspective. First, it minimizes the uneconomic bundling of components. For example, the hardware supplier might have a very competitive price for the system's CPU, but a poor per item price for disk drives and printers. If the prices for these latter items were shown separately the buyer might decide to buy compatible disk drives at a better price from another supplier. This kind of mixing and matching is becoming more common in order to implement cost-effective hardware configurations, but it cannot be done if the main supplier prices its products as a "package deal."

Breaking down the contract price item by item also assists the buyer in exercising a trade-in allowance, assuming the buyer has such a right. This issue is discussed later in some detail. It is enough to say at this point, that in order to operationalize a flexible trade-in-allowance provision, namely, one where the buyer can trade in single hardware or software items rather than only the whole system, the price of each item must be shown separately or at least be referenced in the contract. In a similar vein, if a certain item does not work properly upon installation and the buyer wants to achieve the "surgical" solution of refusing acceptance for that item while accepting the remainder, it is necessary to show a separate price for the item in question.

The price schedule should also indicate the various indirect costs associated with the system, such as transportation, shipping insurance, and installation charges, to the extent that these are part of the all-in price quoted by the supplier. If nothing else the practice of expressly stipulating such costs in advance will likely lead the supplier to secure for the buyer the best possible deal on them (these costs, in the aggregate, can sometimes be quite significant). Finally, just so there are no misunderstandings between the buyer and the supplier, especially an American supplier, the contract should specify whether the monetary amounts quoted in the agreement are to be paid in Canadian or American dollars.

2. PROJECT MANAGEMENT

A central objective of effective contracting is to help the buyer of the computer system meaningfully monitor the acquisition process. Not surprisingly, virtually all standard form contracts of unreasonable suppliers are alike in that they do not contain clauses which might give the buyer the ability to review the timing and manner in which the supplier performs its obligations. This omission might not be serious where the user is acquiring a small system comprising hardware that is readily available and easily installed together with standard software which requires no modification. In a larger project, however, where the hardware might have to be ordered weeks if not months in advance to allow for manufacturing, where installation could require pulling hundreds of metres of wiring and perhaps even the construction of cable conduits in walls and floors, and where software might have to be modified for the particular needs of the user or perhaps created independently on a custom basis, the buyer could be exposed to substantial cost overruns and timing delays if it cannot participate in or at least effectively supervise the management of the project.

Supplier's Personnel

One way in which the buyer can exert some control over the management of the acquisition is to have the supplier agree in the contract to assign only fully trained and qualified personnel to the buyer's project. More importantly it is very useful for the buyer to have the ability to request the removal from the project of any of the supplier's personnel found to be unsuitable by the buyer. Of course a supplier might insist on the buyer having some reasonable grounds for requesting the removal of any of the supplier's personnel. A middle ground might be to enumerate some objective qualifications that at least the senior employees of the supplier must possess, such as academic or professional qualifications, or years of experience working with systems similar to the one being installed for the buyer.

It is also helpful if the buyer can insist contractually that certain of the supplier's employees previously assigned to the buyer's project remain with the buyer's project until the implementation of the buyer's system is complete. It often happens that a supplier has its finest technical and business people assigned to a buyer initially in order to win the contract. Once the buyer is secured as a client, some suppliers have been known to effect a change of personnel, with its first-rate employees being shifted to another contract bid, and replaced by less expert people on the buyer's acquisition. This replacement group, in addition to not being perhaps the supplier's best and brightest, are at a distinct disadvantage in that they do not have the same degree of familiarity with the buyer's needs as the initial team which had to get to know the buyer's circumstances thoroughly in order to win the job in the first place. By insisting on a continuity of supplier personnel the buyer is helping to ensure that the project is completed in a timely fashion and without untoward incident.

If the buyer cannot convince the supplier to agree to these personnel management provisions, then at the very least the supplier should be amenable to appointing a project co-ordinator who can be the buyer's contact person throughout the acquisition process. Such a person should be quite senior and have enough clout within the supplier's organization to ensure that the buyer will have the full attention and consideration of all the supplier's personnel. Again, the buyer may wish to insist that the supplier's project co-ordinator be the same individual who initially orchestrated the supplier's winning bid for the buyer's acquisition project, and who thereby gained both a detailed knowledge of the project and the confidence of the buyer, both of which will improve the chances of a trouble-free implementation of the system.

Implementation Schedule

No buyer should sign a contract for the acquisition of a computer system without the supplier's first having agreed to a schedule that sets out the dates by which the supplier is to perform certain obligations. Such a project implementation schedule may be as brief as setting out two dates: the date the hardware and software is to be delivered to the buyer's premises (more on this later in section B.4, "Delivery Date"), and the date the system will be installed and ready for the commencement of acceptance testing. In a more complex acquisition the implementation schedule could include a host of other dates relating to preparation of the installation site, commencement and completion of training of the buyer's personnel, or commencement and completion of the conversion of the buyer's data to run on the new system. If there is a software development component to the project it is also essential that the implementation schedule list the dates by which both the functional specifications and the system design specifications for the software are presented to the buyer for approval (more on these specifications in section C.4, "Software Development").

Such an implementation schedule should not contain "target" or "estimate" or "best efforts" dates. They should be firm dates which, if not met, will allow the buyer to take certain steps, including exercising certain remedies if the delay exceeds a certain period (more on this in section B.15, "Remedies"). Being hard and fast dates they will also be realistic dates, that is, the supplier will have to take a good, detailed look at the project and predict, as objectively and honestly as possible, how long it will all take. Many buyers are sorely disappointed when a project they were initially told would take eight months is still barely half-way complete eighteen months after its commencement. A contractual implementation schedule backed up by firm remedies has an uncanny ability of making actual performance conform with predicted performance.

Periodic Meetings and Reports

Especially for larger system acquisitions a buyer is well advised to have in place a mechanism for monitoring the supplier's progress against the dates contained in the implementation schedule. This can be done by requiring at least the project coordinator of the supplier to attend a periodic meeting, perhaps bi-weekly or even weekly on a major project, in order to give a progress report and answer any questions the buyer might have. The report could be quite detailed — it might list all activities completed by the supplier since the previous meeting, all items of hardware and amounts of cabling installed, and the degree of completion of any software customization; it could also include an estimate of work to be done in the next bi-weekly or weekly period.

A key objective of such meetings and reports is to enable the buyer to ascertain whether the supplier is on schedule with the implementation of the project. If there is a slippage in deadlines the buyer can be informed promptly, can inquire as to the cause, and perhaps can even help in solving some of the problems that are causing the project to fall behind schedule. There is nothing more disconcerting to a buyer than to be told by the supplier a month before the planned start-up date for the new system — a date agreed to perhaps six months before when the contract was signed — that the equipment will not be up and running for another three months due to a lengthy list of cumulative problems and delays. The buyer may have no interim or alternative plan, and in extreme cases a delay could mean the difference between success and failure of the buyer's ventures. It is far more conducive to harmonious buyer-supplier relations for the former to hear from the latter about any hitches in the implementation timetable immediately as they arise.

Depending on how closely the buyer wishes to supervise the supplier's activities, the buyer may want written progress reports, or at least written minutes of the oral reports given at the periodic meetings. Such documentation is particularly useful in chronicling the buyer's objections to any supplier tardiness. This is an important consideration. There is no point in having a supplier agree to a strict implementation schedule if when the dates on this timetable are not met the buyer does not reprimand the supplier, but instead merely lets the supplier continue to fall behind schedule. Indeed, having a detailed implementation schedule and then not objecting and taking other appropriate action when milestones on this schedule are not met may leave the buyer in a worse situation than if no implementation schedule was ever made part of the contract.

This is so because of a legal rule known as the "doctrine of acquiescence." If a supplier, for example, fails to meet a 1 April hardware delivery date and the buyer does not object to such nondelivery until 1 July (the date on which the equipment is finally delivered), the supplier can argue that the buyer acquiesced in, or accepted, the late delivery and in fact did not really care when the hardware was delivered. In essence, a judge might be very reluctant to permit the buyer to sue the supplier for late delivery on 1 July if the buyer exhibited concern about the breach of the contract by the supplier for the first time only three months after the delivery should have occurred.

The essential point to grasp from this discussion is that important rights secured by a buyer, after sometimes long and painful negotiations, in effect can be diluted or even abandoned or rendered worthless unless enforced promptly. A buyer can give up rights if, once granted, they are not exercised. This point will be made several times in this book, but it cannot be emphasized enough. It is perhaps easy to sympathize with the buyer that does not know any better and hence signs without amendment a standard form contract of an unreasonable supplier which gives the buyer precious little in the way of contract rights. It is, however, difficult to feel sorry for the buyer who, having acquired certain rights — such as having the supplier install the system in accordance with the timing of events listed in an implementation schedule — loses those rights and the remedies they trigger through failure to exercise them when it was appropriate and necessary to do so. This point is taken up in greater detail in section D.2, "Administering the Contract."

3. PREPARATION OF THE INSTALLATION SITE

Computer hardware, especially of the minicomputer and mainframe variety, is very sensitive. Too much dust or humidity, or too little power (or too much power when there is a power surge!), and even the most solid-looking computer component can stop functioning properly. Accordingly, suppliers of hardware generally publish "power and environmental specifications" which stipulate the type of power source and the heat, humidity, ventilation, and other conditions required for optimum (or indeed minimum) performance of the system. It is useful on larger projects to list the power and environmental specifications in a schedule to the contract. It is important that the space set aside by the user (often called the installation site) to house a minicomputer or mainframe CPU and other data storage components of the hardware conform to the power and environmental specifications. (Microcomputer CPUs generally are more rugged and don't need too much in the way of special environmental conditions.) If the specifications at the installation site are not appropriate, the equipment installed there is apt to malfunction or become altogether inoperable much more frequently than would otherwise be the case. Indeed, some suppliers insist that their warranty and subsequent service obligations are valid only if the installation site is prepared and maintained in accordance with the supplier's specific environmental standards.

Renovating an installation site to conform to a supplier's environmental specifications can be expensive. It has happened more than once that a data manager with a fixed computer budget, say $500,000, spends all this amount on hardware and software only to find out later that preparing an adequate room to house the CPU of the computer will cost perhaps an additional $20,000. This revelation tends to result in an embarrassing request for further funds from the treasurer of the company. To avoid this, the data manager should inquire very early on about the relevant environmental specifications and determine the additional cost.

Whatever the cost involved in preparing or renovating an installation site, an accurate record of these expenses should be kept by the buyer (or the supplier if the supplier is responsible for performing such renovations and then bills the buyer for such expenses). This is particularly necessary if the buyer is able to negotiate a remedy with the supplier whereby certain of these costs will be borne by the supplier in the event the supplier's system does not pass its acceptance test. This remedy is discussed in detail below under "Remedies" (B.15).

After the issue of cost, the next question is who will implement any necessary changes to the installation site so that it conforms to the supplier's requirements. There are three options. First, some suppliers will do the work, either directly or by contracting the work out to another company. This is usually the costliest option, but it can also be the safest in the sense that if there is a problem subsequently with the installation site, or with the performance of the computer due to some fault with the installation site's environmental specifications, then there is little doubt that the supplier is at fault and should bear full responsibility (and expense).

The two other options are for the buyer to hire a contractor or do the job itself. The latter may be a cheaper alternative if the buyer has the expertise, but in each of these two cases responsibility for any problems with the installation site shifts to the buyer. The buyer can allocate some of this risk to the supplier — even when the supplier does not prepare the installation site — by including a contract clause, typically in the hardware purchase agreement, stating that after the buyer (or its contractor) has prepared the installation site, the supplier shall review the site in order to approve or disapprove the site from the point of view of compliance with the supplier's environmental specifications. If the site is not approved, the supplier must notify the buyer, who then undertakes whatever changes are necessary to obtain the supplier's approval. The buyer is protected in that once the supplier approves the installation site the supplier is unable to raise the issue of power or environmental conditions as a cause for poor performance of the computer system. The supplier's inspection and approval will turn up any flaws in the installation site early on in the acquisition process, when it is most useful for the buyer to hear about them. Then, the flaws can be corrected before the computer system is installed (rather than six months after it has been operating, only to crash completely because of, for example, an inadequate air conditioning system in the user's installation site).

4. DELIVERY DATE

It may well surprise buyers that suppliers' standard form contracts seldom state exactly when the supplier is to deliver the computer equipment in question. Buyers are often unaware of this critical omission when they sign the standard form agreement, with the result that a buyer can still be awaiting delivery long after the date the supplier may have mentioned over the telephone has come and gone. Some supplier agreements do not mention delivery at all, while others use phrases such as "the supplier will deliver the equipment in accordance with the supplier's delivery schedule." Still others will state "an estimated delivery date" subject to the critical proviso that such date is an estimate only and that the supplier is not really obliged to deliver the goods on this or any other particular date.

Suppliers will often argue that they have some good reasons why they are generally hesitant to commit to firm delivery dates. For example, with respect to products that are currently in existence, it is generally the exception rather than the rule that the supplier will have the appropriate equipment in stock at its Canadian warehouse. Even smaller-ticket items such as microcomputers are typically not kept in inventory in great quantities because of the expense involved. Rather, it is usually only after a supplier has entered into a computer contract with a buyer, and received a deposit of anywhere from 10 to 40% of the purchase price, that it places the order with the affiliated manufacturer in the United States, Japan, or Europe. The filling of this order can take time, particularly where the item must be first manufactured and not merely shipped from the relevant factory or warehouse, which is often the case for larger computer systems. Unforeseen delays can also creep into the acquisition process at this point. For instance, the order of the Canadian supplier may be bumped back to satisfy a supposedly more important customer of an American or other foreign supplier, the thinking being that the Canadian purchaser will wait quietly until another machine comes off the assembly line, however long that may take.

If the period of time between ordering and delivery of equipment can be lengthy for currently existing technology, it can sometimes be an eternity when a user orders a product not yet being manufactured for general sale. The following scenario is an increasingly familiar one. A reputable supplier, confronted with a number of aggressive competitors snapping at its heels with new product offerings, feels pressured to "announce" its new product and to state publicly that it will be available in nine months time, even though such a delivery time-frame would require every employee at the company to work twenty-five hours a day, eight days a week. In short, the announced first shipment date is more a marketing ploy to meet the competition than to satisfy buyers.

This practice of announcing new products for unreasonably optimistic delivery dates has become so widespread in certain sectors of the computer business that the terms "vapourware" and "brochureware" have been coined by the computer industry and the press to describe it. Several years ago *Time* magazine ran an article on the phenomenon, and more recently a piece in *Computerworld* documented fourteen cases of vapourware involving software for microcomputers. In half of these cases almost a year or more had elapsed since the original product announcement and still the software offerings were unavailable. On the same note, a recent press report indicated that a major computer supplier's profit during a particular quarter was lower than expected because of late deliveries of a new product. More recently, a computer manufacturer was fined $275,000 as a result of a claim that it advertised a software program as available for sale which in fact was not yet available.

Even a number of software suppliers have admitted that certain industry players are less than ethical in their use of unreasonably early product announcements and other variations of vapourware. As a result, the Software Business Practices Council (SBPC) was created in the fall of 1990 to establish a voluntary code of marketing conduct for members of the software sector. The SBPC encourages software companies, for example, to make a distinction between the announcement of a general product direction, on the one hand, and the announcement of the release of a specific product, on the other hand. The latter announcement, argues the SBPC, should not be made until the particular software product has been submitted for Beta testing, whereby a software product, after being developed and tested internally by its developer, is subjected to further testing by a few of the developer's current customers. This is a sensible recommendation from the SBPC, and one that prospective purchasers of announced but not yet available software products should keep in mind; that is, there should be some comfort for would-be purchasers of an announced but not-yet-released product in knowing that the product has reached the Beta-testing stage.

Vapourware and brochureware would not cause problems if data managers were never to base their procurement decisions on "soon-to-be-available" hardware or software products. But they often do so. Of course the motivation of the buyer is understandable; why take one supplier's currently available computer system if in two short months the buyer can have a cheaper, more powerful system from another supplier? Why indeed, unless of course the new system will not actually be available for twelve months rather than two. The buyer can take

a relatively simple step to avoid being the victim of vapourware
or any similar form of over-zealous or overly ambitious marketing by a supplier. The buyer should insist that the computer
contract include a firm delivery date — not a target date to be
hopefully met by the best efforts of the supplier, not merely
sometime in the first half of a certain year, but a specific date
such as 15 April 1992.

The following acquisition case study, which actually happened several years ago, shows how the stipulation of a firm
delivery date can expose a supplier engaging in the sale of
vapourware. A large organization decided to replace its existing
telephone system with an advanced telecommunications system (essentially a very sophisticated telephone system with
voice, data, and video signals transmission capacity). When it
called for tenders, one of the suppliers that responded indicated
it had available a new software product that controlled the
telecommunication system's switch, its central component. This
new software product was far superior to any competitor's
offering and, partly on the strength of this feature, the buyer
chose its developer as the supplier for the organization's
telecommunications system.

About eight months before the date that the new system was
to be installed, or "cut over" as it is termed in the telecommunications industry, the organization presented to the supplier the
first draft of a written contract which stipulated a firm delivery
date for the whole system, including the new switch-control
software product. The supplier had several comments on this
draft contract, including the revelation that the much heralded
new software device would in fact not be available for delivery
until many months after the organization's intended cutover
date because of unforeseen delays caused by design and production problems at the supplier's research facility.

This news came as a complete shock to the prospective buyer,
but fortunately the problem came to light sooner rather than
later, thereby affording the organization some time to come up
with an alternative solution. The plan they worked out essentially required an interim software product to be obtained from
another supplier until the delayed software item would be
installed. Not surprisingly, however, the organization, in its next
draft of the contract, required the supplier of the telecommunications

system to foot the bill for this interim switch-control software product. Upon being confronted with this requirement, the supplier changed its tune once again and admitted that the senior research and development officials of the supplier "recently" decided to discontinue work on the new software product altogether.

The buyer organization was aghast. This new software product had been a major reason for choosing the particular supplier, and now the product had vanished, a classic example of vapourware. At least, however, through the mechanism of the initial contract drafts the buyer became aware of this problem relatively early on in the procurement process. The organization was then able to plan for an alternative software product to serve the same functions as the supplier's ultimately nonexistent one, and the bulk of the cost of this alternative was shifted onto the supplier's shoulders. It was not the ideal outcome for the organization, but it was a workable and relatively inexpensive solution. In this case effective contracting had achieved its intended objective, namely to bring to light supplier weaknesses as soon as possible so that the buyer could find reasonable and cost-effective solutions.

Even where the particular computer hardware or software has definitely been developed and is ready for shipment and installation, there are still good reasons from the buyer's perspective for insisting on a precise delivery date and providing for serious remedies if the date is missed. Indeed, the need to specify an exact delivery or installation date is particularly acute for some buyers in regard to certain types of technology. Consider the following true story about a hotel's acquisition of a new telecommunications system.

For a hotel the actual technical activity of cutting over to a new telecommunications system typically occurs on a weekend during which the hotel and its guests will be without phone service or have only skeletal services. Inevitably many guests will complain, a number of business people will move to other hotels, and the hotel generally will lose some business. To minimize its loss, the hotel in this particular case decided to schedule the cutover for the weekend of the year with the lowest occupancy rate, which fell in late October. The next slowest weekend was in mid-April. As well, it should be noted that the new telecommunications system would allow the hotel to lease fewer telephone lines from the telephone company, so some important cost savings would accrue as soon as the new system was installed. In short, the hotel needed the October weekend cutover, and if this date were not met the hotel would incur significant costs waiting until the next possible date in mid-April.

The hotel chain of which this particular establishment was a member had very recently implemented telecommunications systems cutovers at three other hotels with the same equipment supplier. No written agreement was signed for these other installations. For each hotel the cutover was scheduled for a particular slow weekend, and each time cutover failed to occur on the scheduled weekend, resulting in significant extra costs, expenses, and headaches to the relevant hotel. For the fourth hotel, the one with the cutover set for late October, a written contract was entered into for the first time by the hotel and the supplier, stipulating clearly the desired cutover date. More importantly, the hotel insisted on specifying in the contract what would happen if cutover did not occur during the late October weekend, namely that the supplier would be responsible for the hotel's costs and expenses associated with postponing the cutover until the following April, to a maximum of several hundred thousand dollars (essentially the likely profit margin of the supplier on the sale of the system). Sure enough, for the first time in the hotel chain's history, cutover occurred exactly as planned on the intended date.

Two lessons can be learned from this example. First, if a buyer really needs or wants a particular computer system, or a particular item of hardware or software, by a certain date, this date should be specified. The buyer might be a bank that wishes to start to offer a certain point-of-sale banking service to its customers on a particular day and requires sophisticated software to support such a product. It might be the case that changes in government regulations require companies to institute on a specific date certain changes to the way they administer payroll deductions. In such circumstances the new software reflecting the new government rules simply must be up and running by the required date — and no later. Similarly, the user may be coming to the end of a service bureau contract and simply has to have the new in-house computer system up and running by the specific date on which the service bureau agreement expires.

Or it may just be that the buyer wants to have the particular new computer installed and operating by a certain date. In all such cases the user should specify clearly in the hardware purchase or software licence agreement the date by which the relevant hardware and software is to be delivered to the user's installation site.

The second lesson learned from the hotel cutover example, as well as the earlier one involving vapourware, is that in addition to a specific delivery date, it can be extremely useful for the buyer to provide in the contract what will happen if this delivery date is not met. In short, the contract should provide an express remedy for nonperformance if the supplier is unable to deliver the specified goods on the promised date. This question of remedies is extremely important and readers are encouraged to consider carefully section B.15 which is entirely devoted to remedies and includes remedies for nondelivery.

Postponing or Cancelling Delivery

At times a buyer may wish to delay delivery. For example, the buyer may have contracted with a third party to prepare the computer room and such preparations may have fallen somewhat behind schedule. As a result, the buyer is not yet able to accommodate the supplier's delivery on the previously agreed-upon date. In anticipation of such circumstances buyers often negotiate a clause in the supply agreement that permits the buyer to postpone the scheduled delivery date unilaterally. Typically the postponement is subject to several limitations such as that the new date cannot be later than a certain number of days, usually no more than ninety, after the original date, and that the buyer can exercise this postponement right only a specified number of times (usually no more than twice).

In a similar vein, it is useful to include in the contract the requirement that the supplier give the buyer advance notice (a minimum of perhaps five or ten days) of actual delivery of the system. This will allow the buyer to schedule the availability of its personnel, to finalize any insurance issues, and to attend to any related matters necessitated by the actual delivery of the system.

It should be noted that some suppliers will allow a buyer to cancel a procurement contract at any time up to the delivery of the equipment. Of course a cancellation charge may apply depending on when actual notice of cancellation is received in relation to the scheduled delivery date. Typically there is a graduated cancellation fee based on how much advance notice is given; for example, the buyer would pay no cancellation fee if it notifies the supplier ninety days or more before the scheduled delivery date; the buyer would pay a cancellation fee of 10% of the price of the system if notice is given between eighty-nine and sixty days before the scheduled date, and so on up to a 30% cancellation fee if notice is received the day before the planned delivery date. At first glance such a provision seems quite favourable to the buyer as it does allow some flexibility on the buyer's part in terms of making sometimes difficult computer systems procurement decisions.

There is also, however, a real danger to these cancellation clauses in standard form agreements. They can be used as a marketing device with the unsure buyer. The buyer may not be really certain what kind of computer system it wants. The supplier, keen to make a sale, settles the buyer's fears by stating, rightfully, that with such a cancellation clause in the contract the buyer can order the equipment now, but because delivery is slated for, say, four months from the contract signing date the buyer has one month in which to think about the system. Within thirty days of placing the order the equipment purchase can be cancelled. Unfortunately, these specific "do something or else pay the consequences" clauses often end up costing buyers dearly. The period of grace, in this case thirty days, is often not adequate to allow the buyer to make a meaningful decision, or sometimes it lapses before the buyer gets around to making its intentions known to the supplier. In short, a cancellation clause can be useful once the buyer has an otherwise effective computer contract, and only if the buyer is able to monitor the contract closely in order to remember when the important free cancellation period expires. Such a clause, however, is not a substitute for an effective contract and a buyer should not let a supplier convince the buyer of the contrary.

Phased Delivery

It often happens with computer systems, particularly larger ones, that not all the system's components will be delivered simultaneously. For example, a buyer may be obtaining hardware, standard applications software, and custom applications software from a supplier (the case with the plastics manufacturer whose disastrous acquisition was detailed on pp. 5–10). The first two items are ready for immediate delivery while the custom software may take many months to design, develop, and implement. In such a case it might be advantageous for the buyer to have the hardware and standard software delivered early so that, for example, the buyer's information systems personnel can begin to become acquainted with the hardware and some software aspects of the new system. This might be very valuable training time if the custom software will be complex and more difficult to assimilate.

Such a phased delivery presents a real risk to the buyer if the procurement's objective is that the custom software must also be acceptable before the buyer is willing to accept and pay for the hardware and standard software. In other words, if the buyer intends to purchase a complete system, and doesn't want to keep any single component of it unless all the components function together as an integrated whole, then the buyer must be careful that its conduct with respect to the previously delivered hardware and standard software is such as to permit the buyer to return these components if the custom software is unsatisfactory. To guard against such a risk the contract should state very clearly that the early delivery of items and their use by the buyer in no way shall constitute acceptance of such products, and that such acceptance shall occur only after all parts of the system have been delivered, installed, and passed their applicable acceptance tests.

5. TRANSFER OF TITLE; RISK OF LOSS; INSURANCE

Most standard form hardware purchase agreements contain a clause setting out at what point title in the equipment passes to the purchaser, that is, when the buyer becomes the owner of the hardware. Some standard forms state that title passes to the buyer as soon as the equipment leaves the supplier's factory. These forms typically then go on to provide that the buyer is responsible for any loss or damage to the equipment after title has passed to the buyer. This essentially means that the buyer, rather than the supplier, will be responsible for arranging shipment of the equipment as well as shipping and other insurance from the time the equipment leaves the supplier's factory, or that the buyer will reimburse the supplier for these costs.

Other standard form agreements have ownership passing to the buyer only upon payment in full of the purchase price for the system, which, as discussed below (B.11, "Price and Payment Schedule"), should not occur until some time after delivery, and usually only upon the successful testing of the equipment at the buyer's premises. When the transfer of ownership occurs upon payment in full, the supplier tends to be responsible for shipment, risk of loss and damage during shipment, and shipping insurance, although these activities may also be shifted to the buyer in some standard form agreements. In any event, when title does not pass until payment in full there is usually a requirement in the contract for the buyer to maintain insurance for the equipment in favour of the supplier from the time the equipment is delivered to the buyer's premises until payment is made in full.

Several observations may be made about these various provisions respecting transfer of title, risk of loss, and insurance. In most cases buyers will not be overly concerned with exactly when title passes, largely because the period between shipment and acceptance (and hence payment in full) should not be all that long in most procurement situations. Of course, if the supplier argues that with title passing upon delivery to the shipping company the supplier also requires payment in full for the equipment, then the buyer in most such cases should resist having title pass so early. Payment for the hardware should be based on a more meaningful performance milestone, such as that the hardware — or better, the whole system — must pass an acceptance test (see section B.11, "Price and Payment Schedule"). An exception to this might be made where the supplier is a smaller entity that is not financially sound, in which case the buyer may want to take title to the equipment as soon as possible so as to preclude the secured or other creditors of the supplier making claims against the equipment once it is installed at the buyer's premises.

Risk of loss and shipping insurance generally ought to go hand in hand in that whichever party bears the risk for loss or damage to the equipment should usually be the one to procure the requisite insurance. Thus the essential question ought to be which party can obtain insurance at the least cost in any given situation (assuming that in either case the buyer will bear the cost of insurance, either directly or as a cost passed on by the supplier). It may be the supplier if it is a larger entity that procures insurance regularly and who, based on its superior knowledge of the relevant risks and procedures of common carriers, is best able to obtain cost-effective insurance. In some circumstances, however, a buyer that is a larger organization may be able to secure a better rate for shipping insurance, in which case the buyer may want to assume responsibility for the equipment from the moment it leaves the supplier's plant. Whatever the outcome on the question of transit insurance, the buyer should review early on its insurance policies for the premises that will house the equipment to ensure that these policies will adequately cover the new equipment once it is delivered to the buyer's site.

6. INSTALLATION

The agreement between the supplier and the buyer should set out clearly who is responsible for the installation of the system. Many standard form contracts are silent on this point, which generally means the buyer ends up paying extra fees when it needs assistance in installing the system. This might not be a major problem if the item being purchased is a standard application software package that is easy to load on the buyer's existing system. But when the system comprises a significant amount of hardware which requires extensive wiring and cable hookups and related activities, the standard form's silence on the issue of installation may cost the buyer several thousands of dollars in unanticipated costs.

In the case of large telecommunications systems, such as a large private branch exchange telephone system, the installation exercise may include pulling many metres of cable or even building cable conduit. This can be a very expensive exercise and, again, the buyer clearly will want to know what the supplier will charge for it. Moreover, at the bidding stage the buyer should also find out whether the supplier is going to use a third-party subcontractor for this work. If so, in addition to checking out the subcontractor to ensure its acceptability to the buyer, the buyer itself might want to get some quotes directly from contractors for this installation activity. The buyer may be willing to shoulder such responsibility if the cost saving justifies it. Of course, as was discussed under "Preparation of the Installation Site" (see above, B.3) a higher bid by the supplier for the installation work is offset by the comfort of knowing that any problems related to the installation of the system — which may include on-going operating problems as well — will be the supplier's headache and not the buyer's.

7. CONVERSION OF DATA

It is a rare standard form agreement that even mentions the issue of converting the user's data from its existing form into a form that can be used on the new system. This silence is sometimes in contrast to the supplier's sales representative's assurances that, for example, the data on the user's current computer system (which will be completely replaced by the supplier's system) can be easily transferred to the new system by means of readily available conversion programs. This is usually not an unimportant issue to the buyer, given that transferring possibly thousands of data-bearing tapes and cartridges to the new system represents a big job and a large concern to the buyer. The sales representative's oral assurances may be comforting, but they should not be left as merely spoken promises. They should be written into the agreement, together with an appropriate remedy if they prove to be inaccurate in order to ensure that the unreasonable supplier does not underestimate the magnitude of the conversion project or overestimate the capability of the conversion programs. For instance, the remedy might consist of the supplier's having to pay for the manual conversion of the data —essentially keying it into the new system — if the conversion programs extolled by the supplier in fact prove to be inadequate for the job.

Such a clause has on more than one occasion led a supplier to investigate more thoroughly the actual qualities of the relevant conversion programs, with the result that prior to signing the purchase contract the supplier admits that these conversion programs in fact will not do everything required by the user.

Such a timely revelation at least permits the buyer to better ascertain the total cost of the new system. At times the supplier may bear part of such unanticipated costs if the buyer can convince the supplier that the buyer's budget, based on the initial information about the availability of suitable conversion programs, will not allow for the acquisition, now that it is clear that significant sums must be spent on conversion, unless some price concessions on the hardware or software are made by the supplier.

8. EDUCATION AND TRAINING

Another issue that often gets short shrift in the heat of computer contract negotiations is the education and training of the buyer's personnel on the new system. This issue is usually inadequately addressed in the standard form agreements of most suppliers. Some standard form contracts don't mention education or training at all, while others say only that the user will get so many hours of education and training at no extra cost. Although some systems may not require a significant investment in education and training, most do, and the buyer is therefore well advised to consider raising the following issues with the supplier before signing the contract.

First of all what is the buyer's objective with respect to education and training? The spectrum of choices ranges from merely acquainting the buyer's personnel with the supplier's manuals (documentation) so that they can teach themselves, to giving a thorough grounding in all aspects of the operation of the system so that the buyer's people can properly operate it without the supplier's assistance. If the buyer leans towards independence from the supplier, then the buyer might consider including some or all of the following in the contract: the supplier's training staff will teach all the buyer's operations personnel, and not just one or two who would then be responsible for training the rest of the buyer's staff; the members of the supplier's training staff will be subject to the buyer's prior approval (to ensure that only experienced people are made available by the supplier); the buyer will participate in customizing the supplier's training course to meet the buyer's precise needs; the buyer will approve the schedule of training, given that some people might take training earlier than others to ensure adequate expertise at the installation site when the acceptance tests are conducted; and, if the buyer will be looking to maintain the system to any degree after the expiry of the relevant warranty period, the buyer may want to require that some of its staff be able to attend the education courses run by the supplier for its own field technicians.

This is by no means an exhaustive list of educational and training issues, and it should be tailored to meet a buyer's particular circumstances. For example, in the case of a large new telephone system installation for a major corporation or public institution, the education and training provisions of the agreement, which might be set out in a separate schedule given their comprehensiveness, might include training the switchboard operators at the supplier's site a week or two before cutover and having a good number of supplier trainers on site on the next business day following cutover — perhaps one supplier representative for every department in the buyer's organization — to assist in answering inquiries of and attending to problems encountered by the buyer's staff. The education and training regime for such an installation would be markedly different and more complex from that required for a minicomputer system to be operated by only a handful of the buyer's people. In either case the objective is to think through what the education and training needs will be and to have these needs reflected in the contract. In this way the parties will clearly understand each other's responsibilities, and the user can quantify the cost of such education and training, which will likely be lower if negotiated as part of the whole deal rather than purchased as an add-on after completion of the installation of the system.

9. ACCEPTANCE TESTING

The two most important contract control checkpoints for the buyer of technology are delivery and acceptance. Delivery, which entails ensuring that the computer arrives at the buyer's premises in a timely fashion, was discussed at length in section B.4, "Delivery Date." Acceptance, from the buyer's perspective, involves ensuring that the delivered computer operates properly and lives up to the marketing promises of the supplier before the buyer is irrevocably committed to purchasing the system. It is worth discussing in some detail because it constitutes a critical phase in the acquisition process.

Acceptance is very important in that once a buyer has "accepted" a computer system, or a particular software program or other item, the buyer usually gives up the right to return the item for a full refund if it is found to be defective. The buyer should therefore be sure that the system or item works as promised by the supplier before officially accepting it. Prior to accepting, the buyer can argue for a refund of all the monies already paid to the supplier in return for the computer system or item in question. After acceptance the buyer can usually claim only to recover any damages, quantified as a monetary amount, it might have incurred because of the poor performance or nonoperation of the equipment. Acceptance is also important because in many procurement situations a significant portion of the purchase price — usually a large last instalment — is, or least should be, payable upon the buyer's acceptance of the system (see section B.11, "Price and Payment Schedule").

Many standard form agreements stipulate that the buyer has accepted the system as soon as the buyer begins to use it, or sometimes even earlier, namely, once the supplier has installed it; the standard form agreements of some unreasonable suppliers even stipulate that acceptance is deemed to occur upon mere delivery to the buyer of the hardware or software! Having acceptance triggered by any of these events is usually unfair to the buyer in most circumstances, particularly where a larger, more expensive or complex computer system is involved. Rather than be governed by such one-sided provisions, the buyer must obtain the right to conduct a test of the system, a so-called acceptance test, once it has been delivered to the buyer but before the buyer has decided to keep the system.

The need for an acceptance test and for a clear statement in the agreement that the buyer does not accept the system until the successful passing of such test exists not only to override the often high handed provisions in standard form contracts of unreasonable suppliers. These two provisions, and especially the second, serve to rebut the presumption in Canadian law relating to the sale of goods, which provides generally that a buyer has accepted goods if the buyer acts in a way as to imply that the supplier no longer owns the goods or if the buyer keeps the goods without telling the supplier that the buyer has rejected them within a reasonable period of time.

The risk posed by this legal rule regarding the acceptance of goods is perhaps most clearly seen in the context of a phased delivery (see section B.4, "Delivery Date"). For example, if the buyer is acquiring a system comprising hardware, standard applications software (i.e., applications such as general ledger or payroll which do not require modification in order to operate in the buyer's environment), and some custom applications software (i.e., applications which will be developed, or substantially customized, specially for the buyer), the buyer may want to have the hardware and standard software delivered immediately so that its staff can begin to familiarize themselves with these aspects of the system. Consider the result if eight months later the supplier notifies the buyer that it had underestimated the difficulties inherent in producing the custom software, something that happens with disturbing regularity, and therefore it is cancelling that portion of the project, or is requesting a significantly greater payment than was initially contemplated. At the same time, the supplier announces that, notwithstanding this failure, it considers the buyer to have "accepted" the hardware and standard software and that it will simply retain the amounts already paid in respect of these two items, which amounts happen to equal the full price of the hardware and the full license fee of the standard software.

This may not be devastating news to the buyer if there are other software developers who can complete the custom software, or who have programs that serve the same purpose as the unsuccessful custom software and will operate in conjunction with the hardware and the standard software already delivered. It is just as likely, however, that a second supplier of custom software operates in a hardware environment completely different from that of the initial supplier, rendering the initial supplier's installed hardware and standard software useless to the buyer. In such a case the buyer would like to return all the hardware and standard software for a full refund. This may be difficult if the supplier can argue that by having used these items for almost a year, and by having paid for them, the buyer has effectively accepted them under the relevant sale of goods laws. To avoid having to defend against such a claim, the buyer should not have paid the full amount due in respect of the hardware and standard software until the whole system — these two items plus the custom software — had passed its acceptance test. Furthermore, the buyer should have provided in the agreement that only upon the successful passing of this acceptance test would acceptance occur for any component of the system, regardlesss of when it was delivered or how long it was used before the acceptance test. Armed with these provisions, the buyer could approach the failure of the custom software with the choice of either keeping the hardware and standard software if another supplier can be found to complete the custom software, or returning the two items for a full refund. This second course of action would be that much easier if a refund remedy were also included in the agreement (see section B.15, "Remedies").

Hardware Test

Before turning to a discussion of the various aspects of an acceptance test, it should be noted that such an acceptance test is quite a different thing from the diagnostic tests that suppliers often perform on hardware upon its delivery to the buyer. A diagnostic test generally involves the running of routine checks to ensure the hardware is properly installed and in good operating condition — it almost never entails running the hardware in conjunction with all the relevant application software for an extended period of time to ensure that the system operates in accordance with the performance criteria previously specified by the buyer. The reader is cautioned that such a diagnostic test is often called a hardware acceptance test, but is not really a test relating to acceptance at all. The agreement should state that the only result of a successful hardware acceptance is that the actual system acceptance test may commence.

Testing in all Circumstances

Suppliers will often argue, in response to a request to subject a certain computer system or item to an acceptance test procedure, that the system or item is a longstanding, proven model made with very stable technology and therefore requires no further testing; instead the buyer is invited to see the system in happy operation at any number of other sites. Buyers should resist this argument for several reasons and should insist on tests in virtually all cases. First, if there is any amount of customization to the system then, no matter how stable and proven the core of the system, the particular custom changes may be implemented incorrectly, even in a manner that negatively affects the otherwise proven components of the system. More to the point, even if the system is an unaltered standard package that has been marketed for some time, there may be manufacturing defects in the actual system delivered to the buyer, or it may have been damaged during shipment. Although there is less need for testing functionality with such a system, the requirement remains to check that the buyer is not being sold a "lemon." For example, a recent story in the press told of silicon semi-conductor chips in a particular supplier's printers that heated up and charred the paper as it was being printed; this defect in design and/or production was caught during the testing of the product at a customer's site.

Scope of the Acceptance Test

The system acceptance test should afford the buyer an opportunity to review thoroughly all aspects of the system in order to confirm that everything the supplier said about the system is true. The buyer will want to test the functionality of the system together with its performance and possibly its reliability as well. In fairness to the supplier, the testing criteria should be objectively and readily ascertainable and should be clearly enumerated in advance in the contract. Such criteria would comprise, at a minimum, the supplier's published documentation relevant to the system, any representations about the system set out in the proposal made by the supplier in response to the buyer's request for proposal, if any, and some or most of the warranties referred to below under "Warranties" (B.13). Also, the criteria might usefully include the statements describing the various features of the system set out in the supplier's marketing literature.

Perhaps the best way to document the acceptance test criteria in an orderly fashion is to set out in a schedule or appendix to the contract all the functionality and performance aspects that the buyer considers must be proven to exist in the system before accepting ownership. For example, if the computer is an on-line system that must be able to respond to the buyer's clients within a specific and short period of time, such as an automated bank teller machine, then the test criteria should include certain response times that the system would have to meet during the test. If the particular equipment must be able to operate in conjunction with another computer system of the buyer, the acceptance test criteria would include the ability of the new system or equipment to exchange data in an effective manner with such other system. In this regard, the reader is referred to section B.13, "Warranties," which sets out some other aspects of the functionality or performance of the system, such as its ability to be expanded, which could also be made part of the acceptance test criteria. That is, the acceptance test criteria could incorporate, by a cross reference in the contract, the promises set out by the supplier in the contract's warranties provisions such that proving that the system had these capabilities during the period of the acceptance test would be a prerequisite to the successful passage of this test.

The acceptance test criteria may be very short, or they may be quite lengthy if the buyer has high expectations for the new system. In any case, the preparation of acceptance test criteria merits significant attention, a great deal of care, and, on occasion, substantial creative thinking. Compiling a list of acceptance test criteria will require reducing to writing all the qualities of the system extolled by the supplier during the marketing phase of the acquisition process; the test itself will show whether they pan out. If the supplier has made certain representations or warranties about the system, and the buyer's decision to purchase is based wholly or even partly on the strength of these statements or promises, the buyer must ensure that they are included in the acceptance test criteria or elsewhere in the agreement (see B.26, "Entire agreement"), because if they are merely oral promises and not expressly written down within the four corners of the contract, they cannot be relied upon with any certainty.

As noted above, however brief or extensive the acceptance test criteria, they should in all cases be objectively ascertainable, or based on specific factors that can be measured easily. A phrase such as "the system must operate to the satisfaction of the user," or any similar vaguely and broadly defined subjective criteria is not a good acceptance test benchmark. In fact, it is downright dangerous from the perspective of both parties because it signifies that neither the buyer nor the supplier has given much serious thought to what the system must be able to accomplish for it to be acceptable to the buyer. Buyers sometimes prefer such subjective criteria in the belief, probably mistaken in most cases, that such criteria will permit the buyer to remain in control of the acquisition process. It is, however, just as unreasonable for a buyer to insist on such subjective test criteria as it is for a supplier to refuse an acceptance test based on reasonable objective criteria.

Suppliers will often stipulate that a system will work "substantially" in accordance with the relevant criteria, or in accordance with the criteria "in all material respects." These qualifiers of "substantially" and "in all material respects" are demanded by suppliers so that they do not fail acceptance tests for extremely minor problems in the system. Where a buyer is nervous about the inclusion of such qualifying phrases, rather than spend a lot of time negotiating their removal, it is a better idea to concentrate on having the supplier agree with the buyer as to what specific features of the system must work in a particular way for the system to be considered to be working "substantially" in accordance with the acceptance test criteria. In short, the more specifically the contract deals with these issues, the less likely it is that either party will be disappointed upon implementation of the system.

In some circumstances there may be a need for multiple tests. Consider the buyer who has ordered several custom software programs, each of which has a separate function but all of which must ultimately operate together. In such a case there might be a two-part acceptance test. First, each program is tested separately, and only when all programs are found to be acceptable individually are they tested together as one integrated system. This dual-phase approach to testing can greatly benefit the buyer in that additional time and opportunity are provided in which the buyer can become familiar with the programs and therefore conduct a more meaningful acceptance test.

Testing Reliability

Along with functionality and performance, the buyer may want to test a system's reliability, especially in a situation where the system will be required to be up and running virtually continuously. For example, a buyer that is a bank's information systems division may have contracted with the bank's retail services division to provide automated teller machine service on the basis that the service will be unavailable no more than 3% of the time during any one-month period. Accordingly, the buyer will require that the supplier's system achieve similar uptime performance before it accepts the system.

This can be done by providing in the contract that the system, during perhaps a three-month acceptance test, must achieve an "effective level of performance" of 97% during each of the last two months, with effective level of performance being calculated as follows:

$$\frac{\text{effective level}}{\text{of performance}} = \frac{\text{operational use time} - \text{system failure time}}{\text{operational use time}}$$

where "operational use time" is the time that the system is scheduled for operation, and "system failure time" is the time during which the system fails to perform in accordance with the acceptance test performance criteria (or any other predetermined standard).

A buyer intending to include such a reliability criterion in its acceptance testing protocol ought to calculate what, for example in this case, 3% downtime over a month means. If the automated teller system is scheduled to operate twenty-four hours a day (on a thirty-day month), a 97% effective level of performance would allow the system to be inoperable for about twenty-two hours each month. In a case where the system is required for twenty hours per day, the same effective level of performance would allow for eighteen hours of downtime per month. Is the benchmark aimed at too onerous, or not stringent enough? Perhaps the bank needs an effective level of performance closer to 99%. Each buyer must carefully consider what is appropriate under the circumstances.

The buyer may wish to confine system failure time to major conditions of inoperability, rather than including in the calculation every outage, however minor. A good idea here is to define failures in terms of outputs or uses of the system, such as the inability of the system to run a certain day-end calculation or print a particular report. Again, the general goal of keeping acceptance test criteria clear and objectively ascertainable ought to be kept in mind.

Another aspect of reliability is the duration of any single period of downtime. The buyer may wish to stipulate that no single major outage can exceed a specified period of time, say five hours. This is intended to test the so-called recoverability of the system. Again, the definition of "major outage" should be directly related to some functional characteristic of the system so that both parties can judge easily and clearly whether this aspect of the acceptance test is passed.

Duration of the Acceptance Test

An acceptance test is typically run for a predetermined period of time, usually anywhere from thirty to ninety days, though shorter and longer periods are also quite common. The length of the test should be dictated in large part by the degree of complexity of the system being acquired. Generally speaking, the larger and more complicated the computer, the longer the test ought to be to afford the buyer a full opportunity to compare actual performance to the acceptance test criteria. The duration of the test may also be contingent upon any particular needs of the system or the buyer. For example, if the system is going to be used to process the buyer's end-of-quarter financial statements, it would be useful to stipulate that the acceptance test period shall include at least one quarter end; this might be only a month end for a different system that also has financial accounting applications.

When should the test occur? Should it be held before or after the buyer commences to use the system in a live, operational production mode? Many buyers feel that a system cannot be rigorously tested unless it is operated in an actual setting, processing real data. The counter argument to this is that if there are problems with the system, actual data may be destroyed or a business's day-to-day operations negatively affected, perhaps even completely disrupted. Some of these dangers can be avoided by having a test run before going live with the system. Some buyers and suppliers have found it useful to work out an acceptance test plan together, at the contract negotiation stage, and even to devise some test data in order to simulate as closely as possible live conditions in an acceptance test. It is, however, up to the buyer in each case to ensure that the testing regime established is feasible as well as meaningful.

The duration of the test may be, and quite often is, extended past the scheduled period. This typically happens when certain deficiencies or problems become apparent during the test, but they are not of such magnitude as to lead the buyer to refuse the system; rather, the buyer agrees to extend the test period to allow the supplier some time to correct the errors. This raises the extremely important question of remedies: what rights ought a buyer to have if the system does not pass its acceptance test? A whole section (B.15) is devoted to remedies for poor performance or nonperformance.

Who ought to judge whether an acceptance test has been successfully passed? In the absence of a specific provision dealing with this question (as is the case when, for example, the parties stipulate that an arbitrator will decide whether a system has passed its test), it may be said that the buyer is the judge so long as it acts reasonably. In other words, a buyer who thinks the system does not work as it should, will likely put off accepting the system and, equally importantly, will not make the required (and usually last) instalment payment for the system which is due on acceptance (see section B.11, "Price and Payment Schedule," as to the usefulness of this last instalment payment).

Of course if the supplier disagrees with the buyer's assessment of whether the acceptance test has been passed, the supplier can take the buyer to court for breach of contract on account of its failure to pay. Most suppliers, however, do not take this step, preferring to try to solve whatever problems the buyer may have with the system. At some point, though, if the supplier still has not been paid and it believes the buyer's objections to the system are unreasonable, then the two parties may indeed have a rendezvous in the courtroom.

If a supplier and a buyer have a serious falling out about the ability of a system to pass its acceptance test, and they end up commencing legal proceedings, they will have chosen a dispute resolution mechanism that can be very expensive and slow to yield results (a case can easily take two years to get to court in a large Canadian city). Once in court, the parties may be facing a judge who has no expertise whatsoever in computer matters. For these reasons, parties to a computer contract containing an acceptance test should consider providing that any dispute as to whether the acceptance test has been passed is to be submitted to a predetermined person or institution for arbitration, with this arbitrator determining who is right and wrong and in what proportion. The advantages (and disadvantages) of using an arbitrator in such circumstances, or for other purposes with respect to computer contracts, are discussed at length below in section B.22, "Arbitration."

Deemed Acceptance

A supplier will often request that the acceptance test clause of the agreement contain the provision that if the supplier has not heard from the buyer about any deficiencies with the system during the acceptance test period, then upon the expiry of this period the buyer will be deemed to have accepted the system. Buyers should be wary of such a provision. Ideally, as discussed above, a buyer will only have accepted a computer system after taking some positive act which signifies that the buyer has tested the system and found it acceptable; for example, signing a certificate which states that the system has passed the acceptance test provided for in the relevant agreement. If, however, a buyer agrees to such a deemed acceptance clause — which may be the *quid pro quo* for securing a comprehensive acceptance test provision — the buyer should be extremely vigilant during the test period, the buyer should not forget to bring deficiencies with the system to the supplier's attention during the test, and the buyer should notify the supplier that the acceptance test will not be passed unless the problems are cleared up to the buyer's satisfaction before the acceptance test period expires. And in turn any approval of such repairs implemented by the supplier should equally be subject to the buyer's written acceptance.

An Acceptance Test Case Study

In order to illustrate the issues discussed above concerning acceptance testing it is worth considering the following actual computer acquisition experience that occurred several years ago. In this case a public institution in Ontario was acquiring a local area network, often called a LAN, comprised of two components, namely, a series of work stations (personal computers and word processors) and a sophisticated communications network which was to link the work stations together. The buyer was quite confident that the supplier's work stations could operate the particular application software intended for use on the system. But what was very much in doubt was whether the communications link would work at all. This was a key requirement for the buyer. It had several offices in different geographic locations and the prime objective in the acquisition was to permit, for example, one office to send a document that was stored on one of its work stations to a work station at a different location. While the work-station technology had been around for several years and had a proven track record, the communications link was a brand new product.

The buyer had grave misgivings about the supplier's ability to install a complete system that would work, but because of the constraints of government purchasing, the buyer in this case was not free to choose another supplier. The buyer therefore resolved to make sure that if the system did not work, the failure and any remedial action would be squarely the responsibility of the supplier. To this end the buyer insisted on a two-phase acceptance test as part of the contract. First, each individual work station would be tested as to its functionality. As expected, every work station passed this test. The second phase was to test the communications link with an average data load on the system. Everyone knew this would be the tough test, and sure enough the system as delivered could not pass this second phase. To arrive at the main performance criteria for the second part of the test, the buyer's technical people set out very clearly what the communications link should be able to accomplish (i.e, one work station at 50% data storage capacity must be able to transmit a document of a specified length to another machine within a specified number of minutes). The buyer provided in the contract that if the acceptance test was not passed, the buyer would have the right to return all the equipment and receive a full refund — a very strong remedy indeed.

The supplier's initial reaction to the performance criteria was quite revealing. The supplier's technical representatives admitted that they had not conducted such tests themselves and hence simply did not know precisely what the communications portion of the system was capable of, notwithstanding that the supplier's marketing proposal was quite confident that the networking features of the system constituted proven technology and could meet the buyer's needs. This response only served to reinforce the need for the acceptance test. In the end, the supplier's technical personnel conducted a whole new battery of tests on the system even before the procurement agreement was signed so that they could truly operationalize, by reference to specific performance parameters, what had been merely bold, but technically unfounded, assertions in the supplier's initial marketing document.

As it turned out, the supplier's engineers also had greatly overestimated the ability of the particular communications product delivered to the buyer. The supplier manufactured two different models of the communications system, one much more powerful than the other. The supplier had initially advised the buyer to choose the less powerful one (which was also cheaper by tens of thousands of dollars and hence was a factor in submitting a price-competitive bid). In fact, this less powerful (and less expensive) communications link was wholly inadequate and miserably failed the acceptance test. Fortunately, the computer agreement permitted the buyer to terminate the agreement at this point. With this leverage, the buyer succeeded in having the supplier install the much more expensive network communications product at absolutely no extra cost to the buyer. The supplier also agreed to stay on the job for several months ironing out problems, all at no charge to the buyer because it was made very clear that the supplier would be solely responsible for any such problems. In short, through effective contracting and a strong acceptance test provision coupled with a powerful remedy, the buyer ended up with a Cadillac of a local area network even though it paid for only a Chevy.

10. LICENCE OF SOFTWARE

Software is usually marketed to end-users, as already stated, pursuant to a licence. Under the licence, ownership of the copy of the software program remains with the software developer; the user is given the right only to use the software subject to certain restrictions. These restrictions generally include the following: the user may use the software to process only its own data (and not the data of third parties); the software may be used only on a single CPU which is located at the premises of the user; the user cannot copy the software nor disclose or allow access to it by any third party; nor can the user transfer physical possession of the software to any third party.

These restrictions in favour of the software developer are generally reasonable and their rationale is readily apparent. The software developer is attempting to protect its market for an extremely valuable asset, one that may be easily undermined if the software developer is not careful. This is particularly the case with unauthorized copying of the supplier's software, but all the restrictions imposed by the supplier have the same objective, which is to allow the software developer to earn an economic return on its investment in research and development. A software developer will simply not countenance the wholesale removal of the licence and related protective provisions in its standard form agreement, and justifiably so. This is not to say, however, that users should not suggest modifications to the supplier's conditions if they are overly restrictive or cumbersome, provided the user can suggest a creative alternative that both meets the needs of the user and affords the supplier adequate protection. Several such alternatives are suggested in the following discussion.

Restrictions on Use

Most standard form license agreements provide that the user can use the software to process only the user's own internal data. By this restriction, the software developer is attempting to protect its commercial market. If the software developer did not insist on such a restriction the user could establish itself, to use an extreme example, as a service bureau to process the data of many other companies, while the software developer would receive no financial return from this increased exploitation of its product. Of course, software developers regularly permit service bureaus to use their software, but the licence fee paid by a service bureau is far greater than the usual one-time fee paid by the typical corporate user; in addition, the service bureau often remits to the software developer a percentage of its fees generated by the software developer's program.

While it is reasonable for a software supplier to restrict the use made of its program by a licensed user, a user may want to consider whether certain contractual restrictions proposed by the supplier are not too onerous, and whether alternative safeguards exist which might adequately protect the software developer but at the same time permit the user to exercise greater flexibility.

For example, for perhaps a slightly larger licence fee the user may be able to obtain the right to process not only its own data but the data of its present and future subsidiaries and affiliates as well. This is a particularly useful arrangement where a group of companies has designated one affiliate to supply computing services for all the others in the group. Of course such an enlargement of the use parameter ought to be accompanied by a clear delineation of what entities will qualify as subsidiaries and affiliates. A standard practice is to use the definition of subsidiary and affiliate found in many business corporation statutes. Such a statutory definition, however, must always be reviewed in light of the actual (and potential) make-up of the corporate group to which the user belongs, because it may not include, for example, certain companies that are related only indirectly to the user. In some cases it may be necessary to develop a customized definition of "affiliate" in order to capture clearly all entities in the user's group.

Another restriction on use found in many supplier standard form agreements requires the user to operate the software program on only one specified CPU located at the user's premises. This restriction might have made sense, or at least have been workable, years ago when most software was run on a mainframe computer and access to this mainframe was achieved by a single keyboard and video display terminal. Today's computer networking technology permits some software programs run on a mainframe, or "server" computer, to be "down loaded," or transferred, to several minicomputers or microcomputers simultaneously, or merely to be accessed by several terminals all at once. In many cases, therefore, this restriction to a single CPU is a technical anachronism, but it is still found in many standard form licence agreements. Users confronted with this single CPU restriction should strongly resist it, or at least require that if the designated CPU is temporarily inoperable then the user shall be entitled to operate the software on another CPU (at the user's regular site or some other location) on an interim basis until the original CPU is back in operation.

As an alternative to the single CPU restriction many users are turning to a "site licence" or even the "institution licence." Under a site licence a software supplier permits the licensee to use the particular program on any hardware located at designated premises of the user. The software developer then prices the fee for a site licence on the basis of what equipment would be making use of the program at the specific site. An institution licence grants the user the right to use a program on any hardware located on all the geographically diverse premises of the user. Again, the software developer analyses the potential use the organization will make of the program in order to determine an appropriate licence fee. The intent of site and institutional licences is to assure the software developer a suitable rate of return on its product while granting the user greater administrative and operational flexibility. In the past few years several software developers have announced formal site licence programs for larger institutional and corporate users, but there is much to be gained from such an arrangement by even smaller businesses, and they should not hesitate to explore the possibility of obtaining a site or institutional licence when acquiring computer programs.

Site or institution licences must be carefully drafted so that it is clear how may copies of a program the user may make and how many of its personnel, or its computer terminals, may have access to the software concurrently, if any of these factors is a relevant limitation. These can be tricky issues when dealing with networked configurations of personal computers, such as local area networks. The particular "site" or "institution" must also be specified with precision in order to avoid potential disputes between the user and the software developer; for example, an institution licence for personal computer software should address whether employees of the user may use authorized copies of the software at home to work on data related to the user.

Another usual restriction on licensed software relates to whether the licensee will want to modify the software itself rather than rely solely on the supplier to make any required modifications. Many users insist on having the right to make their own modifications because they have particular, unique needs not adequately addressed in the standard version of the software. These users often have (or at least believe they have) the requisite in-house expertise to make changes to the software in an effective and efficient manner. A user who wants this right should ensure that it is clearly articulated in the license agreement. To make modifications the user will likely require access to the source code of the software program and may need other materials from the supplier not generally distributed to software licensees. The user should also realize that upon making any modifications to the software, the supplier's duty to provide software support for the program may cease, with the result that the user is on its own in respect of on-going software maintenance. A further issue that should be clarified if the user makes its own modifications is who owns these modifications? As discussed more fully in section C.4, "Software Development," this type of ownership question can give rise to significant dispute if not dealt with properly in the contract.

Restrictions on Transfer

In an effort to further protect its potential market, virtually every software developer prohibits users from transferring the licensed copy of the developer's software to another user, with the exception that some developers of personal computer software allow their software to be transferred, provided the original user transfers a single copy of the software and then destroys all other copies of the software (such as back-up or archival copies that may have been made by the original user). Again the concern of the developer can be seen very quickly. If it licensed a certain software program to one user for, say, $20,000 on the basis that it would be used to process, say, twenty thousand transactions a week, the developer would not want the software transferred to another user who might be processing fifty thousand transactions, inasmuch as the developer might have charged this latter user $50,000 for the same software.

Some restrictions on transfer, however, may be unreasonable, and users are often successful in getting suppliers to carve out exceptions for these transfers. For example, a transfer of the software licence to an affiliate within the same corporate group as the original user is regularly allowed, particularly if the initial scope of use and related pricing was also expanded to permit the initial user to process not only its own data but also that of its subsidiaries and affiliates. As well, in some cases an assignment of the operating system program for an item of hardware is permitted by a supplier, but then only when accompanied by a resale of the underlying hardware. For further discussion on this point see section B.24, "Assignment."

If a user does not obtain the right to transfer the software then it must always keep in mind that it does not have the right to allow another entity to use the software. Users often first come to learn of this important rule when they attempt to sell to a third party some computer equipment and related software, in the course of selling the business division that uses these items. If such a sale involves a sale of assets (rather than the sale of the shares of the user), then the user will likely be able to sell the computer hardware, provided the user owns it outright and no leasing or other finance company (such as the user's bank) has a legal interest in it. The software running on the hardware, however, is not owned by the user and can therefore only be transferred to the prospective purchaser if the user has the right to assign its original licence. Many users (and potential purchasers of their assets) are dismayed when they realize the financial implications of not being able to transfer software, and they invariably regret that they did not have the foresight to address the assignment issue at the time they negotiated the original software licence agreement.

Restrictions on Copying

A software supplier will invariably prohibit the user in the software licence agreement from making multiple copies of the program. The rationale for this restriction is twofold. First, the supplier wants to preclude an erosion of its market by a user's making and installing copies of the program on several of its machines, all for a single licence fee. If the user's volume of transactions or operational structure requires additional copies of the program, the supplier will want the user to pay on that basis. Many software developers will grant price discounts for multiple copies. There are also software developers, as noted above, who will permit a user to make, for an appropriate fee, an unlimited number of copies of a program, while restricting their use to a particular installation site or institution.

Another reason for the restrictions on copying is to control the number of copies of the supplier's program in circulation. The more copies there are in circulation, the greater the possibility that the program will be used by an unauthorized third party who has not signed a licence or any other kind of protective agreement with the supplier. Each unauthorized copy of a software program in use represents a financial loss to the developer. This activity, commonly known as "piracy" when it happens on a major scale, is estimated to cost software developers many millions of dollars annually. By making software available only pursuant to a licence, software developers are best able to monitor and control copying by users.

Software developers have been aided in this endeavour by the amendments to Canada's Copyright Act which came into force in 1988 and which, among other things, expressly extended the protection of copyright law to computer programs. As a result of these amendments, anyone convicted of pirating software is liable for a fine of up to $1 million, as well as for a jail term of up to five years. It should be noted, however, that even before the Copyright Act was amended it was generally considered illegal in Canada to make unauthorized copies of another person's computer program. Under the old copyright statute many judges were willing to grant protection against the copying of source code on the basis that it was a literary work, and also generally against the copying of object code, or even a computer program embedded in a silicon chip, on the basis that these latter two software formats are translations or adaptations of the literary work represented by the source code. As well, government authorities had prosecuted blatant unauthorized copiers even under the general criminal law offence of fraud.

It should be noted, however, that the new Copyright Act contains an exception to the rule against copying by allowing a person who *owns* a copy of a software program to make one "back-up copy" of it. Practically speaking, however, this is a very limited right because, as noted above, software developers hardly ever sell copies of software. Thus software suppliers are different from, for example, book publishers who actually sell copies of their books. A book publisher cannot restrict, under copyright law, the resale of a book or its use or disclosure; all the publisher has a right to prohibit is the copying of the book (which right survives the sale of the copy).

Accordingly, it is important for a user to insist in the contract that, as part of its licence to use the software, it can make one back-up copy of the software. Indeed, many standard form contracts permit users to keep such a back-up copy so that if the copy in actual use is destroyed or lost because of any computer malfunction or operator error, the user can resume operations with its back-up copy. Users should not abuse their right to make a back-up copy. A back-up copy is just that, one extra copy to be kept in reserve and not utilized unless and until the main copy becomes unusable. The right to make a back-up copy under a licence agreement does not permit a user to make multiple copies, nor does it allow the user to use the single back-up copy simultaneously with the original copy on another machine to process additional data. Such a practice amounts to obtaining two copies of a program for a single licence fee and likely would constitute a case of unauthorized copying in contravention of the user's software licence agreement as well as the Copyright Act.

This discussion on the prohibitions against unauthorized copying of computer software is not intended to alarm users, but it is hoped it will alert users to the serious consequences of unauthorized copying. A software developer's software is, perhaps after its personnel, its most valuable asset. For anyone to abuse this asset is to inflict serious harm on the software developer. Many users cause such harm seemingly innocently by, for example, not realizing that when they license one copy of a certain application program for their personal computer users they cannot simply take the paid-for copy and reproduce it for additional users at no extra charge. But this kind of activity occurs all too frequently. It should not, and software developers are increasingly active in ensuring that it does not happen inadvertently or in any other manner.

It is worth considering several actual examples of "innocent" and less than innocent contraventions of software developers' rights regarding the copying prohibition. To start with a blatant case of conscious corporate illegality, there was a report a few years ago of a company that had ordered a microcomputer software program from the software's creator. This particular software developer had a marketing program whereby the prospective customer could try the software for thirty days and if not satisfied could return it for a full refund. It turned out that this particular user had no intention of legally retaining the software, but wanted to make illegal copies of it. This intent came to light because the user, when it returned the software, left an inter-office memo paperclipped to the floppy diskette containing the software. The memo was a routing notice to the various potential users of the software program within the user's company; it read: "Have copy of book and disk. It can be sent back." When the software developer saw this "smoking gun" memo attached to its returned software it quickly brought a claim against the user for copyright infringement.

This kind of unauthorized software copying has been dubbed "noncommercial infringement," because the copies are made for internal use at the corporation, whereas with software piracy copies are made for resale to third parties. It has resulted in a number of legal proceedings over the past few years, particularly in the United States. Lotus Corporation, the maker of the popular 1-2-3 spreadsheet software, has been particularly active in taking action against corporations that engage in noncommercial infringement; other large software developers (such as Ashton-Tate) and small ones as well have also launched law suits against illegal copying of software by corporate and other institutional users. In the last few years Lotus has brought a copyright infringement suit against a company that made unauthorized copies of the 1-2-3 diskette and manual and distributed them to thirteen branch offices across the United States; sued a health-care company for illegally making copies of 1-2-3 for its affiliated hospitals and nursing homes; and sued another company for distributing unauthorized copies of 1-2-3 to its employees. In all these cases the company settled the embarrassing litigation out of court upon payment to Lotus of a sum of money as damages for the unauthorized copying.

The Software Protection Association (SPA), an industry group made up of some seven hundred developers of software, has also been very active in bringing lawsuits against organizations guilty of noncommercial infringement. The following example illustrates how the SPA operates. In the fall of 1990 a former employee of a construction engineering firm tipped off the SPA that this company was making and using illegal copies of software. The SPA, together with local law-enforcement authorities, conducted a raid of the company's premises and performed an audit of the software in use on its personal computers. These actions, which were part of a lawsuit commenced by the SPA on behalf of several of its members, resulted in a settlement in which the guilty organization agreed to pay $300,000, to destroy all previously made illegal copies, not to make further illegal copies, to institute formal internal copy-control procedures at all its offices, and to permit the SPA to conduct annual software audits for two years. By the spring of 1991 the SPA had brought 60 such lawsuits in the United States alone (and had also conducted some 40 software audits in lieu of bringing lawsuits), and had been involved in similar proceedings elsewhere in the world. Similar cases may be forthcoming in Canada with the establishment, in the fall of 1990, of the Canadian Association Against Software Theft (CAAST), a group similar to the SPA.

There are several steps an institution can take to lessen the likelihood of its being sued for copyright infringement and breach of software licence. The organization can educate its computer users about the copyright law and licence restrictions that prohibit the unauthorized copying of software. This education could start with a bulletin or memo being circulated at regular intervals and perhaps by inserting a similar document in the organization's administrative operations manual if such exists. A seminar with senior managers on the subject from time to time also often proves useful. The message to be conveyed by all these means of communication is that the company simply will not condone the illegal copying of software, and any employee wishing to make a back-up copy, or any other copy if they think such copy is permitted by the relevant licence agreement (e.g., under a site licence) must first check with a designated manager. A company should also consider having its information systems people sign nondisclosure agreements (as discussed further in Section C.6, "Proprietary Rights Protection") in order to better protect not only the company's own confidential materials, such as software developed by such employees, but the proprietary rights of software suppliers as well.

For such a policy to be effective the organization must be prepared to enforce it and to take appropriate steps immediately upon learning of any unauthorized software copying activities. Having the policy on paper without enforcing it could be worse than having no written policy at all because it might lead to the conclusion that the written policy was just a smokescreen.

The following American case illustrates well the need to take suitable measures quickly against employees who participate in illegal software copying.

Several years ago a software developer was unable to get full compensation from a person who had been making illegal copies of the software developer's product while an employee of a certain company. As a result, the software developer tried to impose liability on the employer company who had originally licensed the software, mainly on the basis that an employer is generally responsible for the acts of its employees. The judge dismissed the software developer's claim against the company, concluding that the company, under its licence agreement with the software developer, was only required to take reasonably diligent measures to protect the software; that the company did take reasonable steps to supervise the employee's work; that the company uncovered the employee's irregular conduct in a reasonable and timely way; and that the company had acted with reasonable speed and thoroughness to minimize the damage caused by the employee. The point of this case is that for an organization to be in the clear in the event of an employee's unauthorized copying, it is not enough that the organization simply not encourage or participate in the illegal act; nor can an employer merely turn a blind eye to the problem. Rather, employers must take active and effective measures to deal with the problem and try to ensure it does not recur.

Not all misuse of software by corporations or their employees is as blatantly reprehensible as some of the cases noted above. Many computer users, especially in larger organizations, have never seen a licence agreement because they aren't involved in the acquisition of computer resources. They simply do not know that making several copies of a program, for example, the personal computer spreadsheet program licensed by their employer, is a violation of the law and a breach of their employer's licence agreement. There is therefore a need for employers to educate their employees about the rights of software developers and suppliers, as noted above. As well, there are situations where organizations can be said to be almost innocently encouraging illegal software copying by their employees or other members. For example, consider a post-secondary educational institution that, for a particular business course, assigns throughout the term homework requiring the student to work at home on several different spreadsheet programs so that the student becomes familiar with all of them. Each program costs several hundred dollars, so virtually no student will be able to afford to do his or her homework legally. The inevitable result is massive illegal copying of the educational institution's one legal copy of each particular program. In an actual situation involving this issue, the institution decided to reduce the number of programs on the course curriculum as well as to obtain educational volume discounts for multiple copies of certain programs so that students would not be encouraged to break the law in order to do their homework.

A somewhat similar problem can arise when companies institute employee personal computer purchase plans. These programs are becoming increasingly popular. Under such a program an organization in the process of buying a relatively large number of personal computers for its corporate use strikes a deal with the supplier whereby, for the same low, and usually volume-discounted, price, the buyer can purchase personal computers for resale to its employees. The buyer organization may also assist its employees' purchases with low-interest employee loans. There are multiple benefits in such a program. The organization gets a better price on all its purchases because the employee purchases count towards the buyer's volume discount calculation. The employee benefits by being able to purchase a personal computer at a very attractive price. Another benefit to the organization is that the employee can now be more productive by being able to work on company business at home in the evenings on a computer similar to the one at the office. This raises several potential illegal copying problems. First, the computer program used by the employee at work may be subject to a use restriction that does not allow it to be used in the employee's home unless the organization buys additional licence rights. More importantly, there may well be a temptation for unsophisticated or downright unscrupulous employees to make illegal copies of the suppliers' programs to keep at home for the personal use of the employee.

This problem was addressed recently in an actual situation by having the employees agree, in their purchase agreement with the organization, not to use the personal computers they were buying to make illegal copies, and indeed not to operate on these machines any copies that had been made illegally. Of course, in this and similar situations, user organizations ought to be educating their employees, by means of employee memos and internal seminars, about the illegality of making unauthorized copies of software, as noted above. The essential point to be conveyed to employees is that illegal copying is akin to theft, not unlike if the employee went into a computer store and walked out with a personal computer under his or her coat without paying for it. Of course many people don't view the two activities as being identical, just as many people who would never dream of shoplifting a record album have no pangs of conscience about taping a newly purchased record album for a friend for use on the friend's cassette player. In point of fact, the two activities, in terms of law, morality, and economics (the record company is being deprived of a sale), are quite similar and equally objectionable. This is the message that organizations licensed to use software must impress upon their employees.

There are certain activities that, although they may not violate copyright law, may be contrary to the software licence agreement under which the particular computer programs are made available to the user. For example, in a recent situation a user had licensed several copies of a program that were "copy-protected." This means that the programs contained a mechanical device that made it physically impossible to make copies of them. There was, however, a relatively simple way to remove this copy protection and the user wondered whether doing so posed a problem under copyright law. While it could be argued that merely removing the copy-protect devices did not contravene copyright law, because, strictly speaking, it would not have amounted to copying the program (though it may have amounted to contributory infringement), the licence agreement made it very clear that the user was not to remove the copy-protect devices. In short, the proposed activity would have constituted a breach of the user's contract with the supplier. The short lesson of this case is one that has been repeated in this volume several times now: in order to stay out of trouble users simply must read and understand the computer contracts they sign with suppliers.

Restrictions on Disclosure

A supplier will invariably insist that neither the user nor its employees or consultants permit any one else to see or have access to a licensed software program. The program, given its significant value to the software developer, typically constitutes an important trade secret of the supplier and must be kept confidential if the supplier hopes to preserve any exclusive ownership claim to it. The copyright protection discussed above generally protects only against unauthorized copying and does not extend to the concepts and ideas embodied in the software. These may on occasion be protected by obtaining a patent for the software, but this can be a very expensive and difficult process. Accordingly, if a software developer wants to keep its competitors out of its products so that they don't copy the supplier's novel research and development efforts, it generally has to rely on being able to argue that the particular software constitutes one of its trade secrets. And, as noted above, maintaining trade secret protection requires the supplier to keep the software confidential, which in turn results in the supplier's requiring the user and its employees and consultants to keep the software confidential. The restriction on disclosure may go as far as to prohibit the user from decompiling, disassembling, or in any way reverse engineering the object code of the software, that is, taking apart the software to see what makes it tick.

A restriction against disclosure, provided it is clearly articulated and does not attempt to encompass an overly broad scope of protection, is reasonable and ought to be respected by the user. With respect to the supplier's restrictions on both copying and disclosure, the user should not only be willing to agree to contract provisions which protect the legitimate business interests of the supplier, the user should also consider taking steps to carry out its contractual obligations to the supplier regarding these restrictions by having its employees enter into written agreements with the user. Such agreements are discussed in some detail in section C.6, "Proprietary Rights Protection — Employees." At this point what should be noted is that such an agreement, when signed by the user's employees, not only protects the software developer, but also allows the user to guard against the unscrupulous employee who might have designs to sell some illegal copies of the supplier's software to the supplier's competitors.

Such industrial espionage is not new, and if it happens it is useful for the employer to have an agreement in place with which to pursue the irresponsible employee and in so doing help discharge the employer's obligations to the software developer.

11. PRICE AND PAYMENT SCHEDULE

Price

Mention has already been made of the importance of stipulating very clearly in the contract the per unit price and cost of each item (see B.1, "Description of Hardware and Software," and A.2 under "Putting the Whole Deal in Writing"). Once the buyer is comfortable about the actual amounts stated in the contract, a further step might be taken to ensure that these costs will not be increased unilaterally on the supplier's part as the acquisition proceeds. The contract could specify, for instance, that except for the amounts, fees, and expenses expressly stated in the contract, the buyer will not be billed for or have any obligation to pay other amounts. Such a provision, as mentioned previously, will cause the supplier to divulge all potential costs so that the buyer does not encounter financial surprises later in the procurement process, and especially after the buyer is locked-in and unable to jettison the supplier for a "mere" cost overrun. Several other aspects of pricing are also worthy of mention.

Price Protection

In certain circumstances it is appropriate to address the question of price protection in the agreement. Obviously if the item is being acquired immediately as a one-time, one-of-a-kind purchase from a supplier with whom the buyer does little business, then the issue of price protection may be rather unimportant. By contrast, if the order is placed for delivery, say, ten months from the order date, then the user may want to have a provision in the agreement that requires the supplier to pass on to the buyer the benefit of any price reduction in the item generally (i.e., the buyer will pay the lower of the amount set out in the agreement or the list price, including discounts, prevailing for the item at the time of delivery). Many hardware prices tend to fall over time, and such a clause would allow the purchaser to take advantage of any such price decrease that may occur prior to the buyer's taking delivery of the item.

Price protection can also relate to future purchases. Suppose a large organization is in the process of implementing a new telecommunications system in five of its offices. After receiving quotes on what it would cost to upgrade all five offices, it decides that it can only afford to convert three offices now, but may well get to the other two offices within the next couple of years. In such a case the buyer should negotiate with the supplier to protect the price for the equipment slated to go into the two later offices, by obtaining a firm option on the conversion of these offices at specific prices (or lower discounted future prices, as noted in the previous paragraph) over, say, the next two years. After this period the buyer could still, of course, request the supplier to upgrade the remaining two offices, but the prices would not then be fixed in advance. An issue similar to price protection relates to trade-in credits for items purchased previously; this issue is dealt with in section B.21, "Upgrades and Trade-in Credits."

Volume Discounts

Where a buyer will be making several purchases from the same supplier over time it may be worth negotiating a volume discount policy so that the relative price charged the buyer will improve with the amount purchased. From the buyer's perspective, a volume discount policy can mean substantial financial savings. Many suppliers are receptive to volume discount arrangements because they see it as a means of retaining customer loyalty and fostering repeat sales.

A volume discount is generally based on one of two criteria: the number of units purchased of a particular item, or the aggregate dollar value of all purchases. Most discounts tend to be time sensitive, that is, the discount applies to a volume level, whether expressed in units or dollars, achieved within a definite period of time, perhaps a year. Discount clauses should be drafted or reviewed carefully to ensure that they accurately reflect the parties' intentions. For example, if the provision simply reads that after the fifth personal computer purchased from the supplier a 15% discount on the price of personal computers will apply to the buyer, it is not clear whether the discount applies to the five personal computers already purchased: is there a "retroactive" adjustment of purchase price for these machines when the buyer reaches its discount triggering quota? This sort of question should be expressly addressed in the discount clause.

The prospect of benefitting from volume-based price discounts raises the issue of strategically planning computer purchases in order to maximize a buyer's discount. Consider the following example: a particular buyer is installing personal computers at two offices, each requiring thirty personal computers. The agreement with the supplier stipulates that if in any calendar year the purchaser buys fifty or more personal computers, then the price for all personal computers purchased that calendar year will enjoy a 15% discount. Initially, the buyer was considering installing the personal computers at one office in November and at the other office in February, but because of the supplier's discount policy the implementation of the first office was postponed to the following January so that all sixty personal computers would be purchased in the same calendar year. The buyer was then entitled to the 15% price discount (a not insubstantial saving if it is assumed that each personal computer costs around $3,000).

Sometimes individual buyers can take advantage of volume discounts by collaborating with other buyers of the same computer technology. The most typical partners in a volume discount scheme are the corporate affiliates of the buyer. Such affiliates may even be located in other countries, in which case the supplier's affiliates may also have to be involved in administering the discount policy. Affiliates, however, need not be the only partners for a buyer's discount policy. Consider the following actual example of a joint discount scheme among unrelated entities that took place several years ago.

Three organizations in the same Canadian city were in the market for a new financial administration package for their mainframe computers. The three organizations were each at a different stage of the procurement process: one was ready to sign a contract with a particular software supplier, the second was leaning towards the same software supplier but had not yet obtained approval from its board of directors, and the third was considering this same supplier along with some others as well.

Given the possibility that all three might end up with the same software, the executives in charge of the procurement process at each organization agreed among themselves that they would ask the software supplier for the following discount policy: the first organization to acquire the software would pay the regular "discounted" price, but if a second organization among the three acquired the same software then the second organization would get a 15% reduction from the regular price and the first organization would get a refund of 15% of its payment of the regular price. And if the third organization chose the same software it would get a 25% discount off the regular price and the first two users would each get a further refund on the purchase price paid by them. In fact, over a period of a year and a half all three acquired the same software and each organization realized significant savings as a result of this joint discount policy (the regular "discounted" price of the software was around $750,000 per single licence.)

This example involved what may be called a "loose joint discount policy," meaning that none of the purchasers was obligated to procure the particular software; the second and third organizations were free to choose a software supplier different from the first. Of course the potential cost savings had an influence on the other organizations, and this is why the software developer was not averse to agreeing to the joint discount policy. Assuming, however, that the organizations were satisfied with the technical merits of the software, the discount policy had no negative side-effect and indeed resulted in large cost savings. Moreover, in this example the discount option included other benefits, one of which was that if all three organizations chose the software then the developer (who was based in the United States) would establish a technical representative in the city in which the three users were located.

In contrast to the "loose joint discount policy" is what might be termed the "tight joint discount policy." Several buyers agree simultaneously to procure the same computer hardware or software. Co-ordinating such a simultaneous purchase can be very difficult, and hence the attractiveness of the loose joint discount policy, but if the buyers can agree to simultaneous implementations then their discounts may be even more attractive than in the loose joint discount case because the supplier is assured of multiple sales immediately. In any event, buyers should consider the possibility of joint discount policies, of whatever kind, whenever appropriate, given the financial and other incentives for doing so.

Most-Favoured Customer Pricing

A buyer will want to ensure that the prices it pays to a particular supplier, after the application of all price protections and discounts, are no higher than the best price charged by the supplier to a competitor of the buyer for similar amounts of the same equipment. Often called "most-favoured customer pricing," this rule is in fact enshrined in Canadian law. Canada's Competition Act requires that a supplier make available to each purchaser any price concession, discount, rebate, allowance, or other advantage granted to a competitor of the purchaser in respect of a sale of goods — this legal rule does not apply to services —of like quality and quantity. If granting differing prices to similarly situated competitors can be shown to be a practice of the supplier — and not just a one-time unusual sale — then the supplier may have committed the criminal offence of price discrimination.

It is sometimes useful for a buyer to remind a supplier of this legal rule by having a clause inserted in the contract that requires the supplier to state that the prices and other terms in the contract are at least as good as the prices and terms granted to other purchasers of comparable amounts of similar equipment. The clause would then go on to provide for the operationalization of this rule by requiring a retroactive adjustment of such prices and terms in the event the supplier had granted more favourable terms at some time in the past or does so at some time in the future. Of course, even if a buyer is successful in having such a clause included in the contract there still remains the practical reality that the supplier will not likely voluntarily announce to the buyer that it has granted someone else a better subsequent price. In this regard, buyers simply have to keep their own ears to the ground in order to listen for the details of other transactions involving the same supplier. User groups — collections of computer users using essentially the same make or kind of computer — are a particularly good way of finding out how suppliers are behaving regarding nondiscrimination in pricing obligations.

Payment Schedule

A major aspect of effective contracting, from the buyer's perspective, involves negotiating with the supplier a phased payment schedule of the whole purchase price. The amount paid for the hardware, or on account of the software licence fee, should never be paid in one lump sum at the beginning of, or too early on in, the computer acquisition process. Instead, the total should be paid in intervals or "progress payments" upon the successful completion by the supplier of certain predetermined performance milestones; in other words, these so-called progress payments should be made only if there is progress. For example, in a standard system acquisition the user might pay a deposit of 15% of the purchase price on signing the contract, 45% on delivery of the equipment to the buyer, 25% upon successful completion of the acceptance test for the system, and the remaining 15% upon completion of the ninety-day warranty period following the date on which the acceptance test is passed.

Such a phased payment schedule is in stark contrast to the payment terms required by the standard form contracts of many unreasonable suppliers. Some of these require, for example, 10% of the purchase price on signing the contract, and the other 90% on delivery; there is also the relatively common split of 50% as a deposit, and 50% upon delivery. The supplier's aim, of course, is to be paid the contract price as soon as possible. Buyers must resist this pressure, which in certain contracting situations can be extremely intense. Nonetheless, buyers simply must insist that portions of the money will flow to suppliers only upon the system's being delivered, and upon its being able to perform as promised by the supplier.

The rationale for such a phased payment is clear: it is intended to keep up the supplier's interest in the buyer's acquisition for the whole duration of the procurement process. Suppliers have an annoying tendency to lose interest in a buyer once all or most of the purchase price has been paid. Sure, the supplier generally wants happy customers and will try to please buyers to some extent. Not surprisingly, however, a supplier's paramount concern is getting paid. From the buyer's perspective, anxious suppliers are interested, responsive suppliers. So, the rule on payments is relatively simple; buyers should make sure the amount of the purchase price not yet paid at any point in the acquisition generally corresponds to the work remaining under the contract.

By the same token, however, once a performance milestone has been met by a supplier, the corresponding payment should be made promptly by the buyer. False pretenses should never come between a supplier and a payment instalment rightfully due to it. Buyers who withhold payments under some fabricated or untenable excuse are as unreasonable and unfair as suppliers who insist on full or virtually full payment on contract signing before they have actually done anything. In a similar vein, suppose an acceptance test has been 95% passed, that is, the system is virtually flawless at the time the buyer is willing to accept it, and all that remains is to iron out some very minor problems in how certain reports are printed. Then, a buyer should be willing to consider entering into an amending agreement under which the buyer will make a payment of 95% of the amount due on successful completion of the acceptance test, with the remaining 5% to be paid as soon as the minor problems are cleared up.

12. TAXES

There are several taxes and similar charges that may be payable upon a buyer's acquisition of a computer system. These taxes should be identified and quantified in advance so that the parties, in particular the buyer, are not confronted with an unexpected expense after the agreement is signed. In more than one instance the failure to understand the tax aspects of a computer procurement have resulted in much animosity as supplier and buyer fought over who would absorb the previously unanticipated extra costs represented by the relevant taxes.

The following discussion in this section does not address the tax considerations relating to the ability of the buyer to deduct the costs of acquiring the computer system; this issue is dealt with partially in section C.2, "Lease/Rental." Similarly, the relative benefits of claiming capital cost allowance upon an outright purchase of computer equipment, as compared to deducting lease payments, is also discussed partially in section C.2 below in the context of the tax rationale underlying the decision of many buyers to lease rather than purchase computer systems.

Customs Duties

Customs duties are payable on the importation of various computer products into Canada. The amount of such duty, which can be a relatively low 3.9% on some items such as CPUs to a more significant 17.5% on other items such as certain telephone switching equipment, is generally based on the contract price of the relevant item paid by the Canadian buyer. Most suppliers state that their retail prices include customs duties but few buyers will disclose the actual amount of such duty unless they are asked about this.

Under the Canada–U.S. Free Trade Agreement all tariffs between these two countries are being eliminated. Some duties were eliminated immediately when the agreement came into force (on 1 January 1989); others will be phased out over a period of five or ten years from this date. The Canadian duty, however, remains in place with respect to imports from countries other than the United States (e.g., a telephone private branch exchange switching system imported from Sweden still carries a 17.5% duty while a similar product manufactured in the U.S. comes into Canada duty free). In essence, if the item being purchased by a buyer was manufactured, assembled, or otherwise sourced from the United States, it may well be that no duty or reduced duty is payable on such items. This represents a cost saving to the supplier, and Canadian buyers will want to ensure that these cost savings are passed along to them, as is the intent of the Free Trade Agreement. For example, since the 17.5% duty on telephone equipment has been eliminated, the price in Canada of telephone equipment produced in the United States and imported into Canada after 1 January 1989 (the effective date of the Canada – U.S. Free Trade Agreement) should be reduced by at least 17.5% relative to its price a year earlier. If the supplier's price schedule does not reflect the removal of the duty, then the benefit is not being passed along to the buyer. The buyer will want to see a revised price that does reflect the fact that the supplier no longer has pay the 17.5% import duty.

Similarly, if the buyer is entering into a procurement relationship in which products are delivered over several years, the buyer will want to ensure in the agreement that any reductions in customs duties over this period will result in lower prices by an equivalent amount on the products brought across the border when the lower duty rate is in effect. Otherwise, the buyer may not be able to benefit from the duty reductions and removals provided for in the Canada – U.S. Free Trade Agreement.

Goods and Services Tax

The federal Goods and Services Tax (GST) came into effect on January 1, 1991. The GST, which is currently set at 7% of the final selling price of virtually all goods and services, has replaced the federal sales tax (FST) which was a 13.5% tax levied on goods, including certain operating system software, but not on services or the majority of application software. While the GST, therefore, is more broadly based than its predecessor, the FST, most businesses can claim an input tax credit on the GST paid by them, given that the GST is intended to be a consumption tax and is effectively paid only by final consumers.

Some purchasers of computer systems, however, are not permitted to claim an input tax credit in respect of the GST paid by them, while others may claim only a partial credit. Essentially, if a business provides a service which itself is not subject to GST, such as basic financial services provided by banks and other financial institutions, then the business cannot claim the input tax credit on the supplies that were purchased in order to provide such tax-exempt services. For example, a bank cannot claim an input tax credit on the GST it pays when purchasing a computer that will administer its loans portfolio. On the other hand, where the bank provides services that are subject to GST, such as payroll administration services, the bank is entitled to claim the full input tax credit on the GST paid in respect of goods and services purchased to provide those services. Not surprisingly, difficulties can be encountered where a particular asset is used to provide both a GST-exempt service and one that is not; for example, a certain computer of a bank both processes loan documents and supports the payroll administration service offered by the bank. In such a case the amount of the computer's time devoted to each activity must be carefully determined in order that the proper amount of input tax credit can be calculated.

Another class of purchasers of computer resources limited in respect of the amount of input tax credit they may claim are the so-called public service bodies. They include hospitals, municipalities, public colleges and universities, school boards, and other non-profit organizations, and provide services that do not attract GST. Accordingly, when these organizations purchase goods and services, such as computers, software, and related services, they cannot claim an input tax credit on the GST paid by them. In order to cushion the impact of this result, however, the federal government provides public service bodies with a partial rebate of the GST paid by them. Currently, the percentage rebates are as follows: hospitals 83%, schools 68%, universities 67%, municipalities 57.14%, and charities and qualifying nonprofit organizations 50%.

Canadian companies that have computer processing services provided for them outside of Canada (typically in the United States) should note that, generally speaking, the GST applies only to goods that are delivered or made available in Canada and to services that are performed or used in Canada. Therefore, if a Canadian company licenses some software from a British company for use in Canada by the Canadian company itself and for use in the U.S. by the Canadian company's U.S. affiliate, then, to avoid paying GST on the use to be made in the U.S., the software should be acquired under two licences, one for Canada (on which GST would be paid on the full licence fee amount, not just the value of the medium containing the software) and one for the U.S. affiliate (on which GST would not be paid). Similarly, if the Canadian company retains a U.S.-based service bureau to provide it and its U.S. affiliate with computer services, such an arrangement likely could be structured so that GST is paid only on the services provided to the Canadian company and consumed in Canada.

Provincial Sales Tax

The provincial governments, except Alberta's, impose a retail sales tax on the purchase or lease of computer hardware as well as on the provision of certain services related to such items. The provincial governments also take the view that retail sales tax applies to some types of software, but many suppliers and buyers disagree, given that under provincial sales tax legislation the tax is levied on "tangible personal property" and it can be argued that software does not constitute such property (as opposed to the medium, such as the diskette or magnetic tape, on which the software is resident). The retail sales tax levies range from a high of 12% in Newfoundland to a low of 6% in British Columbia; the rates in Ontario and Quebec are currently 8% and 9%, respectively. It should be noted that certain classes of purchasers are exempt from provincial sales tax, as are various goods and services.

All provinces treat systems software as part of the computer hardware when it comes to taxation. Mass marketed applications software, as distinct from custom-developed applications software, is also considered by provincial taxing authorities to be subject to retail sales tax (except that some provinces exempt from sales tax all software that is licensed for use in a business setting). The provinces, however, do exempt custom software from retail sales tax, inasmuch as they consider it a nontaxable service. In this regard, though, it should also be noted that some provinces levy sales tax on the subsequent sublicensing of custom software by its initial licensee.

The distinction for retail sales tax purposes between mass-marketed and custom software is illustrated by the Ontario government's policy to treat as taxable software that is "off-the-shelf," "pre-packaged," or "pre-written," and that is supplied in executable code only and not intended to be modified or changed by, or on behalf of, the purchaser, such software normally being mass-produced and supplied together with a "shrinkwrap" licence. By contrast, Ontario considers the supply of other application software as the provision of a nontaxable service. Nontaxable software includes custom software specifically designed and developed for the exclusive use and special requirements of a customer, as well as noncustom software supplied pursuant to a specifically negotiated and signed licence arrangement, in other words, a customized licence arrangement, between a software producer and a user; however, such noncustom software sold under a standardized agreement signed by a retailer and a purchaser will be considered taxable by Ontario. Ontario further takes the position that charges for the maintenance and upgrading of taxable software also are subject to retail sales tax, but similar charges in respect of nontaxable software are not subject to tax.

Withholding Tax

Where a buyer licenses software from a supplier that is not carrying on business in Canada, yet another tax may be applicable. A so-called withholding tax is levied by the federal government on any rental, royalty, or similar payments made to a person not resident in Canada in respect of the right to use in Canada virtually any type of property, including most forms of intellectual property (such as patents and trademarks). There is, however, some uncertainty currently as to whether this withholding tax applies to the use of software that is subject to copyright protection — Revenue Canada takes the view that it does apply.

A court decision several years ago resulted in lump sum licence fee payments being exempted from this withholding tax requirement. Recently, however, the Canada–United States tax treaty was amended to override this case, so that at least when dealing with software licensors resident in the United States, Canadian licensees paying a lump sum licence fee will be liable for the withholding tax. It should be noted that under this treaty, as under most bilateral tax treaties to which Canada is a party, the regular 25% withholding tax rate is reduced, to 10% with the United States, or to 15% with some other countries.

The responsibility for remitting the withholding tax to the federal government rests with the Canadian licensee. Thus, if the Canadian licensee does not deduct the proper amount and pay it to Revenue Canada, the licensee may have to pay the withholding tax amount later when it is no longer able to reduce the licence fee by a commensurate amount. The safest policy for a user is to pay the withholding tax if there is any doubt as to its applicability. In most cases the foreign licensor will not be overly concerned because it will likely be able to claim a tax credit in its own country for the amount of the Canadian withholding tax.

13. WARRANTIES

Warranty is a legal term meaning "promise." It is in the warranties section of the computer contract that the supplier, as part of the bargain struck between the user and the supplier, makes (or refrains from making) certain promises about the system being purchased by the buyer. Many standard form agreements contain only a single warranty, namely, the warranty against defects (see below). This should by no means be the full extent of the supplier's warranties. All the promises made by the supplier to the buyer in the period before the signing of the contract, when the supplier was extolling the many virtues of the system, should be recorded in writing in the warranties section of the contract. What follows is a list of the types of warranties that would usefully be included in most computer acquisition contracts.

Warranty Against Defects

The warranty against defects is relatively standard, consisting generally of the supplier's agreeing to repair or replace, at no cost to the buyer, any defective item of the system for a period of thirty, sixty, or ninety days. In some cases a longer warranty against defects is provided, which may extend for as long as twelve months. Such a warranty is often provided for software as well, typically as a ninety-day warranty against errors and bugs in the software which the supplier agrees to fix at no cost to the user. These warranties ought to mirror the performance criteria and warranties that were used to judge the acceptability of the system during acceptance testing. The warranty against defects ideally should call for the supplier to fix any hardware malfunction or software error that prevents the system from operating in accordance with its specifications; many suppliers are not averse to giving such assurance if they have already agreed to a form of acceptance test as described above (section B.9, "Acceptance Testing").

The standard language of most suppliers' warranties against defects can usually use some clarification. It is sometimes unclear, for example, what is meant by "at no cost." It generally means the supplier will not charge for labour or parts, but very often "out-of-pocket" expenses are supposed to be borne by the buyer. These include travel, accommodation, and related expenses. If the supplier's service facility is distant from the buyer's installation site, and if the problem or the technology of the particular supplier's computer requires the supplier's personnel to travel to the buyer's premises, these out-of-pocket expenses can quickly mount up. The contract should be quite clear about who pays for these expenses; if it is to be the buyer, consideration should be given to limiting the amount of such expenses on a per diem basis. In a similar vein, a buyer who is expected to pay travel and accomodation for a supplier's technical representative should ensure that the representative is not collecting the same expenses from other buyers for the same trip. It is not unlikely that the supplier's representative will be servicing more than one buyer on such a trip. This might seem like a small point, but it is the sort of behaviour that tells a great deal about a supplier, and a prudent buyer should not hesitate to raise the point in advance. There will be more to say on this and other issues relating to hardware maintenance and software support, during and after the warranty period, in section C.3, "Maintenance."

The main question concerning the warranty against defects is when the warranty period begins. In many standard form agreements the thirty, or sixty, or ninety days begin to run as soon as the hardware is delivered (in some cases even earlier, i.e., from the time the item is shipped). The fact that the equipment sits in a box for two months and is not even installed because a certain part has not yet arrived is often immaterial from the supplier's perspective, but in the case of a ninety-day warranty, two-thirds of it may have expired without the new system's being so much as uncrated. This is not reasonable. Many buyers require that the warranty period commence on the day the equipment is delivered and that it continue until ninety days (or whatever the negotiated period may be) after the successful completion of the acceptance test for the system.

With this type of warranty in place, a rather tidy trilogy of phases can be contemplated in the post-delivery stage of a computer acquisition. First, there is the period between delivery and acceptance in which the focus is on acceptance testing and acceptance, rather than on warranty. This has the beneficial effect of keeping the supplier attentive to the implementation of the system, in some measure at least because of the sizeable instalment payment generally due on completion of acceptance. Acceptance serves as a great divide: the buyer has to make the critical decision whether or not to keep the system. Following acceptance is the warranty period, in which the supplier ought to be obligated to fix all problems with the system at no cost to the buyer; these should be only relatively minor problems inasmuch as the existence of major deficiencies should have resulted in the buyer's refusing to accept the system. When this warranty period has expired, then, at the buyer's option, the supplier should be prepared to provide, for a fee, service and support capability equivalent to that provided during the warranty period.

These three periods — pre-acceptance, warranty, and maintenance — should be kept distinct and separate in the minds of
buyers. By mixing them all together the buyer may be losing
valuable rights if something goes wrong with the system delivered, so attempts by suppliers to blur or overlap the edges of
each period should be doggedly resisted by buyers.

Before leaving the issue of warranties regarding defects, it is
worth discussing what steps a buyer can take to guard against
so-called computer viruses. The computer virus is a relatively
recent, but increasingly disturbing, phenomenon in the computer industry. As noted in Section C.6 below under "Proprietary
Rights Protection — Employees," the primary legal response to
counteract computer viruses has been the prosecution of their
developers — if they can be identified and apprehended —
under criminal laws which prohibit the abuse of computer systems and data. While this is a useful development, it is of little
direct assistance to the buyer whose computer system may be
the unwitting target of such a virus. There are, however, a few
steps the buyer can take in the contract in respect of computer
viruses. There are an increasing number of so-called antidote
computer programs that are intended to screen other programs
to detect any viruses within them. A buyer could require in the
contract that the software developer subject the software to the
latest of such antidote programs at reasonable intervals in an
attempt to uncover viruses. This obligation would be an on-
going one and would also require the supplier to notify the
buyer promptly of any virus actually found in the software and
to absorb the cost of dealing with it, even if the virus is found
after the expiry of the warranty period.

Warranty as New Equipment

There are two aspects to the new equipment warranty. First, the
supplier should guarantee that the equipment being purchased
by the buyer is new, rather than used, unless both parties agree
otherwise. This might seem like an unnecessary provision, but
some suppliers have been known to include less than new parts
in a hardware configuration which is being sold as new equipment. This might not be a terrible thing from the point of view
of performance, inasmuch as certain computer boards, for
example, can be made as good as new with the replacement of a

couple of silicon semi-conductor chips or other minor servicing. The point, however, from the buyer's perspective, is that the buyer wants to know when it is being provided with equipment that contains less than new components so that it can make up its mind independently from the supplier as to whether this is a desirable state of affairs. If the contract allows for delivery of used or reconditioned equipment, then the supplier should be required to notify the buyer of the manufacturing date of such equipment.

The other matter to consider under a new equipment warranty is whether the buyer is purchasing the supplier's most recent technology. With software, for example, if the particular program has gone through several releases over time, each one more advanced in terms of functionality, performance, and error correction, then the user will want to be assured that it will take delivery of the latest release.

With respect to the supplier's existing, already announced product offerings, whether the buyer is acquiring the supplier's most advanced technology is a relatively straightforward question. The issue becomes somewhat more problematic when the supplier, unknown to the buyer, is about to announce a new replacement product just as the buyer is plunking down its money for what will very shortly be old technology. This has happened to many buyers. Consider, for example, the buyer who purchases a certain computer from a supplier in year one. In year three the buyer wants to add a good deal of equipment to the computer system. A month after making this second purchase, the supplier announces a new line of computers which is intended to replace, and which is not compatible with, the computer originally purchased by the buyer nor the very recently acquired accessories. The buyer is hopping mad. Had the buyer known about the new product's imminent introduction, it would not have bought all the new accessories for its now outdated technology; instead it would have used the money towards upgrading to the new technology or simply have leased some old technology accessories for an interim period until it was ready to buy the new equipment.

There are two ways of dealing with such a situation. First, the buyer can have the supplier give a warranty to the effect that the system being purchased by the buyer is the supplier's most advanced system and that the supplier is not planning to introduce a successor to this system for a certain period of time. Some suppliers will give out such information, but others will not. For example, one very large computer maker in the United States never pre-announces its products largely because doing so could be construed as an anti-competitive act by its rival manufacturers.

If a buyer is confronted with a tight-lipped supplier, a further contracting mechanism may be useful, namely the predelivery trade-in clause. Such a provision would allow a buyer who has signed a computer contract in January, for delivery of the equipment in March, to trade-in this equipment against the purchase of any successor equipment offering which is announced by the supplier prior to the March delivery date. In this way, if the buyer really wants the supplier's most advanced system, it can buy what may quickly become old technology with the assurance that it can trade-in, and hence not waste money on, the previous generation of equipment of the supplier. This issue of trading-in and upgrading equipment after it is purchased is discussed in detail in section B.21, "Upgrades and Trade-in Credits."

Warranty as to Ownership

A buyer of computer equipment will want the supplier to warrant that the supplier owns the equipment immediately prior to its purchase by the buyer, and that ownership of the equipment will pass to the buyer free of any security interests or other rights in the hardware. With respect to software, things are invariably more complicated. Particularly with respect to expensive mainframe software, the user will want the software supplier to warrant that the latter owns all aspects of the software and has the right to grant the user the licence to use it. Increasingly, the supplier will not own all elements of the software; rather, one or more modules of third-party software will likely be embedded in the supplier's product. In such a case the user will want the warranty to disclose the precise ownership configuration of the various components of the software, and will want some assurance that the supplier has obtained adequate distribution rights from the respective owners to be able to grant a good licence to the user. Knowing fully what ownership interests reside in the software is also important where the user is obtaining only object code and wishes to have the source code put into escrow (see section C.7); in such a case, it is imperative to understand the precise ownership structure of the software product to ensure that the source codes for all relevant components of the software are made subject to the escrow agreement. Further, where the supplier is merely a distributor of the particular software product, this same review exercise must be conducted, and it will be more difficult because the actual owner or owners of the software components will likely want to have very little to do directly with the user.

Warranty as to Compliance with Laws

A great many application software programs include a government reporting dimension. Employee payroll systems, for instance, have to be able to calculate appropriate amounts of personal income tax and other deductions so that these amounts can be remitted by the employer to the government. Certain pension administration software has to be able to massage employee data in a manner that conforms to legal rules and guidelines. Users will want to be assured that, where relevant, their licensed software complies in all respects with the most recent government requirements. To meet this concern users could demand that the software licence contain a warranty by which the software developer guarantees that the software currently, and always will, comply with applicable government rules and requirements such as certain audit inquiry standards. Such a guarantee is particularly important where the user is considering licensing from a non-Canadian company software that may not yet have been customized for the Canadian marketplace.

The buyer may also want a warranty to the effect that the equipment has been approved by the applicable certification testing bodies, such as the CSA or the local hydro-electric authority in Canada. As well, some equipment has to be certified by a government agency. For example, the federal Department of Communications has to approve certain telecommunications equipment that is intended to be attached to the public network system. When buying such equipment the buyer should receive a warranty that the relevant components conform to the required standards and have been certified as such by the relevant government department or agency.

Warranty as to Compatibility

It is increasingly the case that buyers are acquiring various computer systems from different suppliers with the intent that they all be able to work together simultaneously. Indeed, in some cases the buyer is purchasing technology for the express purpose of being able to tie together its several disparate computers. The risk in these connection activities can be significant. Many suppliers make broad, sweeping marketing claims about the ability of their systems to work in tandem with other computers that simply do not stand up to scrutiny once the systems are installed. Then, too, different suppliers have different definitions of terms such as "compatibility" and "connectivity" with the result that buyers can be sorely disappointed by the failure of a certain product to achieve full integration with another item because the buyer and supplier did not understand what each meant by "integration."

In order to avoid these problems buyers should address the issue of compatibility in a warranty that sets out in some detail what other equipment the supplier's equipment will interact with, and, more importantly, exactly what the technical dimensions are of such interaction. A supplier's general statement that "our products are all compatible with XYZ computers," should be fleshed out in some detail, and where the buyer has already installed other equipment with which the new equipment is to interface, then of course the detailed promises as to compatibility ought to be tested during the acceptance test as part of the overall suitability of the new system. In many instances, however, the additional equipment will not be acquired for some time, but the buyer still wants to ensure that its current purchase will work in conjunction with its future acquisition. In such a case a forward looking warranty as to compatibility is appropriate.

If a buyer is acquiring an application computer program separately from the supplier of the hardware on which the application is intended to operate, then again the buyer should ask for a warranty from the software developer that its program will operate on the designated hardware configuration. If possible such a promise regarding compatibility obviously should be made part of the acceptance test. It may also be useful to obtain an on-going warranty from the application program supplier regarding any future changes that may be made to the hardware's operating system. That is, the buyer might require the application to be modified within a certain period of time after the announcement of a new operating system or hardware feature if it is the case that the buyer can take advantage of these developments only by having the application program modified.

Warranty as to Capacity

Consider the following scenario. A particular buyer is an organization whose data processing requirements are expected to grow about 10% every six months for several years. When looking for a new computer system this buyer is anxious to acquire a system with sufficient speed and data storage capacity to meet its needs not only for the next six months, but at least for the next five years. The buyer approaches two suppliers, Supplier A and Supplier B. Supplier A has a regular system for $100,000 and a larger system for $300,000. Supplier B has a regular system, which is about mid-way between Supplier A's two systems, in both capacity and price; it sells for $200,000.

The buyer knows it will never need the larger system from Supplier A, so it has to decide between Supplier A's smaller system for $100,000 and Supplier B's somewhat larger system for $200,000. Supplier A, knowing that the buyer is strapped for cash, makes general statements to the buyer at several meetings to the effect that "why pay more for Supplier B's system when our smaller system can meet all your data processing needs for years to come." The buyer is tempted to go with Supplier A because of the $100,000 cost saving, but is worried about whether the smaller system from Supplier A will be big enough in the long run.

One way to tackle this problem is to put a capacity warranty into the acquisition agreement: Supplier A warrants that its smaller system will process, for example, up to 200% of the transaction volume generated by the buyer at the time the system is installed. The clause could also stipulate that if this promise later proves to be untrue, Supplier A will replace its smaller system with its larger system at no additional expense to the buyer, or perhaps be subject to a somewhat lesser remedy as noted below.

Operationalizing the capacity warranty requires a bit of flexibility by both parties' technical staff. The supplier will want the capacity test to be conducted as soon as possible after delivery, perhaps as part of the acceptance test. The buyer, of course, will have enough on its plate in testing for functionality and performance; if capacity testing is confined to the acceptance test period, it may well have to wait until very late during the acceptance test, and may not get done at all. More importantly, it will often be impossible to test the capacity warranty until several months after the system is up and running so that sufficient data can have been loaded onto the system.

Accordingly, a buyer may well want to be able to run a capacity test on the system for some discrete period of time — perhaps two weeks — at some point, say twelve months, after acceptance of the system. If this aspect of the approval of the system is moved out beyond the acceptance test, it may be appropriate that the remedy for failure to meet this capacity test be somewhat less than the return of the system and a refund of the purchase price, inasmuch as for such a remedy it is not unreasonable to require *all* testing to be conducted during the acceptance test. Instead, a reasonable remedy for failure of the capacity test might be that the supplier will provide the buyer, at no additional cost to the buyer, with all the necessary hardware (typically extra memory such as disk drives) or software required to bring the system up to warranted capacity.

In the above example, if Supplier A deliberately or inadvertently recommended its smaller system (for $100,000) when really its larger system (for $300,000) was required, and if to meet the capacity warranty an additional $125,000 of equipment has to be added to the smaller system, then Supplier A ought to pay for the required additional equipment (if not provide its larger system at no additional cost to the buyer, as noted above). This would bring the ultimate cost of Supplier A's smaller system to $225,000. Had Supplier A's original bid been $225,000, the buyer might have chosen Supplier B's $200,000 system. The application of the warranty clause to have Supplier A absorb the additional $125,000 would therefore not be an unfair outcome.

Warranty as to Expansion

An expansion warranty is very similar in its objective to the warranty concerning capacity; both are inspired by the dynamic nature of computing, the fact that computer technology and most users' computer needs are constantly changing. An expansion warranty is indicated when the buyer and the supplier both know that the supplier's system will be sufficiently large only for a certain period of time, after which the buyer will want to expand the system by adding extra data storage capacity or by other means. In such a situation it is not unreasonable for the buyer to ask the supplier for a relatively detailed picture of the additional hardware or software required to undertake the contemplated expansion. The key here is to flush out sufficient knowledge about the operational aspects of the system so that the buyer will be aware of and prepared to deal with any problems associated with future expansion.

Accordingly, a warranty clause reflecting such an approach would provide that the computer system is capable of expanding to a capacity required to process, say, 300% to 500% of the current monthly transaction volume of the buyer. The clause would go on to list, completely, the specific hardware and software required for the expansion (a schedule could be attached to the agreement for the purpose). The corresponding remedy would provide that if equipment or software in addition to what is so listed is in fact required when the buyer undertakes the expansion, it shall be supplied by the supplier at no cost to the buyer.

The warranty may also state that a certain number of terminals can be added to the system without adversely impacting the system's performance; an instance of this would be longer response times after expansion. Yet another warranty may focus on the precise requirements, in terms of equipment, software, and services, to migrate from one system of the supplier's to another, or from one particular model of a system to another model. Such a warranty clause may well list the relevant items as well as their current prices, which, coupled with some price protection as discussed above (see section B.11), would give the buyer the comfort of knowing that the chosen system expands readily and in a cost-effective manner.

14. WARRANTY DISCLAIMERS

The law in all Canadian provinces relating to the sale of goods affords to buyers certain rights called "implied warranties." These warranties are binding upon the seller of the goods, even though the warranties may not be written in the contract between the seller and the buyer; the law automatically imposes them on the buyer and they are therefore considered to be implied terms of every contract for the sale of goods. Two of these warranties merit special attention: the "warranty of merchantable quality" and the "warranty of fitness for a particular purpose." The former means that the goods sold will be fit for the ordinary purpose for which they are sold; that is they will operate properly and generally be of good condition. The latter means that where the buyer is relying on the seller's skill and judgment to select or furnish certain goods, and where the seller has reason to know the particular purpose for which the goods are required, the seller is responsible for ensuring that the goods are fit for that purpose.

Buyers should be aware that virtually all suppliers contract out of these two implied warranties. They can do so under the law, but only if the buyer is not a consumer, that is, someone buying the equipment for personal use rather than for use in a corporate or similar environment. The way suppliers negate the implied warranties in respect of nonconsumer purchases is by having a "warranty disclaimer" in the contract that states very clearly that the implied warranties and conditions of merchantable quality and fitness for a particular purpose shall not apply to the sale of the computer system being purchased under the contract. In the context of a computer system acquisition these two warranties, if in fact they were applicable, would mean that the system would have to be, first, of good quality generally. Second, and perhaps more importantly, with respect to fitness for a particular purpose, it would mean that where a buyer said to a supplier, "Here are my accounting, inventory, and other requirements, now sell me a system that meets these requirements," the supplier would have to provide a system that indeed met those needs; otherwise the system arguably would not be fit for its particular purpose. Such a standard of performance places a rather heavy burden on the supplier, one that virtually all suppliers refuse to bear, at least on such open-ended terms; this is why they use the warranty disclaimer provision.

Whether or not a warranty disclaimer is reasonable is usually a moot question; the fact is suppliers simply will not delete or modify the disclaimer. Having such a provision in the agreement, therefore, makes it all the more imperative that the express warranties in favour of the buyer, such as those discussed in the previous section and under "Acceptance Testing" (B.9), are included in the agreement. There is an essential difference between the express warranties discussed above and the implied warranty of fitness for a particular purpose. The express warranties tend to be promises related to objective, readily ascertainable criteria (e.g., "if the system is expanded from two to four data entry terminals, the response time of the CPU to an on-line enquiry triggered by a keystroke will be the same"). By contrast, the implied warranty of fitness for a particular purpose has a certain element of subjectivity that, were it applicable, could lead to many misunderstandings between a supplier and a user (e.g., "if over the next two years the business grows, the computer must be able to grow with the business"). The imprecision of the latter statement, if it were made by the buyer to the supplier and thus invoked the implied warranty, likely would not assist the supplier or the buyer in mapping out a realistic computer system growth plan and costing it properly. In effect, buyers are better served by express warranties as to system performance, functionality, and reliability than if they had to rely solely on the implied warranty of fitness for a particular purpose with its amorphous sentiment, even if this implied warranty were not disclaimed by suppliers. By disclaiming this implied warranty a supplier shifts a significant amount of responsibility for the choice of an appropriate system to the buyer, in the sense that the buyer has to determine whether the system will meet the buyer's needs. The buyer can shift some of this responsibility back to the supplier, however, by having the supplier agree to important express warranties that relate directly to the system being acquired.

Similarly, suppliers will sometimes state in their agreements that they do not warrant the system to operate error free or uninterrupted. Such a provision merely reflects the bug-prone reality of computer technology. Thus, rather than waste time debating with a supplier the appropriateness of this type of provision, a buyer's efforts would be better spent on determining how much hardware and software maintenance will be required. Is servicing between 9:00 a.m. and 5:00 p.m. on weekdays enough, or does the buyer need coverage twenty-four hours a day, seven days a week? A provision that confirms the fallibility of the system should caution the buyer to institute appropriate daily data back-up procedures as well as manual contingency procedures in the event the system is down for an extended period. In short, a worthy result of implied warranty disclaimers and other similar provisions is that buyers are prompted — if they adhere to the principles of effective contracting — to secure much better protection than that afforded by the implied warranties.

15. REMEDIES

There is an old saying in the law that there is no right without a remedy. What this essentially means in the context of a computer contract, from the buyer's perspective, is that it is often not enough to get the supplier to agree to, for example, a fixed delivery date or specific performance criteria that must be met during the acceptance test. What the buyer also needs is a remedy, or several remedies, at its disposal in the event the supplier does not live up to its obligations.

One remedy that is almost always available to the buyer, particularly with respect to nondelivery, is a straightforward breach-of-contract lawsuit, based on the general law of contract. For example, assume a supplier has agreed to deliver a certain computer on 1 April 1992. If the supplier does not deliver on this date, on 2 April 1992 the buyer could start a legal action against the supplier for failure to honour the agreement. This is not an easy task. Court papers have to be drawn up, and the buyer has to be able to show that it has suffered damages. Immediately following the nondelivery the buyer's damages may be quite minimal, though they will mount as time goes on. Most importantly, there is a good chance that the supplier will try to cure the contract breach by making the delivery some time after the lawsuit is commenced but before it is heard by a court (which, as mentioned above, can be two years in most Canadian cities, given the backlog in most courts). This could throw a wrench into the buyer's plans to seek and purchase an alternative system. Finally, perhaps the biggest problem with suing a supplier for breach of contract on the basis that a delivery date has not been met is that it represents such a blunt, unfocussed, draconian option which cannot be tailored to meet particular circumstances. It is an all or nothing option, which in practice often amounts to nothing.

The need for sensible and precise remedies is further accentuated at the acceptance test stage of the computer acquisition process when buyers often feel the need for recourse. Consider the computer system that has been delivered on time and during its acceptance test performs 85% of the functions required of it. Is the missing 15% really worth suing over, as far as the buyer is concerned? If it is a crucial 15% it may well be worth a lawsuit. The buyer will have to convince a judge of the great importance of this 15%, because the supplier surely will argue that at most the buyer is entitled to a partial refund to compensate for the 15% loss of functionality. Again, the buyer does not have sufficient flexibility in formulating its strategy towards the supplier if all it can rely on is the major step of the full-blown lawsuit for breach of contract.

Express Remedies in the Contract

Some of the problems inherent in the general legal remedy of breach of contract can be alleviated by providing expressly in the contract for certain remedies. Three remedies are particularly useful. The first involves what are called "liquidated damages"; the buyer receives a predetermined amount of money as damages or credits against the purchase price of the system in the event the supplier fails to perform in a timely manner (e.g., the supplier is late in installing the system). The second remedy, if the problem is nonperformance, entails having the supplier solve the problem at its own expense by whatever means necessary, including the cost of any additional hardware and software needed by the buyer in the interim. The third remedy is not unlike the general legal remedy of suing for breach of contract in that it represents a significant lever in the hands of the buyer, but it is intended to be more specific and efficient in terms of application. It involves a termination of the agreement by the buyer, but only after all amounts previously paid to the supplier are returned to the buyer.

Consider these remedies in a situation of nondelivery. The contract provides that upon the supplier's failure to deliver the system on schedule, the buyer has two options. The buyer (and only the buyer) may extend the delivery date, whereupon the purchase price is reduced by 2% for each week or part thereof that delivery is delayed, or the buyer may give notice of its intention to terminate the agreement, whereupon the supplier immediately must return all monies to the buyer; upon such return of monies the contract is terminated. Armed with such a flexible remedies clause, if the supplier has delivered 90% of the system and has satisfied the buyer that the additional 10% will arrive in two weeks' time, then the price reduction remedy may be quite sufficient. If, however, on the delivery date the buyer realizes it has become a victim of "vapourware" and that the intended system has not even been fully designed yet, let alone manufactured or shipped, then it will be quick to exercise its full termination remedy. This latter option, being more specific, is easier to administer and enforce than the general legal remedy for breach of contract, and because the parties already agreed to it when they signed the agreement, a court should be far more ready to enforce it.

Consider also the usefulness of express remedies for poor performance during the acceptance test. Again, assume the contract provides that upon failure to pass the acceptance test the buyer may opt to extend the test for one or more additional periods, during which time the supplier shall correct errors and deficiencies at no cost to the buyer, and upon any such extension the purchase price is again reduced, say by 2% per week or part thereof that the test is continued. The buyer also has the option to give notice of its intention to terminate the agreement, whereupon all monies must be returned to the buyer. Upon return of monies the contract is terminated. The remedy provision may stipulate that the buyer has a third option: to designate certain portions of the system as acceptable and to keep (and pay for) those items while returning the rest. A final clause might provide that in the event of termination the whole system will not be removed until such time, perhaps to a maximum of twelve months, as the buyer has had an opportunity to install an alternative system.

Assume that the buyer who has these remedies has contracted for the installation of a large computer system consisting of a mainframe CPU with dozens of terminals wired to it. During the acceptance test the system falls 10% short of what was promised. In this case the buyer may simply require the supplier to bring the system up to the acceptable level, at the supplier's expense, and allow the acceptance test to run a second (or third, or more) time. If, however, it was found that the mainframe was hopelessly inadequate, but that the wiring and the terminals were fine, then the buyer might elect to return the mainframe for a full refund of its purchase price while keeping (and paying for) the wiring and the terminals. This type of remedy demonstrates the need for unit prices for the equipment and other items being acquired to be set out clearly, in an unbundled way, in a schedule to the contract. As an interim measure the buyer might continue to use the original mainframe until it finds the best of several compatible mainframes to work effectively with the original supplier's wiring and terminals.

There are all sorts of other remedies that the buyer can use to construct an appropriate incentive structure to ensure proper and timely performance by the supplier. For example, a buyer orders a certain computer technology that requires environmental conditions markedly different from most competitive computers in the marketplace. In designing and outfitting the room for the new CPU, the buyer will have to install many expensive devices which can be used only for this particular equipment (see section B.3, "Preparation of the Installation Site"). This worries the buyer. It means that if the new system is not delivered, or if it is delivered but ultimately cannot be made to work, all the unrecoverable costs of preparing the installation site would be borne solely by the buyer. Some buyers, believing they should not carry this risk themselves, have negotiated clauses in their agreements to the effect that if delivery of the system does not occur by a certain date, or if the acceptance test cannot be successfully completed within the time allotted for it, and if as a result the buyer terminates the agreement, then the buyer will not only be refunded all amounts previously paid on account of the system, but also be reimbursed by the supplier for those costs of preparing the installation site that were unique to this supplier's system (the supplier would not pay for a change or renovation that could be used by the buyer with an alternative computer system).

Two Case Studies

Several references have already been made to actual situations where express remedies in the computer acquisition agreement have enabled the buyer to achieve a successful outcome when the supplier's equipment failed to live up to the supplier's promises. In particular, reference is made to the case of the acquisition by a public institution of a local area network (discussed in section B.9, under "An Acceptance Test Case Study"). In that situation, when the supplier's communications link product failed to perform adequately, the buyer was able to have the supplier replace it with a more expensive model at no additional cost, largely because the buyer was armed with an express remedy in the contract that allowed it to receive a complete refund for the system if it did not work. Faced with such a remedy, the supplier opted to save the deal by installing for free the more expensive product.

Another actual case, the facts of which are set out in a recent court decision, illustrates well how useful express remedies can be when properly administered. A Hawaiian telephone company contracted with a California computer company to develop and implement for the utility a computerized directory system. The contract had very detailed specifications for the system (e.g., it was required to handle fifteen thousand calls per second while maintaining a response time of one second) as well as very specific delivery dates for the various components of the system. The contract also provided three key remedies to the buyer: (1) if the delivery of the system did not occur by a certain date then the supplier would deduct $1,000 from the purchase price for each day installation was delayed, to a maximum credit of $100,000; (2) if installation was delayed past a certain point the supplier would have to provide an interim back-up system by a further date; and (3) if, after installation, the system did not work in accordance with the specifications during an acceptance test, the buyer could reject the equipment.

Two months prior to the scheduled delivery date the supplier informed the buyer that major difficulties were being encountered in developing the system. When the scheduled delivery date was missed, the buyer notified the supplier that the $1,000 a day credit had been triggered accordingly. A little bit later the supplier notified the buyer that it proposed to modify certain key specifications of the system. These proposed changes were unacceptable to the buyer. Soon after, once the credit reached its maximum of $100,000, the buyer visited the supplier's site to observe what progress had been made in the development of the system. Convinced by this visit that the supplier would not be able to complete the system as specified, the buyer cancelled the agreement and claimed damages. The court found that the buyer was entitled to $600,000 in damages, which included the difference between the purchase price of the first, unsuccessful system and the higher amount the buyer eventually ended up paying another supplier to develop a working computerized directory system.

This case confirms how important it is, from a buyer's perspective, to include effective remedies in the computer contract, and how critical it is to administer those remedies in a timely manner. By contrast to many procurement situations where buyers are slow to exercise their contractual rights — thereby running the risk that these rights will be diluted — in this case the buyer acted quickly and decisively once it determined on the basis of strong evidence that the supplier would be unable to perform its obligations. Compare the effective response of the buyer in this case to the wholly inadequate response of the buyer in the sad acquisition story referred to at length in section A.1 under "Computer Acquisition Disasters." The need to administer contracts in such an effective manner is discussed further in section D.2, "Administering the Contract."

When providing for express remedies in the contract, the buyer should be careful to retain all its other rights and remedies as well. For example, consider the situation where a particular system fails to pass its acceptance test and the buyer elects to return the equipment for a full refund under a clause providing for such a remedy (such a situation is analogous to the Hawaiian telephone company case discussed above). The buyer now goes back to its original second choice supplier to inquire as to the acquisition of a system to replace the failed equipment. The price of this second system may have increased since the buyer first inquired about it, and this increase in price would be in a real sense a damage suffered by the buyer on account of the first supplier's system not being adequate. If this difference were significant, the buyer might consider seeking to recover it from the first supplier; to this end the remedies clause in the agreement with the first supplier should state expressly that the specific remedies provided in it shall not detract from the buyer's other remedies available at law, such as a claim for damages for breach of contract to recover these additional costs, which could include extra salaries, supplies, and outside services.

16. INTELLECTUAL PROPERTY RIGHTS INDEMNITY

The computer system acquired by a buyer will invariably be subject to one or more forms of intellectual property rights, such as patents, copyrights, or trade secrets. "Intellectual property" denotes property rights, such as ownership or exclusive use, in certain intangible items, as opposed to real property or personal property. For example, the hardware may contain a number of subcomponents on which there are patents. A patent is a legal right granted by the government for new inventions. If a manufacturer has a patent for Canada on an invention, then for twenty years no one else is permitted to utilize the idea or concept implemented by such invention in this country, unless the patent holder licenses others to use the invention. Patents are expensive and time consuming to obtain, but they can be extremely important for the competitive advantage they confer, and literally hundreds of patents have been granted on various components of all types of computer hardware.

While some software is patentable, software is typically subject to copyright law protection. Generally speaking, if a patent protects an idea or concept that is reduced to a useful and novel invention, copyright protects only the form of expression of an idea that has been created as, in the case of a computer program, a so-called literary work. Several recent court cases in the United States, however, have decided that copyright law in that country also protects the "sequence, structure and organization" of a computer program. Such an expansion of the scope of protection afforded by copyright for software may be adopted by Canadian judges as well, and it is arguable that one Canadian judge has already done so. Some commentators have argued that this broader interpretation may have the impact of affording almost patent-like protection for a copyrighted work. They go on to argue that there is a potential danger in this development because copyright is much easier to acquire than a patent: essentially, an author — or software developer — merely has to put pen to paper and copyright arises in the resulting work product. As well, copyright protection, which prohibits the unauthorized copying of the copyrighted work, lasts much longer than the patent law's twenty years of exclusivity. The term for a copyright is generally the life span of the author plus an additional fifty years. As the writers of software tend to be quite young, the term of software copyright protection for any particular program could easily extend eighty or more years.

A trade secret is an item of commercially useful information, such as a formula, concept, idea, or in certain circumstances a computer program, that gives a competitive edge to a business and is not generally known in the industry (indeed, as its name implies, it must be kept a "secret" by its originator). A trade secret affords a very broad scope of protection inasmuch as algorithms and scientific theorems can be protected by trade secret law, while such items would not qualify for copyright, and in some cases not even patent, protection. The trouble with a trade secret is that it must be kept secret, and the protection dissipates once a trade secret becomes known generally; conversely, the protection afforded by trade secret law, namely, that unauthorized persons are prohibited from using the trade secret, continues for no set time period as with patent or copyright protection but rather extends for as long as the trade secret is a secret. In this regard it should be noted that some courts have decided that certain software marketed only pursuant to a licence agreement that contains restrictions on copying and disclosure (see section B.10, "License of Software") may retain its trade secret status.

Given the heavy reliance of hardware manufacturers and software developers on intellectual property rights to protect their valuable corporate assets, a buyer of a computer system will want some assurance that the supplier either owns the relevant patents, copyrights, trade secrets, and other intellectual property rights, or has been granted the right from the owner, directly or indirectly, to use, copy, or distribute the relevant intellectual property. The buyer would not want to pay the supplier a large licence fee for the right to use certain software if some time later a total stranger were to claim to be the rightful owner of the copyright in the software and demand another licence fee of the buyer. Disputes between suppliers over rights to intellectual property, while they are very common in the computer industry, do not always affect buyers directly. A supplier who claims, however, that a second supplier's hardware and/or software infringes the intellectual property rights in its own high technology goods may take action against the second supplier's customers. Buyers should therefore always seek assurance from a supplier that the supplier's computer system will not land the buyer in hot water over someone else's intellectual property claims.

This assurance can be given in the form of a warranty that the supplier has sufficient rights to enter into the computer contract and carry out its obligations under the contract, including granting the buyer a licence in the software. More common than such a warranty is an "intellectual property rights indemnity" clause in the contract which provides that if a claim is brought against the buyer on the basis that the computer system infringes the intellectual property rights of a third party, the supplier will defend such a lawsuit and reimburse the buyer for any costs and expenses incurred in respect of such a claim.

From the buyer's perspective, the good news is that virtually all standard form agreements contain such an indemnity clause. The bad news is that the actual wording of many of these clauses greatly cuts down the protection that should properly be afforded the buyer. For example, some clauses mention only patent and copyright and therefore should be expanded to cover claims brought against the buyer on the basis of trade secrets or "any other intellectual property rights." In respect of this latter category, for example, in the United States and some other countries (and likely soon in Canada) there is legal protection available for the so-called mask works embedded in semiconductor chips. This protection is somewhat similar to copyright, except it arises under a special statute and the term of protection against copying mask works is only ten years.

In a similar vein, particularly where the supplier is an American company, the standard form clause will often state that the indemnity covers only those claims where the computer system infringes United States patents or copyrights. This is inappropriate in the case of a Canadian buyer, given that any claim against a Canadian buyer would come under a Canadian patent or copyright. Because copyrights and patents are national in scope, a computer system located and used in Canada could never infringe an American patent or copyright, it could only infringe a Canadian patent or copyright. Either the reference to the United States should be replaced by one to Canada, or, better still, no reference at all ought to be made to a particular country. Even if a reference to a country is made for patents and copyrights, no such national reference should be made for trade secrets because a trade secret is not founded upon a national system of statute-based intellectual property rights, and its protection need not be limited to the territory of the country in which it originates. That is, a Canadian user may be required to stop using a purely American-based trade secret.

Another shortcoming of many standard form intellectual property indemnity clauses is that they require the supplier to reimburse the buyer only for any award of damages against the buyer made by a judge. In fact, most intellectual property disputes are settled out of court, and therefore the indemnity should cover all costs and expenses incurred by the buyer, including settlement costs and reasonable legal fees. By the same token, however, it is usually reasonable for the supplier to require prompt notice from the buyer of any intellectual property claim brought against the buyer on account of the supplier's computer system, and to reserve the right to conduct the defence of this claim, with the buyer possibly having such right only if the supplier fails to take reasonable actions itself. Similarly, it is sensible for a supplier to insist that it will be liable to reimburse only those settlement costs which are consented to by the supplier. For the buyer's protection, the contract should state that the supplier's consent ought not to be unreasonably withheld.

Some intellectual property indemnity clauses in standard form agreements contain provisions allowing the supplier to take certain actions if the computer system becomes the subject of an infringement claim. These actions typically take the form of the supplier's being able to make technical modifications to the system to make it noninfringing, and procuring the right for the buyer to continue using the infringing item. These are generally fine from the buyer's point of view, except that the buyer may want to stipulate with respect to the former that any modification has to result in the system meeting the same specifications and performance criteria as the initial system.

In addition to these two options, many suppliers add a third: if neither of the first two options is available then the supplier can terminate the contract and software licence (if there is a

software licence). Some suppliers try to make this alternative
more palatable by providing that upon such termination the
supplier will refund a portion of the original price to the user —
typically the whole purchase price less 20% or 25% of such purchase price for each year the buyer has used the system. Even
with such a partial refund, the possibility that the system may
be taken out from under the buyer should cause serious concern to buyers. Buyers should try to have this provision
removed, or at least circumscribed so that it may be invoked
only after the supplier has tried its best to deal with the claim in
a manner that would allow the buyer to continue to use the system. In addition, particularly if the system will become a critical
resource to the buyer, the buyer may want to explore the ownership rights of the supplier in, for example, the software, by finding out who actually developed it, whether it was all done by
employees of the supplier, which would give some comfort to
the buyer, or whether it was created by outside programmers or
consultants. In this last case the buyer should ensure that ownership of the copyright has been transferred to the supplier by a
written agreement; for the rationale behind this requirement see
section C.5, "Consulting."

17. LIMITATION OF LIABILITY

A malfunctioning or completely inoperable computer system can
cause a buyer serious grief and damage. Consider the following
example: a large advertising agency's brand new computerized
accounting system is responsible for, among other things,
preparing the invoices for services provided to the company's
clients. During the second month after the acceptance test, but
before the expiry of the contract's warranty period, the computer malfunctioned (ostensibly because it was the busiest month
in the agency's history and the extra volume simply over-
whelmed the system). The invoices were prepared by the computer and mailed, and it was not until several unhappy clients
called about their invoices that the company realized that the
computer had malfunctioned. It had inserted an incorrect
amount on each of the agency's 350 invoices sent out for that
month. The agency ended up suffering the following so-called
direct damages: the cost of retaining the services of an expensive

outside computer expert because the system's supplier could not find the problem at first; the cost of hiring temporary additional accounting staff to deal with all the complaints and to manually prepare correct invoices; and the cost of a service bureau for the agency's computing needs for six weeks until all the bugs were ironed out of its own system. These costs amounted to $45,000.

As well, as a result of the invoice mix-up a relatively new client that had not been all that impressed with the agency's creative work called up and said it was taking its work elsewhere, citing the outrageous invoice as the "last straw." The agency was looking to earn $100,000 in profits from this client over the following year. More significantly, during the two weeks that the agency had no computer resources at all — its own system was down because repair people were trying to fix it and the service bureau hook-up was not yet complete — the agency lost the opportunity to bid on a major government advertising job; the agency missed the bid submission deadline because they could not access in time the financial numbers trapped in the computer in order to estimate the cost of the project. The agency later heard it was a shoo-in to win this job — had it bid — because its previous work was superior to all the other entries. The agency lost a certain $300,000 in profits in respect of this government project.

It is because computer systems can easily be the cause of these sorts of damages and costs that suppliers, in their standard form agreements, limit the extent of their liability. First, there is a provision that states that under no circumstances will the supplier be liable for consequential damages, that is, damages that flow as a consequence of the supplier's fault, such as the lost profits suffered by the agency when it was unable to bid on the government contract. As well, most standard form contracts limit the amount of direct damages a supplier will be liable for, typically to the cost of the computer system. Thus, if the advertising agency was subject to such provisions, and the system's cost was $150,000, the agency might be able to recover its direct damages of $45,000, but it would not be able to make a claim in respect of the government contract or losing the disgruntled client, because these would not be considered damages directly related to the computer's malfunction.

As with warranty disclaimers (section B.14), it is rather a moot question whether limit of liability provisions are reasonable or not: they simply will be insisted upon by the supplier. While removing them altogether is probably out of the question, a buyer should review the actual wording to ensure that the supplier does not limit liability too much. For example, some standard form contracts state that the supplier is not responsible for any damages, including direct ones. This is unreasonable. A supplier should be liable for at least what may be termed a buyer's interim replacement costs if the supplier's system breaks down. And the extent of recovery for such damages should be at least the amount of the purchase price of the system. Some suppliers, after stating they will be liable for direct damages, limit recovery to the cost or value of the particular component which caused the damage. This may be reasonable in some circumstances, for instance, under a long-term master supply agreement in which each component is defined to be a separate system. In a typical one-system procurement situation, however, such a per-component limit is arguably on the meagre side.

The supplier's rationale for such limitations on its liability is that a limited economic return on the sale of the system simply cannot be accompanied by an unlimited liability exposure in the event the system malfunctions. An accompanying argument to this one is that the supplier has little or no knowledge of, and no control over, what the buyer will be doing with the computer system, and whether these activities will be particularly risky or risk free. Regardless of the merits of these arguments, even most suppliers admit they are not applicable, and that the general limitation of liability provisions ought not to apply, to situations where damages are incurred by the buyer because of patent, copyright, and other intellectual property claims brought against the buyer as a result of the system. Similarly, these justifications should not be relevant where the buyer's damages flow from a disclosure by the supplier of the buyer's, or its customers', confidential information (see section B.20, "Buyer's Confidential Information"). Equally, the contract's limit of liability clause ought not to affect recovery from the supplier where the supplier or its employees cause physical injury or property damage to the buyer's employees or premises. If a supplier employee, while soldering some cables for the installation of a $200,000 computer system, starts a fire at the buyer's site which causes $500,000 in damage, the buyer should not be limited to recovering only $200,000 inasmuch as this activity, which invariably will be covered by the supplier's insurance, was completely in the control of the supplier. Accordingly, the contract should state clearly that the limit on liability provisions do not apply with respect to claims for intellectual property infringement, unauthorized disclosure of the buyer's confidential information, or personal injury or property damage.

For those situations in which the limit of liability would apply, the buyer should consider what steps might be taken to reduce the amount of damages upon the occurrence of a computer breakdown. A thorough assessment of maintenance and support needs for the system should be undertaken so that the optimum level of assistance is available whenever malfunctions occur (see section C.3, "Maintenance"). As well, consider the advertising agency example, where keeping a back-up tape of daily data might have been enough to permit the generation at a temporary site of the necessary financial information to submit the bid to the government. As well, a manual review of a few of the invoices prior to their mailing as a form of quality control before mailing might have caught the computer error before it caused the damage to the agency's relationship with its clients. In short, the limit of liability clause in a computer contract should lead a buyer to consider the various operating and business risks that go along with the acquisition of the computer system and to take positive, cost-effective steps to minimize these risks.

Another device often used by certain suppliers to limit liability is the shortened limitation period. One party to a contract can normally bring a breach of contract or negligence claim against the other party any time up to, generally speaking, 6 years after the breach, and in some cases of breach of contract even 20 years after. Some suppliers do not wish to have the possibility of a lawsuit hanging over them for so long, so they provide in the computer contract that the buyer cannot bring a lawsuit after a much shorter period of time — typically one or two years — has elapsed from when the facts giving rise to the suit first developed. Many buyers do not mind agreeing to such a provision, provided it is made reciprocal (i.e., the supplier is also subject to the same shortened limitation period in respect of any lawsuits contemplated against the buyer). As well, the buyer must be very careful to ensure that it commences a lawsuit within the shortened period for any problem that it may consider taking legal action in respect of, even where it has allowed a supplier to try to fix the problem, because the limitation period will not likely be extended by the amount of time the supplier spends trying to fix the problem. The buyer should commence a lawsuit to keep all options alive, and can then agree to postpone taking action under the claim for the period of time that the buyer allows the supplier to attempt to fix the problem.

18. EXCUSABLE DELAYS

Virtually every standard form computer agreement contains a clause that exonerates the supplier from responsibility where the supplier is unable to perform its obligations because of events beyond the reasonable control of the supplier. For example, the computer to be delivered to a buyer cannot be manufactured in time to meet the predetermined delivery schedule because an earthquake in California — the manufacturing plant is in the Silicon Valley — has destroyed this plant. This type of occurrence is often called an event of *force majeure,* an intervening act outside of the reasonable control of the supplier which prevents the supplier from performing its contractual commitments. The provision in the agreement excluding the supplier's liability in such circumstances is known as the *force majeure* clause, or in some cases the "excusable delays" clause.

It is usually reasonable for a supplier to have such a clause in the contract, provided it is not overly broad in its scope. For example, some such clauses contain a list of events that would qualify as acts beyond the reasonable control of the supplier. The standard list would include occurrences such as earthquakes or governmental acts (i.e., the Canadian government suddenly and without notice closes the border to American computer imports). Some lists, however, mention less excusable events, such as "an inability of the supplier to obtain adequate supplies." This latter event may reasonably be prevented if the supplier keeps a large enough inventory of component parts, and therefore its failure to perform because of a parts shortage should not be excused under the contract.

Many *force majeure* clauses are also inadequate from the buyer's perspective in terms of what they fail to include. One useful provision is that the supplier, in order to be able to rely on the clause to excuse its delay in performance, must notify the buyer immediately upon the occurrence of any event which will cause such delay and from that point the supplier must take all reasonable steps to work around the event causing the delay, including obtaining materials from other sources or using services of other suppliers. As well, the buyer should have the option to terminate the procurement agreement if delivery of the system is delayed by an event of *force majeure* for, say, ninety days. That is, at some point the delay, regardless of its cause, will prove to be an unreasonable hardship on the buyer and the buyer simply must have the right to turn to another supplier. To take the earthquake example, if the manufacturing plant is not rebuilt within three months, the buyer should be able to take its business elsewhere. Of course, if during these three months the buyer believes the supplier will be in operation relatively soon after the ninety-day period, then it may wish to stay with the supplier. If, however, it takes three months for the supplier merely to process its damage claim with the insurance company, and if after such time the original plant is still a scrapheap of rubble, then on the ninety-first day after the earthquake (if not sooner) the buyer ought to be able to pursue other procurement options.

19. TERMINATION

Most standard form contracts contain a termination clause that permits the supplier to put an end to the agreement if one or more of several events occur, such as the failure of the buyer to pay any amount when due or for any other breach of the agreement by the buyer. In the case of a software licence, the events triggering a termination option in favour of the supplier might include the user's unauthorized disclosure of the supplier's software, or bankruptcy of the user. As with the warranty disclaimer and limit of liability clauses, a buyer should probably not try to negotiate a wholesale removal of such a termination clause because virtually no supplier will delete it. What a buyer ought to do, however, is review the clause closely and if necessary request appropriate amendments to it.

One essential addition is the concept that whenever the supplier believes the buyer to be in default under the agreement the supplier must give the buyer written notice of such default and a reasonable time, say thirty days, to cure the problem before termination can be triggered. It may be, for example, that an invoice of the supplier has not been paid because the particular buyer, a major company, has misplaced the invoice in its large accounts payable department. Such a "default" should not present a pretext upon which the supplier can terminate the contract; rather, notice of such nonpayment and an opportunity to cure this oversight ought to apply.

The other useful addition to the supplier's termination clause should be that only "material" or significant defaults by the buyer will give the supplier the right to terminate the agreement, and, again, only after notice of the material default has been given to the buyer along with a reasonable period to remedy the default. Once more, the objective of such a modification is to ensure that the supplier is not tempted to use a rather minor problem as an excuse for putting an end to the relationship. Such a temptation may arise, for example, where the supplier realizes after the contract is signed that it underestimated the work required of it, and that the project will therefore be less financially rewarding than the supplier originally contemplated. At this point any device able to jettison the contract — including the seemingly unreasonable, but legal, application of a poorly drafted termination clause — would be welcomed by the supplier. Incidentally, a buyer might be tempted to engage in the same exercise, in which case if the termination clause is to apply to both parties, it is not unreasonable for the written notice, cure, and material default provisions to also apply mutually.

With respect to the principle of mutuality, many buyers mistakenly assume that they are suitably protected if the standard form's termination clause is merely made mutual. In many cases, however, the remedy of termination is not all that useful to the buyer. For example, where a buyer has accepted a software program (and hence arguably is satisfied with it and wants to use it for as long as possible), but the supplier fails to provide appropriate service under the contract's warranty provisions, terminating the agreement and the software licence may not do anything positive for the buyer. A more effective remedy for the poor warranty service may be for the buyer to

accumulate credits against future maintenance charges, or ultimately the buyer may claim its direct damages incurred in having a third party complete the supplier's obligations. In either
case, the buyer will want the agreement to continue.

If the supplier goes bankrupt the buyer may well want the software licence to continue; indeed, the effective remedy in such a
case may be to have an escrow agent release to the user certain materials relating to the software so that the buyer can maintain the
software in the absence of the supplier (see section C.7, "Source
Code Escrow"). This may be contrasted with the supplier's usual
preference for the remedy of termination upon the bankruptcy of a
buyer. This example illustrates well that certain remedies may not
be symmetrically applicable to both parties to a computer contract.
In each case the user should give careful thought to what remedies
make practical sense if the supplier is in default of its obligations.

In some cases, however, the buyer may well be able to make
use of a termination remedy. Termination for nondelivery or
nonacceptance of a computer system was discussed in section
B.15, "Remedies." Another situation in which termination might
be indicated arises when a buyer contracts with a service bureau
for the provision of certain computing services. If the service
bureau's level of service is inadequate or it otherwise breaches
materially the service bureau agreement, the buyer should have
the option to take its business elsewhere. In such a case, however, the buyer should not only ask for the remedy of termination,
it should also give some consideration to practical questions
such as how its data (and possibly its software) will be transferred from the defaulting service bureau to another service
bureau and what related transition services the first service
bureau should be required to perform upon a termination of the
agreement. These requirements should then be written into the
agreement so that in the event of the buyer's move to another
computing solution, transfer occurs in an orderly fashion.

20. BUYER'S CONFIDENTIAL INFORMATION; PUBLICITY

The importance of the buyer's keeping the supplier's software
confidential and not permitting unauthorized persons to have
access to it or copy it was discussed at some length in section B.10,

"Licence of Software." Although many buyers fail to realize it, a need for confidentiality may arise when information and data owned by or in the possession of the buyer is provided to the supplier. This is particularly true in respect of a software development agreement where the supplier must delve deeply into the inner workings of a buyer, but it can also be relevant in a hardware/software acquisition where the supplier may well require substantial information and data from the buyer, as well as its customers, to understand the computing needs of the buyer. The contract should expressly require the supplier to treat any such information in a confidential manner and not to disclose, use, or copy it except as required to perform its obligations under the agreement. Moreover, if the nature of the buyer's information warrants it, the buyer may also require that the supplier's personnel who work on the project sign nondisclosure agreements with the buyer.

A somewhat similar issue relates to the desire of some buyers to control the manner in which suppliers might publicize the fact that a buyer is a client of the supplier. Suppliers tend to keep customer lists which they advertise generally or make available on some other basis to prospective customers. There may be several reasons why a buyer would not like to appear on such a list; for example, the buyer might have security or competition concerns. Even if a buyer does not mind being listed as a customer of the supplier generally it may object to certain types of advertising on which the supplier's customers' names may appear. To meet these concerns a buyer could have a clause in the agreement that stipulates either that the supplier shall keep confidential the fact that the buyer is one of its customers or that the supplier may reference the buyer as a customer but only on marketing and advertising literature that has been approved by the supplier prior to its distribution.

21. UPGRADES AND TRADE-IN CREDITS

In the dynamic, ever-changing world of computer technology buyers likely will want to continue automating previously manual procedures (assuming their computer acquisition experiences are positive ones!), or to upgrade automated procedures as new functionality and performance features come onto the market. Suppliers are continually expanding their product lines with new devices, capabilities, and improvements to existing products. The only constant in the computer industry is change. Therefore, an effective computer contract, from a buyer's perspective, should assist the buyer in coping with, and indeed in taking advantage of, such change. The contract must contemplate not just the immediate system being procured but also the next purchase several years later so that the transition from the present system to the following one is as orderly and cost effective as possible.

Two issues are especially important in this regard. In the first place, in the contract the buyer should have the supplier commit to provide the buyer with meaningful and organized information about the supplier's new products that may be used in the future in conjunction with the system currently being purchased. The supplier will likely do this to some degree in any event as part of its follow-up marketing effort with the buyer, but what the contract ought to guarantee is that the supplier will provide a written analysis of how each new hardware or software development might be integrated or added to the existing system, what the new item's impact will be on the performance of the system, and what the new item will mean in terms of increased (or decreased) on-going maintenance costs. Such information will be needed for the buyer to make an informed and timely decision about when to replace or upgrade the system.

The buyer should also think now about how to get the best value for the system it is about to purchase when the time comes, as it inevitably will, to upgrade this system. The quick obsolescence of computer technology should lead buyers to consider such matters. The equipment can be sold as used hardware, an increasingly viable option as a rather robust used-computer market is developing, particularly for certain models of mainframe computers.

Another option (not inconsistent with selling the used equipment) is to negotiate a trade-in credit mechanism with the supplier that assures the buyer a market for its current system for a particular period of time. The trade-in mechanism offers to the buyer some security against obsolescence. If, for example, the reasonable useful life of a particular system is five years, the buyer might secure a trade-in credit to be used against the purchases of additional equipment or software from the supplier, calculated on the basis of 100% of the purchase price of the item during the first year after the acceptance of such item, 80% for the second year, and so on, until at the end of the fifth year there would be no further credit.

Some suppliers tend to be receptive to such trade-in schemes because they create a significant incentive for the buyer to stay with the original supplier. Of course, if at the relevant time a used-computer broker offers a better price, then the trade-in credit will not be used. The reality may be, however, that a toughly negotiated trade-in clause up front as part of the overall deal, when concessions from the supplier may be quite forthcoming, will produce a far superior trade-in value for the buyer.

22. ARBITRATION

Arbitration is a method for settling legal disputes that takes place outside the court system. Two parties to a contract, for example, can decide that in the event they have a dispute arising out of the contract — perhaps they cannot agree on the interpretation of a very important clause — they will submit the issue to an arbitrator who will decide the question. There are several reasons, particularly in the context of a computer contract, why arbitration might be chosen over the regular court process for settling contract claims.

First, the parties can appoint the arbitrator (there may be more than one); they can choose someone who has particular expertise in the matter which is the subject of the dispute, for example, where the buyer and the supplier cannot agree on whether the system has passed the required acceptance test. Another example might be where the contract calls for the development of documentation of a certain quality and the buyer disagrees with the supplier as to whether the documentation delivered actually meets the required standard. In any such impasse, the parties might usefully call in a neutral expert in data processing — perhaps a professor of computer science from a nearby university — to make an objective assessment. An expert in the relevant technology would be much better prepared than a judge to come to a quick decision. In addition to providing for greater technical expertise, arbitration may also be a faster route than a judicial proceeding, given that in major Canadian cities a lawsuit can take two years to come to trial. A further benefit of arbitration is that the supplier and buyer can keep their dispute private inasmuch as the papers filed with the arbitrator setting out each side's arguments, and all supporting material, need not be made publicly available. This is in contrast to the official record of a judicial proceeding which usually is open for anyone to see at the court house.

Notwithstanding these benefits, arbitration does have its disadvantages. One is cost: the government pays the salaries of judges and the rent for the court house, whereas the parties to an arbitration have to foot the (often substantial) fees of the arbitrator — or often three of them — and the cost of the hotel meeting room where arbitration hearings typically take place. As well, while arbitrators may have technical expertise, they probably do not have the same experience as judges in holding hearings, taking evidence, and writing decisions; this means that the legal procedures that protect the parties to a lawsuit may not be as carefully followed in an arbitration. Now while some find an arbitrator's ability to be flexible when it comes to procedural rules a further benefit of arbitration, others are more comfortable with the more certain rules of the court system. As a compromise, many parties to an arbitration insist on having three arbitrators rather than one so that there is less chance of the arbitration getting derailed on procedural grounds. Thus an arbitration panel may have, in addition to a technical expert, a lawyer and a business person to ensure that all aspects of the dispute are properly aired. Of course a three-member arbitration panel significantly increases the costs of the arbitration; it would also cause the arbitration to move at a slower pace as it is that much more difficult to schedule commonly available times for three typically busy people.

Arbitration, then, is not a panacea, but for the reasons noted it is becoming increasingly popular for settling computer contract disputes. This is particularly true where the supplier and the buyer reside in different countries. In such a case each party may feel uncomfortable about using the other's domestic court system, and therefore they establish their own mechanism for handling disputes through arbitration. In these circumstances, as well as where the supplier and buyer are both Canadian, the parties should set out clearly in the contract who the arbitrators will be, or at least who will appoint them if the parties cannot themselves agree. They should also set out the city in which any arbitration is to take place, which should typically be the city where the buyer's installation site is located, inasmuch as that is where the bulk of the evidence regarding the system's performance and related witnesses will be. And if the parties' personnel do not normally function in the same language, then the arbitration clause in the contract should also stipulate in what language the arbitration will take place.

23. GOVERNING LAW

Virtually every standard form agreement contains a clause that sets out which jurisdiction's laws will govern the interpretation of the agreement. Such a clause generally presents no problem to the buyer where the buyer and supplier are in the same jurisdiction. For example, if they are both in Quebec, then the standard form will invariably provide that Quebec law will govern the agreement. This is fine from the buyer's perspective. It wants Quebec law to apply because it, or its counsel, knows Quebec law, and if there were a court proceeding or arbitration, it would likely take place in Quebec where the system was installed, so it makes sense for Quebec law to apply. If, on the other hand, the parties chose the law of British Columbia and the arbitration took place in Toronto, the arbitrator would have to go to the trouble and expense of getting a law professor or some other expert in British Columbia law to give testimony in Toronto as to the applicable law of British Columbia.

If the supplier is in a jurisdiction other than that where the buyer is located, the supplier may nevertheless, and usually does, agree that the law of the buyer's jurisdiction will govern the contract. A problem arises, however, when the supplier is from another jurisdiction and wants the law of its home jurisdiction to apply. For example, it is very common for an American supplier, say from California, to provide in its standard form agreement that the laws of California will govern the agreement, even where the buyer is in, for example, Alberta.

There are several reasons why the buyer should require this reference to California law to be changed to Alberta law. The first, as noted above, is that any arbitration or lawsuit will likely be brought in Alberta and it would be cumbersome and expensive to have to apply California law in an Alberta proceeding. As well, if the Alberta buyer were to agree to the California law clause it would have to retain a lawyer in California to review the contract, given that the buyer's Alberta lawyer would not be qualified to give advice on California law. This would constitute an extra cost to the buyer of dealing with this particular Californian supplier.

Now, the supplier might respond that it would have to incur similar costs if it agreed to abide by Alberta law. This is true, but surely it makes more economic sense from a global perspective to have the supplier conduct this review once than to require each of the supplier's Alberta customers go through the same exercise, which would be a costlier and more time-consuming exercise if indeed the supplier were planning on doing a significant volume of business in Alberta. In effect, the supplier who is seriously interested in marketing its product in Alberta or any other jurisdiction outside its home base should consider it a cost of doing business to review the law of such foreign countries and to amend its standard form contract so that it is these various foreign laws that will govern its agreements.

Also with respect to contracts with foreign entities, the buyer and the supplier will have to decide if they wish the rules of the United Nations Convention on Contracts for the International Sale of Goods to apply to them, or whether they wish to opt out of this international convention (which they can do by expressly excluding the applicability of the convention in their contract). A further issue related to the legal rules governing computer contracts is the law regarding the regulation of high technology exports. Canada, together with its NATO allies, Japan and Australia, has implemented a regulatory system of export controls which is intended to prevent certain goods, especially items like certain computers and software, from being delivered to the Soviet Union and several other formerly or currently communist countries, such as Vietnam. The effect of these rules is that a Canadian buyer of computer equipment and software should not relocate, resell, or otherwise transfer such products outside of North America without first reviewing the export licensing requirements for such a sale or transfer. This also applies to inter-group transfers of equipment where, for example, a Canadian company intends to send some hardware to an affiliate in France. Indeed, American suppliers will often remind Canadian buyers of these export control rules by providing, in their standard form agreements, that the export of the equipment to certain countries requires the approval of the United States government! American suppliers insert this provision into their standard form agreements to discharge the export control regulation duties imposed on them by the American government.

24. ASSIGNMENT

Assignment is the legal term denoting a transfer of all or some rights under, for example, a contract. In the context of a computer agreement, the concept of assignment may be important in several different ways. First, the buyer may want to have the power to transfer — or assign — the entire agreement to an affiliated company, if, for instance, another company in the corporate group is given the new mandate to provide all of the group's data processing services. If the buyer wants the flexibility of effecting such an assignment at some point in the future, it should carefully review the standard form contract's assignment clause, which typically prohibits any type of assignment of the contract by the buyer.

There are other assignment possibilities that a buyer may want to address in the agreement. The buyer should secure the ability to assign the licence for the operating system software to any entity that may eventually buy the hardware from the buyer. Similarly, where the equipment purchased by the buyer contains software embedded in the hardware, the buyer will want to provide in the contract that such hardware-based software may be transferred without the consent of the supplier to the person buying the equipment from the buyer. That is, the buyer may want to sell the hardware as used equipment but the equipment may not be very marketable if the would-be purchaser cannot obtain a licence to use the related operating system software or the software embedded in the hardware. In such a case, the items of hardware can be labelled, in computer jargon, "boat anchors" inasmuch as the hardware is quite useless without the relevant software to operate it. If the buyer cannot itself assign the software, a second-best solution is for the buyer to have the supplier agree to grant a licence to the new owner of the hardware, although the supplier may agree to do this only for a fee equal to or approximating the original licence fee, in which case the cost of the used system to the new purchaser is increased. The necessity to assign in the context of lease and maintenance agreements is discussed more fully in Part C.

While the buyer should seek to expand its assignment rights in the contract, it may also wish to restrict the supplier's right of assignment. For example, in most cases it is not unreasonable for a buyer to insist that the supplier not subcontract to any third party any of the supplier's contractual obligations without the consent of the buyer. This is especially important when the supplier is a hardware manufacturer who will retain the software developer under a "turn-key" system implementation agreement. (Under a turn-key agreement the hardware manufacturer supplies all components of the computer system — hardware, operating system software, and application software.) Before signing the contract the buyer agrees on which software developer will be utilized, and the hardware supplier should not be able to replace this critical component of the project without the approval of the buyer. Readers will recall that just such a substitution was a critical factor in contributing to the system implementation fiasco involving the Vancouver buyer described at length in section A.1 under "Computer Acquisition Disasters."

Another situation in which the buyer will want to restrict the supplier's right of assignment arises where the supplier has some on-going obligations to the buyer in respect of the software licensed to the buyer, such as warranty, maintenance, and support services. In these circumstances, the buyer should require the supplier to agree that it will not sell the ownership rights to the relevent software program unless it first obtains the agreement of the new purchaser to also assume the buyer's warranty, maintenance, or support services agreement. The buyer should explain to the supplier that the intent of such a provision is not to restrict the ability of the supplier to sell its software assets, but is merely intended to ensure that such sale does not leave the buyer without on-going services, at perhaps the very favourable rates negotiated with the original software owner, simply because the software itself has been sold to a new owner (who may not want to assume voluntarily the buyer's services agreement if its terms are very favourable to the buyer).

25. NOTICES

Most standard form agreements contain a so-called notices clause, which sets out the addresses of the parties to which all notices or other communications required under the agreement must be sent. Such a clause also often contains what is called a deemed receipt provision, which stipulates that a party is deemed to have received a notice within a certain period of its being delivered (typically the same day as the delivery of a notice sent by courier or transmitted by facsimile machine) or of its being mailed (generally three to seven days after the notice is put in the mail). These deemed notice provisions are important because they can start time periods running under the agreement even if the buyer is unaware it has received any notice. For example, if the supplier delivers a notice of termination by courier, and the buyer's receptionist signs the receipt for the courier package, from that moment the cure period (of perhaps thirty days which, as noted above, ought be provided for in the agreement) will begin to run, even if the courier package is misplaced in the buyer's mailroom and never does get to the buyer's project co-ordinator.

By the same token, a deemed receipt provision in the notices clause can work to the advantage of the buyer where, for example, the buyer wishes to give notice to the supplier that a system acceptance test has not been passed. The provision, however, must be used carefully. Consider a situation where the acceptance test provision requires the buyer to notify the seller of any errors or deficiencies in the hardware or software before the thirtieth day after the start of the test or otherwise the system is deemed to be accepted. On the twenty-eighth day the buyer decides there are in fact serious problems with the system and it wishes to notify the supplier accordingly. In such a situation, if the notices clause states that a notice is deemed to be received when it is delivered by courier or facsimile, or five days after it is mailed, the buyer should only use same-day or overnight courier or facsimile transmission to give the notice; if it uses the mail the date on which the supplier will be deemed to have received the notice will fall outside the thirty-day acceptance test period and the buyer will be deemed to have accepted the system! As already noted, and as more fully discussed below in section D.2, "Administering the Contract," computer contracts must be administered with great care.

26. ENTIRE AGREEMENT

Virtually every standard form computer contract includes a statement that such contract contains the entire agreement between the supplier and the buyer with respect to the subject matter of the contract, and that the contract supersedes any other negotiations, proposals, or other communications between the parties. Such a clause may be viewed as a simple housekeeping mechanism; that is, the negotiations may have gone through multiple stages with several earlier drafts of the agreement and much correspondence containing offers and counterproposals for various terms and conditions that are different from the ones eventually agreed to in the final contract. The entire agreement clause simply makes it clear that the last, signed version of the agreement is the only one intended to be the legally binding document. A less charitable but perhaps more cautious interpretation of the entire agreement clause sees that it is also a mechanism to help protect the supplier by ensuring that all exaggerated, unauthorized, and unfounded statements about the system made by the supplier's salespeople are excluded from the contract and therefore are of no binding effect.

For both of these reasons, the existence of an entire agreement clause makes it essential for a buyer to ensure that all the various remedies of the buyer and the warranty, price, and other concessions agreed to by the supplier are expressly referenced in the agreement. The buyer must ensure that all specifications and performance criteria and anything else relevant to the system are included within the four corners of the agreement; if any oral promise or portion of the supplier's proposal is not put into the agreement (at least by cross-reference in the case of the proposal) then the buyer likely will not be able to rely on it.

There are some legal avenues for introducing before a court evidence about matters not included in the contract. It could be argued, for instance, that the supplier (or supplier's salesperson) fraudulently or negligently misrepresented a key factor related to the procurement and that this induced the buyer to enter into the agreement. In such a case a court may set aside the agreement, particularly if fraud were involved. This is, however, a very difficult task, and courts generally prefer to uphold the entire agreement clause, especially where the buyer and supplier are sophisticated, larger entities that have gone through extensive negotiations to arrive at a mutually satisfactory agreement. Accordingly, the general rule that the buyer ought to follow is that if the buyer really wants the supplier to comply with some promise of the supplier or some wish of the buyer, the promise or wish ought to be expressly reflected in the agreement.

27. AMENDMENT

Standard form agreements usually include an amendment clause which provides that any changes to the contract may be made only by an instrument in writing signed by the authorized representatives of the buyer and the supplier. An amendment clause serves the same function as the entire agreement clause: it excludes any oral promises or claims made by either party. As such, it is a reasonable mechanism for imposing discipline on the parties so that they conduct their mutual dealings in an orderly manner. The danger, particularly from the buyer's perspective, is that one party will receive an oral promise at some point in the procurement relationship but neglect to see it written into the agreement and then be unable to rely on it later when the party who gave it denies having done so. Perhaps there was misrepresentation, but perhaps the parties simply misunderstood one another in conversation; later they are both sorry they did not reduce their understanding to paper in order to avoid confusion at a later date. The upshot of this discussion is that the buyer simply must get in writing any subsequent changes to the contract if the buyer intends to be able to hold the supplier to any such additional agreements.

28. GUARANTEE OF AFFILIATE

Buyers should always be concerned about the longevity prospects of their suppliers, particularly with the aquisition of larger computer systems which will serve critical functions and which will necessitate a long-term relationship with the supplier. The buyer wants some assurance that the supplier will be around for at least as long as the buyer needs maintenance and support for the current system — and possibly even for the buyer's next system. The bankruptcy rate among small software developers is notoriously high, but even large hardware manufacturers have gone out of business over the relatively short but stormy history of the computer industry. A thorough check of the supplier's credit rating, financial history, and prospects is in order. Coupled with the real possibility of the supplier's future insolvency is the extremely prevalent risk that the supplier will discontinue the very product line that has become vital to the buyer.

A buyer can take steps to help avoid these situations, or at least to try to minimize the risk and the disruption caused by them. One device is to have the contract state that source code for licensed software will be deposited with a neutral escrow agent who will release it to the buyer under certain conditions, such as the bankruptcy of the supplier (see section C.7, "Source Code Escrow"). It is vital to learn whether the supplier itself owns the intellectual property rights in the computer system being sold. It may be that the supplier is only the Canadian subsidiary of an American manufacturer of the system, or that the Canadian supplier is a nonaffiliated distributor of a Canadian manufacturer. In such cases, or in any other situation where the buyer is nervous about the financial future of the supplier, the buyer should request some form of contractual commitment from the ultimate manufacturer to the effect that if the Canadian supplier goes out of business or in any other way ceases to perform its obligations under the contract, the manufacturer (Canadian, American, or other) will undertake to fulfil the obligations of the Canadian supplier in accordance with the original contract. Such guarantees, which may take the form of a separate agreement or may consist of the guarantor jointly signing the main contract with the supplier, are rarely volunteered by the affiliate or other backer of the supplier, but they are regularly given when a buyer asks for them. The essential rationale for asking is that the manufacturer or other party giving such a guarantee is assumed to be much larger, more stable, and more likely to survive the vagaries of the computer marketplace than the supplier.

PART

C

Additional Contract Provisions

Part B discussed contracting issues relevant to hardware purchases and software licences. Part C focuses on issues relevant to other types of computer contracts. Of course, many of the issues raised in Part B are also relevant to the agreements discussed in Part C, but are not repeated here. The reader is referred to the appropriate checklist in Part E which lists and cross-references the relevant issues for each type of agreement. The contract issues checklist for "Software Development Contract," for instance, refers to numerous issues discussed in Part B which apply to other agreements as well; it also makes reference to issues unique to software development agreements discussed below in section C.4.

1. MASTER SUPPLY

Some buyers of computer technology have equipment procurement plans that involve them with a specific supplier over a long period of time. Consider the following example: a large retailer plans to install a point-of-sale cash register/computer system at each of its sixty stores across Canada. If the pilot test involving three stores in Halifax is successful, the retailer will acquire systems for the rest of its stores over a period of three years though it may take a slower or quicker implementation path depending on how well the technology is being accepted by the retailer's sales force.

For this acquisition program the buyer should negotiate a so-called master supply agreement. Such a contract follows the basic form of hardware and software acquisition agreements, but contains several extra provisions in light of the phased procurement plan. For example, the agreement should contemplate the completion of individual purchase orders, the form of which would be set out in a schedule to the contract, for each unit of equipment and software to be installed at a particular store. Each purchase order would also contain the purchase price and maintenance fee for the particular unit, which in turn would be based on a price and fee schedule set out in the master agreement. As well, the implementation schedule might be divided into a specific fixed schedule for the first few store installations, especially those involved in the pilot test, with subsequent units being delivered in accordance with the dates set out in the relevant purchase orders.

The master agreement would provide that each unit would be subject to an acceptance test (see section B.9). What differs from the regular hardware purchase contract, however, is the remedy options available to the retailer. That is, if the three units involved in the pilot test do not pass the acceptance test, which test would assess each unit's performance as well as its ability to communicate with the head-office computer, then the buyer should have the option to terminate the master supply agreement and obtain a refund of the monies paid to the supplier to that point. This remedy is similar to the one discussed earlier for a single system acquisition. At some point after the pilot test, however, the buyer will likely have to give up the remedy of termination of the master supply contract, probably once the pilot system proves to the buyer that the supplier's technology will operate adequately when installed in all sixty stores. The buyer may then have to restrict itself to terminating individual purchase orders if individual units do not work. Indeed, a better approach would be to require the supplier to take all possible steps to make each subsequent unit work at no extra cost to the buyer, given that, in a real sense, the buyer may be locked in to the supplier's technology after the pilot test.

The pilot test, then, represents a critical watershed in this buyer's procurement relationship with the supplier because after the successful passing of the pilot test the buyer is for all practical purposes wedded to the supplier's technology. Since at this point the buyer loses the ability to terminate the whole agreement, some additional remedies may be in order. If the delivery of a subsequent unit is delayed past its scheduled date, for instance, then significant credits against the purchase price of the delayed unit might be triggered. If any individual delivered unit fails to pass its acceptance test, significant credits against the purchase price of the unit may be triggered for each day that the acceptance test has to be extended beyond its original period. After the pilot test the buyer has lost its major bargaining chip with the supplier, namely, the possibility of switching to another supplier. These additional remedies may therefore be useful to keep the supplier continually attentive to the buyer during the term of the master supply agreement.

Another major issue for buyers to consider is the question of volume discounts, given that the buyer may be acquiring significant quantities from the supplier over time. Accordingly, the buyer entering into a master supply agreement will want to consider carefully the points about volume discounts discussed in section B.11, "Price and Payment Schedule." And of course the upgrade and trade-in provisions dealt with in section B.21 are also of importance to a buyer entering into a master supply agreement.

Another way to modify a master supply arrangement is to modularize the provision of maintenance services on a per-unit basis. The buyer should have the right to terminate maintenance service for any particular unit or units, while having the supplier maintain the remainder of the units. This would be useful, for instance, if the maintenance facility of the supplier, in the foregoing example of the national retailer, in Winnipeg was not up to the same standard as its Montreal service office. In such a case, if there was an alternative provider of maintenance service in Winnipeg, the buyer could have the units in its Winnipeg stores serviced by this third party while keeping the original supplier in place everywhere else. If the maintenance fees were a lucrative source of revenue to the supplier, as they usually are, this flexible remedy might be just the nudge the supplier needs to bring its Winnipeg service operation up to the mark, which is all the buyer really wants in any event.

2. LEASE/RENTAL

Some users of computing resources prefer to lease (or rent) computer equipment rather than to purchase it. (The difference between leasing and renting is usually only in the duration of the agreement; rental terms are typically less than a year while leases can run for several years.) Not least among the reasons for leasing is the avoidance of significant initial payments, which can be particularly attractive to a company that is just starting up and has not yet established a strong cash-flow situation. When a user leases a computer it does not obtain ownership of it — title in the equipment does not pass to the user, unless it exercises an option to purchase, which is provided in many leases. Ownership resides in the leasing company, usually a finance company that buys the equipment from the supplier or the buyer. The user merely has a right to possession and exclusive use of the system provided it makes the required periodic rental payments to the leasing company.

One of the benefits of leasing computer equipment is that the user generally can deduct its lease payments as a business expense. By contrast, if the user were to purchase the system it generally would be entitled to write off the purchase price as capital cost allowance. This difference in treatment makes leasing more attractive to some users. A lease, however, often contains an option in favour of the user to purchase the equipment. The danger in such an option, from a tax perspective, is that if the purchase price in the option is unreasonably low, such that it does not reflect the fair market value of the equipment at the time the purchase option is exercised, and the equipment has effectively been paid for by this time, then there is a risk that Revenue Canada will characterize the original lease transaction not as a lease but as a conditional sale. If this happens, the user will not be able to deduct the previous lease payments and the possibly less favourable capital cost allowance treatment will be imposed instead. In short, great care must be taken when structuring purchase options in computer leases. The actual drafting of the option to purchase must also be done with precision, so that there is no doubt as to when the option to purchase arises or as to how it is to be exercised, or as to the purchase price and how it is to be paid.

The standard form lease or rental document invariably shifts all responsibility for the maintenance, insurance, and related services and costs onto the user. From the finance company's perspective, although it is the owner of the equipment it has nothing to do with the day-to-day operation or upkeep of the system. Most leases contain what is known as the "hell or high water" clause, a colourful expression that describes a provision whereby the user must continue to regularly pay the periodic leasing fees regardless of operating problems that may befall the computer system. As a result, it is up to the user to ensure that the lease agreement contains a provision in which the finance company, as owner, transfers (or assigns, to use the legal term) to the user all the warranties and rights in respect of the equipment to which the owner is entitled. It is also a good idea for the user to obtain a written acknowledgement from the supplier that the user has been assigned and will be exercising directly all the rights and remedies in respect of the supplier's warranties and other obligations to the owner. In addition to the lease, the user will generally enter into a maintenance agreement for the equipment and a licensing agreement for the operating system software, probably directly with the hardware supplier.

With respect to the lease agreement itself, the user will want to ensure that it can assign the lease (and the underlying equipment) to another user without any cost or penalty, provided that this other user agrees to assume all the obligations of the original user and is equally or more solvent financially. The assignment clause might go on to say that assignment can still proceed with a less financially stable new user if the original user stays as a party to the lease and guarantees the payments of the new user. These assignment provisions are useful from the user's perspective because often the key rationale for a lease in the first place is that the user cannot predict accurately its own future data processing requirements, and hence when circumstances change it will be handy to be able to pass the lease along to another party.

Most standard form lease agreements have rather draconian termination-upon-default provisions in favour of the finance company, and lease agreements are notorious for failing to require that the user be given written notice of a default and be allowed a period to cure the default before the lease is terminated (the importance of these provisions, from the buyer's point of view, was discussed in section B.19, "Termination"). If the user is in default under the lease (usually for nonpayment) most leases allow the finance company to repossess the equipment as well as to collect payments for the full term of the lease. If in the case of a four-year lease the user defaults at the end of the first year, the finance company can repossess the equipment and collect the lease payments for the next three years. This is a rather rich recovery — possibly amounting to almost double recovery — depending on how soon the lease company can place the machine with another user, which it likely can do. Accordingly, users should have the default provisions reworked so that they are liable, if they default, only for the interim portion of the lease until the equipment is re-leased to another user, as well as for any financial loss to the owner occasioned by the default and termination. The equipment, since it is used, might not now command payments equal to the original lease, and of course the finance company has to expend some effort to find another user. The finance company should be required to make reasonable efforts to place the equipment in as advantageous a lease arrangement to the finance company as possible, as soon as possible after the termination.

An equally unreasonable provision that users should be wary of in leases requires the user, upon a termination of the lease, to return the machinery at the user's expense to any location in Canada designated by the finance company. Such a provision ought to be pruned to require the user to pay the relevant shipping charges only to a delivery point within a reasonable distance from the user's site, such as another location in the same city.

The equipment needs of some users can best be served through a so-called master lease, similar to a master supply contract for buyers (see section C.1). A single master lease applies to all the equipment leased pursuant to a number of so-called equipment schedules made under the master lease. Each equipment schedule will list the specific items of equipment to be leased as a particular unit, the monthly fee for each unit, the relevant purchase option for each unit, and any other details applicable to the specific unit. When entering into such a master lease the user should require that the various schedules be treated, in effect, as separate leases such that if the user fails to pay the monthly fee for one unit the finance company can take action in respect of that unit only and not the others which remain in good standing.

3. MAINTENANCE

Whether a computer system is purchased outright or is leased, the buyer or user will want to ensure that there is adequate maintenance and support for the system, either from the system's supplier or suppliers, or through some other company. As noted earlier, software by its very nature contains errors and certain other deficiencies, many of which cannot be found beforehand and come to light only when the software is in use. The result can be inconvenience, or even chaos when a software bug makes itself known. Hardware, although it is becoming generally more reliable over time, also tends to contain components that break down or malfunction. In short, the technical fallibility of computers requires that buyers and users have at their disposal sufficient maintenance and support expertise to get a system back in working condition in short order, particularly where the organization greatly relies on the continuous operation of the system.

Term of Maintenance Agreement

Most standard form maintenance agreements are for a period of one year, and typically can be terminated by either the customer or the maintenance company on ninety days notice. The short term and early termination option may be convenient for many buyers of maintenance services, but the buyer should consider seriously whether a longer term commitment — at least from the maintenance supplier — would be more convenient. If the estimated useful life of the system is five or even ten years, then the buyer should have the option to require the supplier to provide maintenance for the whole of this period. The buyer should still have the right to terminate the maintenance agreement on specified notice, but the supplier should agree contractually to provide service, if called upon, for virtually as long as the system is installed and being operated.

Given the lengthy nature of the maintenance relationship, the buyer will also want to negotiate some price protection against unreasonable increases in maintenance fees; although in some cases at least the costs for parts of hardware are decreasing, labour costs will no doubt continue to rise. Many suppliers of maintenance services will agree to limit their fee increases to the rise in the consumer price index for at least the first few years of the term of the agreement, but thereafter service is typically provided at "prevailing rates." To get the best price on maintenance services, the buyer ought to negotiate the maintenance agreement at the time it negotiates the hardware acquisition and software licence agreements. Unfortunately, it is often the case that the buyer treats the maintenance agreement as a poor relation to the other two contracts. Not surprisingly, once the purchase and licence deals are already negotiated and signed, the buyer has precious little negotiating leverage left in respect of the maintenance agreement. When all agreements are executed simultaneously, the buyer knows up front — and can negotiate more effectively — all prices, terms, and conditions, including longer term price protection, for all three agreements.

After the expiry of any price protection, the rates for maintenance may rise dramatically, in which case the buyer will also want to explore whether a third party maintenance supplier, of which there are a growing number, could do the job as well and for less money; indeed some buyers utilize the services of third-party maintenance suppliers from the beginning because of their cost effectiveness. The buyer's freedom to change to another maintenance supplier should be addressed in the initial maintenance or perhaps purchase or licence contract: the buyer may need to obtain certain manufacturer's diagnostics maintenance manuals and other specifications and information to be able to service the system (or permit a third party to do so). Some suppliers have been reluctant to release such information, so much so that some third-party maintenance firms in the United States have brought anti-trust legal proceedings against suppliers, arguing that their actions in refusing to permit access to such materials have the effect of blocking competition in the after-sale maintenance services market. In order to avoid such a problem, a request for access to such materials ought to be made before any contracts are signed so that maximum persuasive force may be brought to bear on the supplier.

Some suppliers request a whole year's worth of maintenance fees to be paid in advance. A buyer who agrees to this should get in return a deep discount on the maintenance fee. Furthermore only solvent, large suppliers should receive substantial payment in advance; many buyers in the past who have made advance payments to smaller, financially strapped maintenance organizations have ended up losing many months' worth of maintenance fees when the suppliers went out of business. This point can be expressed by the following seemingly ironic rule of thumb: a buyer should pay maintenance fees well in advance only to those companies that really don't need all the cash up front.

Description of Services and Exclusions

Most standard form maintenance agreements give an adequate description of the services to be provided by the supplier. In some cases, however, the buyer will want to enumerate these services in greater detail. For example, when a supplier says it will perform preventive maintenance for a minicomputer, it may be enough to state that such preventive services will include lubrication, adjustments, and parts replacement as required. By contrast, for a large telecommunications system the buyer may want to spell out exactly what tests and checks the supplier will perform daily, weekly, and monthly, given that such preventive maintenance may include traffic studies and other forms of "strategic" maintenance that are intended to permit the buyer to make better use of its system.

All standard form maintenance agreements set out a long list of services that are *not* included as part of the maintenance and support program, such as electrical work external to the system, repairing damage or malfunction caused by the negligence of the buyer's employees, or in the case of applications software, fixing problems caused by or related to modifications made to the software by the user. In many respects this list merits greater attention from the buyer than the list of services provided; the exclusions should be scrutinized carefully. For example, one common exclusion is the reconditioning of the hardware if the supplier concludes that remedial maintenance is no longer cost effective. A buyer should at least have the maintenance supplier clarify what this means and receive some assurance — in the contract — that under no circumstances will such reconditioning be deemed necessary by the supplier for at least a certain number of years. The best alternative, of course, is to have this clause deleted because it does seem to call into serious doubt the economic value of an expensive all-parts-and-labour maintenance program.

Performance Guarantees

Many standard form agreements do not adequately describe the level of performance the buyer can expect from the maintenance supplier. The buyer should exact from the supplier one or more of the following possible performance guarantees as they apply: when the buyer calls for remedial assistance because of an "emergency" failure of the system, a representative of the supplier will arrive at the buyer's site within two hours, twenty-four hours a day and seven days a week; the system will maintain an "effective level of performance" (see section B.9, "Acceptance Testing," for a discussion of this concept) of 97%

during each calendar month; if the system experiences more than two major failures any month, the supplier must completely replace the faulty components rather than attempt to repair them at the buyer's site; if the main switch on a major private branch exchange of a large telecommunications system becomes seriously inoperable and cannot be fixed within twelve hours, then the supplier will install a temporary switch until the buyer's switch is fixed; if a major problem is not fixed within a certain number of hours, the buyer can call the supplier's American parent to report the problem; the supplier will fix bugs brought to the supplier's attention not only by the buyer, but by other customers of the supplier as well. This list is not exhaustive and there are many variations or combinations of each of these performance standards. For example, while emergency failures might carry a two-hour response time, "major" failures might allow for a four-hour response, while minor (all other) failures might wait until the next business day. And of course phrases such as "emergency failure" and "major failure" should be defined in each case, preferably in relation to the operability of functional elements of the particular system.

The buyer's objective is to establish a cost-effective safety net based on how critical the system is to the organization's operations and continued success. That is, most suppliers will grant these types of performance guarantees, but at a higher cost than their standard maintenance offerings. Thus, the choice confronting the buyer is not unlike buying insurance; the buyer must determine how much it needs relative to what it is prepared to pay. The aim is to be neither overinsured nor underinsured. In this regard, the buyer would be wise to monitor its maintenance needs, perhaps starting out with rather more than fewer maintenance services and then cutting some of them if it finds the reliability levels of certain equipment better than expected. And of course, it is worth repeating the by now familiar refrain that the best prices can usually be had by buyers when they negotiate the maintenance arrangements together with the other supplier agreements.

No discussion of performance guarantees would be complete without mentioning remedies. All the performance yardsticks enumerated above should have financial consequences attached to them if they are not met; for example, the buyer would receive a certain credit against the next month's maintenance charges for every time the supplier fails to respond within the required response time. Buyers should remember however that the main objective of these remedies is not to save money but to encourage the timely performance of obligations. There could be a provision, for example, that if credits or other liquidated damages accumulate to a certain point, then the buyer will have the option to switch suppliers, and that the original supplier will make available to the new supplier any technical information required for system maintenance.

However well thought out and expertly crafted the maintenance agreement, the buyer should always consider that the worst possible computer system malfunction could come to pass and that the maintenance supplier might not be able to respond immediately. Again, with respect to source code availability in such a situation, the user should contemplate requiring the deposit of the source code with an escrow agent who would release it to the user under specified circumstances (see C.7, "Source Code Escrow"). Perhaps more fundamentally, the user also ought to think about operational ways of coping with system malfunction; that is, is there a suitable temporary backup, manual or otherwise, if the system collapses? Or perhaps the system is critical enough to the organization to warrant the purchase of a more expensive redundant system with greater reliability in the first place. Of course even a technically far superior system should be covered by an effective maintenance agreement.

4. SOFTWARE DEVELOPMENT

The Risks of Custom Software

Perhaps the riskiest of all computer acquisition relationships is the one involving the development of custom software by a software developer. So many things can go wrong in a custom development project, as can be seen from the computer acquisition disaster involving the Vancouver-based company (see section A.1, under "Computer Acquisition Disasters"), which involved a custom software development project. The user can misunderstand its own needs, or even if it understands them it can convey them inaccurately to the software developer. As a result, the custom software program will be inadequate for the required task. Or the program can be poorly designed or programmed, in which case it may generally serve the user's purpose but have the disconcerting habit of malfunctioning all too frequently. With standard software, users benefit when the developer makes corrections to the program as errors come to light through the reports of other users; no such benefit comes with custom software because the user is, by definition, the only user.

Because of the very high risk involved in the development of custom software, many users go out of their way to try to use a standard software application, even if this means making some modifications in the user's business or other operating procedures. For example, a user may have found a standard inventory control software program that meets 80% of the user's needs, but unfortunately no software on the market meets 100% of this user's requirements. Some users, in such a situation, would implement this software and retain a software developer to create new software to satisfy the other 20% of the user's inventory control procedures. What might be more advantageous, however, is for such a user to modify this 20% of its business practices so that the standard software can accommodate all the user's requirements. While this may be troublesome and costly, the alternative of developing custom software may be even more so.

Some software suppliers strongly discourage users from requesting the supplier to make custom changes to its standard software. One software supplier does this by bringing to light the potentially extensive costs involved in maintaining custom software (in addition to the expense of creating it in the first place). This supplier, in its standard form agreement, states that while the supplier will perform custom modifications to its basic software, the customer should realize the following: (1) The supplier will provide maintenance and support for the custom modifications only on a time-and-materials basis because the standard maintenance fees cover only the standard base software. (2) The supplier's telephone hotline service cannot answer questions concerning the modifications as the staff manning this service are knowledgeable only about the base software; a telephone request for the modifications would be routed to that client's account manager who would deal with the request on a time and materials basis. Again, this service is not included in the general support and maintenance fee while telephone support for the base software is included. (3) It is the user's responsibility to provide documentation and training for the custom software; the supplier provides these for the base package only. (4) The expense of refitting the custom software to new releases of the base software will be borne by the user. "Fix tapes," which contain software corrections to reported problems and minor enhancements between new releases, cannot be implemented automatically in situations where the base package has been modified; these fixes have to be entered manually, again at the user's additional expense. (5) Finally, this supplier admits that the performance of the base software may be affected negatively by the custom changes.

While not all software suppliers are as forthright about their concerns with custom modifications, in most cases some or all of these additional costs and inconveniences arise when changes or additions are made to standard software. If, after all due consideration, it is decided that custom software is really the only solution, then at least these additional cost issues should be addressed in the contract so that the user can better understand all the ramifications of the custom software development project.

Checking Out the Software Developer

Many software developers are smaller companies that are often very thinly capitalized. A user intending to deal with such a company should do extensive homework on its track record and potential prospects to ensure that it will be a viable business throughout the period of the development project and thereafter if on-going maintenance and support will be required by the user. Such a review could include running a credit check, asking former and current customers of the software developer about their experiences, and even requesting to review a copy of the supplier's financial statements. This exercise should give the user a good sense of the company's prospects for longevity. If the prospects are doubtful then proceeding with the company may be a serious error, for even the most effective, ironclad software development agreement from the user's point of view will not shield the user from significant financial and other pain if the software developer goes belly up halfway through the development project.

Development Control Checkpoints

The creation of software typically proceeds through a rather standard development methodology consisting of several distinct stages. The first phase consists of ascertaining the needs of the user and producing a statement of those needs, typically called the "functional specifications." This statement explains the functions to be included in the custom software. In this sense it may be called the "what" statement. The functional specifications are generally jointly produced by the user and the supplier. In the next phase the developer concentrates on how the new custom program will operate so as to perform the necessary functions as set out in the "what" statement. The statement produced as a result of this second stage, generally referred to as the "design specifications," may be called the "how" statement. This statement explains in detail how the program will carry out its various tasks and what the actual operating characteristics of the software will be. It is from the design specifications that the programmers write a "first draft" of the code for the program in the appropriate computer language. The "first draft" is subject to a series of tests to work out any "bugs," or errors. It is often only through rigorous testing that many errors make themselves apparent. With very large software programs, there are that many more system design and programming errors to be corrected in this trial period. It is generally only after a good deal of such testing and refining that the final version of the program is delivered to the user.

Of course not all custom software is the product of these four distinct stages of development. From the user's point of view, however, this orderly, phased development process allows the user to impose a contractual discipline upon the software developer. This requires the user to institute a control checkpoint at each of the stages in the process, typically a review or acceptance test bolstered by a payment milestone. Thus, the first control checkpoint is the user's approval of the functional specifications. Accordingly, the contract should require that these specifications be delivered to the user by a certain date, failing which, the typical sorts of remedies for nondelivery in general (discussed in detail in sections B.4 and B.15), should be available. Upon delivery of the functional specifications, the user should have an opportunity to review them and request clarifications. If satisfied, the user would then approve the functional specifications and pay a portion of the contract price. If the functional specifications were unsatisfactory, the user could allow the developer to try again, or, if the user did not see any hope for the functional specifications, the user should have the ability to terminate the agreement, perhaps in conjunction with a payment to the developer of a certain amount (always subject to a ceiling, and never to include a profit component) for the development efforts expended to that point. In return the user would have the right to own or use all the material created by the developer prior to termination inasmuch as the user's next software developer might find this material useful.

Other control checkpoints should be established for the delivery and approval of the design specifications, the delivery of the programmed software, and the acceptance test for the operation of the software. In short, through a staged development process the user can monitor the progress being made by the developer with a view to dealing effectively with any difficulties as soon as they arise and before they become big, expensive problems. Contrast this process to the sorry software development disaster involving the Vancouver plastics company (see section A.1, under "Computer Acquisition Disasters"). In that case the user did not insist that the development process follow discrete phases, and as a result found it difficult to shut the project down even when it became clear that the software development effort would likely prove to be unsuccessful. That case illustrates what can happen if a software developer is not subject to discipline by means of an effective contract that breaks the project down into several distinct phases and provides the buyer with effective remedies at each stage.

Two additional observations are relevant to the phased implementation of software development. First, if at all possible the functional specification document should be finalized before or at the time the agreement is negotiated, and it should be appended to the contract. While the production of this document can be made a milestone of the project, as noted above, completion of this document before the buyer commits to the project is the preferred route, given that being able to attach a solid technical reference point to the agreement invariably reduces the risk that the project will become derailed at a later date. A recurring problem with software development projects is that both sides underestimate the amount of effort required to develop the custom software. By agreeing on the functional specifications beforehand, both parties will have a much clearer idea of the cost, risk, and time involved to complete the subsequent stages of the project. There will then be less chance of poor performance on the part of the developer, and of the need to exercise remedies on the part of the user.

If the functional specifications are not ready at the time the main software development agreement is to be signed, it is sometimes a good idea to hold off signing the agreement and, instead, to have the user and supplier enter into a consulting agreement under which the functional specifications will be developed on a "time and materials" basis. Then, when the functional specifications are ready, they can be appended to the software development agreement under which the software, to be based on the functional sp ifications, can be developed, possibly for a fixed price. By contrast, it would be foolish for either a user or a supplier to agree to a fixed-price software development contract where the functional specifications have not yet been developed and agreed to by both parties.

Even where the functional specifications form part of the contract, there should be in any software development contract a provision that sets out the process by which changes can be made to the functional specifications as well as the system design specifications (before or after they are delivered by the supplier and approved or rejected by the buyer). An effective process would entail the buyer's delivering a written request to the developer (e.g., the custom software accounts payable program requires a monthly reporting feature which was not previously contemplated). The developer must then respond to this request within a certain period, stating the cost of the additional feature, its impact on the project implementation schedule, its impact on the performance of the software overall, any changes it would necessitate in the maintenance or support obligations of the developer or charges to the user, and any other effects it would have on the project. In short, the developer would think through how such a requested change would affect all aspects of the development project. After receiving a detailed written reply from the developer, the user will have to decide whether the various aspects of the modification are acceptable. If they are, then the contract would clearly provide that upon acceptance of such a change the other parts of the agreement affected by such change will be deemed to be modified accordingly. The essential objective of such a procedure is to provide for a disciplined yet flexible system for changing the scope of a software development project in mid-stream, an activity that can be very dangerous if it is not thought through and documented properly. Indeed, what may be initially an effective agreement, from the user's point of view, can be made virtually useless if the user agrees to subsequent changes that discount or sometimes altogether displace the user's hard-won concessions in the original contract.

Close attention in the software development contract should be paid to documentation — both the user's instructions and manuals and the source code narrative — particularly to its quality and timely delivery. It often happens that a busy software developer, scrambling to meet a delivery deadline, fails to expend the effort necessary to produce quality documentation. Such an omission can adversely affect both the training of the user's personnel and the user's ability to adequately test the software, inasmuch as the user's prime benchmark, the related documentation, is perhaps still merely a glint in the software developer's eye. This is rarely as problematic an issue with standard software; documentation is usually available for standard software (although its quality, too, can sometimes be highly questionable). Accordingly, the development contract should be unequivocal about documentation delivery, both in terms of its timing and its quality.

The user and the developer should agree to the quality of the documentation to be produced. The developer may be a supplier of standard software products for which the documentation is of a suitable quality from the user's perspective; then these existing items can be made the standard to which the new documentation must measure up. Alternatively, the documentation of another software supplier might serve as a standard. If no existing documentation can be found to serve as a general guide, then perhaps user and developer could agree on a functional test for the quality of the documentation and make the test a part of the agreement. For instance, the documentation must be such that a user (or a programmer in the case of source code) of average skill and ability should be able to operate the software based solely on the user's familiarity with the software. This quality requirement for the documentation (including source code) should be rigorously reviewed as part of the acceptance test for the custom computer program.

Ownership of Custom Software

The question of who owns standard software almost never arises because the ownership of the developer is made clear in the standard form licence agreement; users almost never challenge the software developer's right to be the owner of its standard software and are usually perfectly satisfied with a nonexclusive licence to use it. Not so with custom software. The user, having paid for custom development, thinks it ought to own it, while the software developer feels an equally strong sense of proprietorship. As this tends to be a very contentious issue, it is worth reviewing the respective positions of the two sides; often an understanding of each side's essential interests can lead in short order to a mutually satisfactory resolution of the ownership issue.

From the user's perspective, the key issues generally underlying the ownership question are money and exclusivity. Because the user is paying for the development of the software, it feels it should own it (after all, argues the user, isn't that how most every other commercial arrangement works — you get to keep what you paid for?). The user is also concerned, particularly where the custom software is going to give the user a visible edge in the marketplace, that the user's competitors not be able to get access to or make use of the particular software. The underlying thought of the user here is: "We came up with the bright idea for this software, so why should we allow the software developer to permit our competition to have the benefits of our ideas?"

The developer takes quite a different but equally defensible view of the ownership question. The developer's essential concern is that if the user ends up with ownership, and if this ownership means that the developer cannot work on similar software in the future, the developer may be denying itself later work in a whole segment of the marketplace. If this is so, then a developer, particularly one with a narrow line of products, would only agree to ownership resting with the user if the user paid a huge sum of money to the developer so that all the developer's employees could retire immediately after the completion of the user's software, because they might have nothing further to do. This concern of the developer is becoming more acute with the current expansion in the scope of copyright law protection for computer software by some courts (as noted in section B.16, "Intellectual Property Rights Indemnity"). Whereas previously most courts took the view that copyright law protected only the literal form of expression of source code listings, more recently several judges have been deciding in software copyright infringement cases that copyright law also protects a program's "sequence, structure and organization." With this new legal test, a software developer's ability to create software with a similar function to that sold previously to a custom purchaser may be greatly circumscribed if not precluded altogether. In short, the developer responds to the user's arguments in favour of user ownership with the sentiment that development costs would be prohibitive if the user were to become the owner.

To illustrate the different viewpoints, software developers could compare the request for user ownership to a cab company's requesting Ford to produce only for that cab company a special engine that ran on propane. Ford would of course disagree with the exclusivity request because it would want to recoup its development costs over a broad market. The software user might respond that this is an inappropriate analogy, and that a better one is the commissioning of a major sculpture by a company from an artist for display outside the company's headquarters. It would not do to have an exact copy of the sculpture parked outside another company's headquarters just down the street, so the first company buys the sculpture outright — including the copyright.

The question of which party ought to own custom software is a difficult one, but can best be solved by understanding the fundamental objectives of each party. To meet the concerns on both sides, consider the following arrangement that has worked reasonably well in a number of software development agreements.

The developer retains ownership of the software, but subject to two important conditions. First, the developer cannot market, license, or in any other way make the particular software, or any functionally equivalent software, available to any competitor of the user for a certain period of time. And after this period, if the developer does make the software available to a third party, the developer must reimburse the user a certain percentage of the fees already paid by the user for the development of the software, either as a direct cash payment, or perhaps as a credit against on-going maintenance services. In short, without acquiring ownership of the software, the user nevertheless has achieved its essential goals, and the software developer is also satisfied.

In some respects, dealing with the question of exclusivity in such express terms is superior to trying to achieve exclusivity through user ownership of the custom software, given the rather uncertain scope of copyright law protection for software. If a supplier sells outright a custom modification, it knows it cannot produce an identical piece of software for any other customer. This does not, however, prohibit the developer from producing software of similar functionality. And just how close this second program may come to the first is an issue that can never be determined with certainty, except by a judge in an infringement case, which all parties would prefer to avoid. Therefore, by providing for developer ownership coupled with the express prohibition to market the software, or functionally equivalent software, to the user's competition for a certain period of time, the user will have instituted a form of control that gives the supplier far more direction as to what is permissible conduct on its part.

Since the user will not likely acquire ownership, and if it does not obtain a licence to the source code of the custom software, the user will want to take appropriate steps to ensure the on-going availability of the source code. Because the developer may go out of business or cease to support the custom software at some point, the user should see that a copy of the source code is placed in escrow with a third party, who would release the source code to the user under such conditions (see section C.7, "Source Code Escrow").

5. CONSULTING

A user of computing resources often retains a consultant to provide various services, which can include advising the user as to the kind of computer system to acquire and even developing custom software for the user. Consultants and consulting firms come in many forms, from the large, well-staffed advisory groups at large accounting firms and information technology consultants who advise only on computer, telecommunications, and related matters, to the small, one- or two-person software development company.

A user should choose consultants with some care. The user will want to be satisfied, for instance, that the consultant is absolutely objective when giving advice and is not subject to any factors that would put the consultant into a conflict-of-interest situation. This is particularly important where the user is retaining a consultant to assist in preparing a request for proposal (see section D.1 for a discussion of the request for proposal) and then assisting with the selection of a vendor from those that respond to the request for proposal. A number of consultants who provide such vendor-selection-related consulting services may also be suppliers of computing resources in their own right. Accordingly, a user will want assurance from such a prospective consultant that its supplier-related activities in no way compromise its ability to provide totally independent and objective advice, free from even the possible appearance of conflict of interest.

A user will also want to review the professional designation, if any, of its prospective consultants. For example, in Canada certified management consultants are recognized by the designation "CMC," or "Certified Management Consultant;" there are, however, many consultants who practice outside the jurisdiction of a provincial institute of certified management consultants, or some other similar organization, that has been established to provide consumer protection. The CMC accreditation is attained by completing a three-year education program, which includes a practical apprenticeship component and passing a final examination. Certified Management Consultants must practice in accordance with the guidelines of a professional code of conduct which, among other things, requires a CMC to be free of any conflict of interest in carrying out a consultancy mandate. The code of conduct is enforced by the discipline committee of the local institute of certified management consultants. This institute can also provide prospective users of consultancy services with a listing of CMC members by reference to their specialty areas, one of which comprises information technology consulting.

When retaining a consultant, the user should make it very clear what services the user expects from the consultant. A recent court decision illustrates that the consultant should also be eager to specify with precision the scope of the consultancy mandate. In this case a manufacturing company retained a consulting firm in respect of its proposed acquisition of a computer system. The procurement turned into a classic system acquisition disaster, not unlike those described in section A.1. The user, rather than take legal action against the supplier of the computer, sued the consultant, arguing that the consultant had been negligent in failing to provide the necessary system implementation, testing, training, and other services required of it, given that the user had retained the consultant to deliver a "turn-key system," namely, one that would be completely operational when turned over to the user. The consultant, in its defence, countered that it was retained for a much narrower purpose, specifically, to assist in evaluating the client's needs, preparing the request for proposal, and helping with vendor selection. The judge held that the consultant was in fact retained to ensure the implementation of a turn-key system, and as this had not happened the judge found the consultant to have been negligent. The court ordered the consultant to pay the user $82,500 in damages. Such a result, and more importantly the computer acquisition disaster itself, might have been avoided had the user and the consultant agreed at the start of their relationship precisely what each was expecting of the other.

Users should also guard against consultants straying beyond their particular area of professional expertise. For example, some consultants will offer to provide what effectively amounts to legal services by volunteering to review, and in some cases even to draft, the relevant contracts to be used for the computer acquisition. This is a dangerous practice. Reviewing and drafting the specific language of computer contracts are activities that properly fall into the domain of lawyers — preferably ones experienced in computer matters. Just as a user should not look to a lawyer for information technology consulting advice, so should a user not request, or allow, a consultant to draft computer contracts.

When a user retains a consultant, the user must be careful to ensure that the consultant signs a written agreement intended to protect the proprietary rights of the user. Such an agreement should cover at least the following issues: nondisclosure of user information, nonsolicitation of employees, and ownership of work product. (Each of these important issues is discussed below.) If the consultant is a corporation, the user should ensure that the employees or individual consultants hired by the corporate consultant also sign a proprietary rights protection agreement directly with the user. In this way the user can be satisfied that all individuals who may have access to the user's proprietary information through the consulting arrangement are bound by protective provisions. It is inadvisable to rely solely on the corporate consultant to look after this important matter.

Nondisclosure of User Information

The need for buyers or users to state in their computer acquisition agreements that the supplier will take protective measures with respect to the user's confidential information has already been discussed (see section B.20, "Buyer's Confidential Information; Publicity"). In many respects it is even more important to include a confidentiality clause in a consulting agreement, given that a consultant will likely have access to a greater amount of the user's sensitive information. At a minimum, the confidentiality provision should describe what kind of confidential information of the user will be disclosed to the consultant, and state that, with respect to this information, (1) the consultant will not acquire any form of ownership right in it, but shall be able to use it only to perform consulting services for the user and for no other purpose; (2) the consultant shall not copy or use such material except as required to provide the user with consulting services; (3) the consultant shall not disclose such material to any third party without the permission of the user; and (4) access to the material by the consultant's employees shall be permitted only to those employees who sign an additional nondisclosure agreement. This latter point is important because, as noted above, if the consultant is a corporate entity and only it signs the nondisclosure agreement, there is a possibility that the consultant's obligations do not effectively bind its employees. To eliminate this possible loophole the employees of the consultant assigned to the user's project should personally acknowledge their duty of confidentiality by signing virtually the same nondisclosure agreement as their corporate employer.

When describing the type of information that will be subject to nondisclosure protections, the user should specifically reference the information of its customers or clients if this is appropriate. For example, a user that is an insurance company should get a contractual commitment from the consultant to keep confidential the personal and other information of the user's policyholders that the consultant inevitably will come into contact with. Indeed, in some cases the user itself may have a strict duty of confidentiality, whether under law or by contract, with respect to such information, and a key means of discharging this duty is to have others who come into contact with such information through the user, such as a computer consultant and its employees, sign nondisclosure agreements.

In some situations users may decide that simply providing for nondisclosure in the consulting agreement is not enough protection. A user may be concerned, for example, that if the consultant provides services to a competitor of the user while working for the user or soon thereafter, the user may not be able to monitor effectively whether in fact the user's confidential information is being disclosed to the competitor. To avoid such difficult situations, some users require consultants to agree not to perform for a competitor of the user the same services in respect of the competitor's competing products during the period that the consultant works for the user and for a period of, say, six months thereafter. The aim being to protect only the reasonable business interests of the user, the restriction should not be too broad. This security measure will protect the user against the unauthorized and perhaps inadvertant dissemination of its information, and, if crafted carefully, will usually not be objected to by consultants.

Nonsolicitation of Employees

Some consultants stipulate in their standard form agreements that the user cannot solicit the employees of the consultant or even offer them employment if in fact the consultant's employees approach the user. These provisions are intended to protect the consultant from a very common occurrence: after one of the consultant's employees has worked closely with the user over a period of time, perhaps on the implementation of a major computer system, and has built up more expertise in the operation of the new system than anyone on the user's staff, this consultant's employee is offered attractive terms of employment by the user. Software developers share this occupational hazard and often lose valuable personnel to users as a result of the software developer employee's long and sustained contact with the user over the course of a project. It should be noted that employees can flow the other way as well; it is quite common for an employee of a user to join a consultant or software development company.

Dealing with this movement of employees only through a nonsolicitation clause can often be unsatisfactory. Such a clause may, in the first place, be unenforceable at law as being an unreasonable restraint on competition. Even if it were enforceable, or at least neither party challenged its validity, there is still the problem that it can lead to a great deal of discontentment both in its observance as well as in its breach. An alternative approach taken by some consultants is to replace such a blanket prohibition with the more positive and remunerative provision that if the user hires one of the consultant's employees during the term of the consultancy, or for a period of, say, three months thereafter, the user will pay to the consultant, as a form of employment-agency and training fee, an amount of money equal to some percentage of the employee's first year salary with the user. The benefit in this mechanism is that it allows employees to choose freely where they want to work, but it also recognizes to a degree the cost incurred by the consultant in losing a valued member of its staff.

Ownership of Work Product

A critical issue to be addressed in any user-consultant relationship is which party will own the work product — whether it be software, technical specifications, or documentation — developed by the consultant during the consultancy. Unfortunately, because this question often is not dealt with expressly or in writing, many such situations end in protracted and acrimonious legal proceedings.

Consider, for instance, the situation in which a user retains a consultant to develop a small but important software module for the user's much larger software program. No contract of any nature is ever signed between them. The user pays the consultant a monthly fee.

After the project is finished the module proves to be so successful that the user, which is not a software developer and has never marketed any of its proprietary software before, grants several lucrative sublicences for the module to other users. The consultant learns of this licence fee revenue and demands a share of it from the user. The user refuses on the ground that the user owns the software module. The consultant reviews the Copyright Act and realizes that except in the case of employees (discussed in the next section below), the author of a copyrightable work, which includes software, is the first owner of such work and that ownership in a copyrighted work may be transferred only by means of a written contract. Armed with this information, the consultant informs the user that in fact the consultant owns the module and that the user merely has a licence to use it for its internal purposes, but that the sublicensing to other users is not included in the licence from the consultant. The user replies that, given its monthly payments, the consultant had impliedly transferred ownership to the user. And they have the makings of a long, drawn-out lawsuit, which could have easily been avoided by deciding initially, on paper, who was going to own the module once it was created. This agreement might have included, incidentally, a provision whereby the consultant received a 10% royalty on all sublicence fees, if any, received by the user in respect of the distribution of the module, to a maximum of a certain amount.

If the ownership of work product clause in the consulting agreement vests title in the resulting work with the user, then the clause should also include a provision whereby the consultant waives all so-called moral rights in the work. Moral rights are guaranteed by the Copyright Act to all authors and continue in favour of the authors even after they have sold the copyright in the work (unless these moral rights are given up or waived). Moral rights permit the author to object to a certain use of the work if it would reasonably be expected to diminish the reputation of the author. Such rights are more relevant to creative works such as music or artwork. (The Canadian artist Michael Snow exercised these rights a few years ago. His sculpture *Flight Stop*, a series of sixty Canada Geese in bronze, was commissioned by Toronto's Eaton Centre in 1979 and is permanently displayed in the centre's shopping galleria. As part of the 1983 Christmas decorations, red ribbons were tied around the necks of the geese. Snow objected to the ribbons and, although he did not own the sculptures, he was able to have the ribbons removed two weeks later by virtue of his moral rights in his work.) But the application of moral rights to computer software or documentation is not inconceivable. As such, the document by which the consultant (and its employees) assigns its copyright in such works to the user should state clearly that the consultant (and its employees) waive all their moral rights in such works.

6. PROPRIETARY RIGHTS PROTECTION — EMPLOYEES

Many of the protection issues discussed in the preceding section on consulting agreements apply with equal vigour to any number of other situations in which users permit various entities to have access to their computer systems and their confidential material. The most important group in terms of numbers and sustained access to the user's materials is, of course, the user's employees. Accordingly, through either employment agreements or more sharply focused nondisclosure agreements, the user should establish the same kinds of protective measures with employees as with consultants, but with some modifications as discussed below.

A user should have those of its employees that have access to confidential materials sign a nondisclosure agreement that restricts disclosure, copying, and use, and clearly acknowledges that such materials do not belong to the employee. In addition, it is a good idea to explain the rationale behind such a provision at periodic seminars held for employees on the subject of why and how to protect the user's confidential information. The seminars should point out that the user, and by implication each employee, is harmed when the user's confidential information is disclosed in an unauthorized manner. The need to protect third-party information should also be emphasized at such sessions, by reminding employees of the requirement that all employees comply with the nondisclosure and no-copying rules imposed on the user by the owners of the software programs licensed to the user. Software suppliers are with increasing frequency suing users for the improper copying of licensed software by the users' employees (see section B.10 under "Restrictions on Copying"). It is also in order to minimize the risk of such lawsuits that users should have employees sign nondisclosure agreements and undertake to educate staff as to the proper way to handle proprietary and third-party confidential information.

Users may also want to include noncompetition provisions in the employee's employment or nondisclosure agreement for much the same reasons that they impose similar restrictions on consultants. All such clauses, again, must be crafted very carefully because if they go beyond what is necessary to protect an employer's reasonable business interests they may be unenforceable; as a general rule courts are unsympathetic to noncompetition restrictions on employees, and judges have little hesitation knocking down those that are overly broad in terms of geographic scope, temporal duration, or scope of the activity being restricted. It is often preferable, for example, to restrict the noncompetition clause to a more enforceable period of perhaps six months than to possibly overreach with twelve months, only to have the twelve months' period found unreasonable by a court, in which case the employee would not be bound by any contractual period of noncompetition. (The employee, depending on his or her level of seniority, may still have other general obligations under the law which temper prospective competitive behaviour, such as a so-called fiduciary duty to the former employer not to pursue a business opportunity that the employee learned about while working for its former employer in a senior managerial capacity.) Courts are, however, somewhat more receptive to a restriction on an employee's soliciting the customers of the former employer, and often such a nonsolicitation of customers clause is used in conjunction with a noncompetition restriction.

The Copyright Act provides that where an employee produces a copyrightable work in the course of his or her employment the copyright in such work belongs to the employer.

Notwithstanding this legal rule, users should still have employees expressly transfer their rights in any products or materials
they develop to the user in order that there will be absolutely no
question about who owns what. This transfer can most effectively be accomplished in a two-step process. First, upon commencing employment the employee should sign an agreement
that provides that the ownership of all works created by the
employee, including the related copyrights, trade secrets, and
patent rights, will belong to the employer. Second, when leaving
the employment of the user, the employee should sign a document confirming the transfer of such rights to the user. Assuming
that the particular software on which the employee worked is
developed at this point, this second document should refer, by
name, to all the specific items of software covered by the assignment. And as the employer ownership rule in the Copyright Act
does not address the issue of moral rights, both assignment documents should have employees waive their moral rights to any
works produced by them. (For an explanation of "moral rights,"
see section C.5 under "Ownership of Work Product.")

An agreement containing such protective provisions should
always be signed, if at all possible, at the time the employee
commences employment with the user. If this is not possible,
the agreement should be signed when the employee is given a
job promotion or pay raise, and it should be clear in the agreement that part of the consideration for the promotion or salary
increase is the employee's willingness to sign the document.
Having the agreement signed under such circumstances (or taking other measures discussed with legal counsel), decreases the
likelihood that the employee could successfully argue that the
agreement is not binding on the employee because the employee received no benefit from it — it being a basic principle of
contract law that for a contract to be binding both sides must
have received something of value under it.

It is also useful to include in the nondisclosure agreement a
provision whereby the employee acknowledges that by coming
to work for the user the employee is not bringing to the user
any confidential information of the former employer (or of any
other entity) and that there are no agreements which might conflict with the provisions of the employee's new confidentiality
agreement. Such a provision is useful in order to show to the

rest of the world that the user does not even remotely want to be using the proprietary rights of others in an unauthorized manner. Of course it is not enough merely to have this sentiment on paper; if, for example, the user finds a document of a competitor labelled "confidential" on the desk of a new employee, then prompt steps must be taken to return the material and to discipline the employee. In a similar vein, when an employee leaves the user an extensive "exit interview" should be held during which the employee should be reminded of the important nondisclosure and other obligations of the employee to the user that will continue after the employment relationship ceases.

The user may from time to time disclose its confidential information, or allow access to its licensed computer programs, to persons other than consultants or employees. For example, the user may decide to have maintenance performed on the system by someone other than the supplier. In such a case the user should have the third-party maintenance company sign the supplier's standard form nondisclosure agreement. Or the user may want to enter into a relationship with another user to jointly develop some custom software that each user would then be able to use, albeit perhaps in different market niches. In such a situation, where the two users would determine the specifications of the new product and then retain a software developer to create the product or have the work done in-house if they had the expertise, the users should enter into a nondisclosure agreement to cover each party's materials as well as to establish who will own the resulting software. In effect, whenever the user permits anyone to have access to its sensitive information it should ensure that the entity given such access is contractually bound to treat the material in a confidential manner.

Proprietary Rights Protection Policy

By this point it is hopefully crystal clear how vitally important it is for a user of computers to safeguard its own proprietary software assets as well as those only licensed to it. A major element of any protection plan is to have consultants, employees, and others who have access to such materials sign proprietary rights protection agreements as discussed above. In addition, it is useful to provide these people with a document that sets out clearly, concisely, and in easy-to-understand terms the various policies and procedures of the user regarding the protection of proprietary and other confidential information. This proprietary rights protection policy should begin by listing the various types of proprietary information that will come into the hands of employees and consultants. This would include the user's own software and documentation, of course, but would also encompass a number of other items, such as confidential business or financial information, marketing and new-product plans, customer lists, and the confidential information entrusted to the user, such as data regarding the user's customers and software licensed to the user.

After describing the relevant proprietary information, the policy should state how important these materials are to the organization and that, accordingly, all staff are required to protect them by, among other means, the procedures described in the policy. It is important to stress to employees that inadvertent, let alone conscious, disclosure of proprietary information to persons outside the company can cause great harm to the company — as well as to the livelihood of the people employed by it; in short, the protection of proprietary rights is every employee's business, and every employee should take the task seriously.

The policy should note that some of the proprietary information handled by the company, such as software licensed by the company, is actually owned by others and is typically provided to the company for a particular purpose only. The policy should emphasize that it is imperative to treat such material with the utmost care, particularly because the company is invariably obligated by contract — in the case of software, under software licence agreements — to keep confidential this third-party material, and because an improper disclosure of it by an employee could expose the company to a breach-of-contract claim (as noted in section B.10, "Licence of Software").

After noting why the protection of proprietary rights is so important, the policy should describe the actual procedures and practices utilized by the company to ensure such protection. In this regard a key element will be a description of the physical security measures instituted to safeguard trade secrets and confidential information, as trade secret protection can be easily lost if adequate measures are not taken to keep the particular item secret. The following are a few basic examples of such physical security measures: cleaning desks at the end of each day and keeping the proprietary material in locked filing cabinets; locking the doors and otherwise limiting access to areas where proprietary material is kept; utilizing state-of-the-art password and other access security devices for the user's computer systems; and implementing visitor-control procedures, such as keeping a visitors' log, issuing visitor badges, and excluding visitors from areas where trade secrets or other confidential materials are kept. This is not an exhaustive list by any means, and each company should carefully review its own operations and "corporate culture" to institute the right mix of physical security measures. These should then be clearly described in the policy so that all staff know exactly what is required of them in this important area.

The proprietary rights protection policy should briefly explain the terms "trade secret," "copyright," "patent," and "trademark," and how each is obtained and maintained. It should also point out that to obtain and maintain protection for proprietary rights and information certain formal requirements must be met. For example, company documents that contain trade secrets or confidential information should be clearly marked as follows:

TRADE SECRETS/CONFIDENTIAL INFORMATION

THIS MATERIAL CONTAINS TRADE SECRETS AND/OR CONFIDENTIAL INFORMATION OF [name of company] AND MAY NOT BE USED, DISCLOSED, OR COPIED WITHOUT THE PERMISSION OF [name of company].

The policy should also note that, in addition to being properly marked, materials containing trade secrets or confidential information should be treated in accordance with the physical security measures outlined elsewhere in the proprietary rights protection policy. The policy should go on to explain how patent rights are acquired and how trade-marks and copyrights are registered. The policy should also contain the form of copyright notice that should be placed on the company's copyrightable works, including software and related documentation. The notice should contain three elements: the symbol "C" in a circle, not merely in brackets; the year of first publication; and the name of the owner of the material. The copyright notice should appear prominently on the first page of written material and should be embedded in software so that it appears on the first screen visible to a user of the program. While not mandatory, this copyright notice is useful as it makes it difficult for a copier of the software to argue that it did not know the material was copyrighted, and hence greater damages can likely be recovered from the infringer.

The proprietary rights protection policy should encourage employees to strictly limit the number of copies made of documents containing trade secrets or confidential information. The indiscriminate copying of such materials greatly increases the risk that the sensitive information contained in them will be disclosed to unauthorized parties. To this end, such documents should be made available only to selected employees on a strictly "need-to-know" basis. In some circumstances it may also be useful to keep a log of authorized copies and to prohibit the further reproduction of such copies. When such copies are no longer required, they should be shredded or otherwise destroyed rather than merely thrown out with the regular waste. While some of these measures may seem extreme, the policy should explain that these and other measures, such as the physical security measures discussed above, are required in order to help the company protect its valuable information-based assets. The company should also take great pains to ensure that computer software licensed by it from others is strictly controlled so as to prevent its unauthorized copying, as discussed in section B.10 (under "Restrictions On Copying").

The proprietary rights protection policy should address the problem of software viruses, which are causing increasing concern among both users and suppliers of computer resources. The term "software virus" was coined to describe the destructive bits of a computer program that malicious employees of software developers can purposely implant within software, usually in a manner so that the consciously programmed error will be triggered at some time in the future, often long after the particular employee who implanted it has left the software developer. The word "virus" refers to the way these high-tech boobytraps can spread themselves from computer to computer by means of telecommunications links or otherwise.

Employees are not the only ones who can perpetrate damage with computer viruses. In a highly publicized case recently in the United States, Robert T. Morris, a former graduate student at Cornell University, was convicted under the U.S Computer Fraud and Abuse Act for letting loose a "worm," a certain type of virus, into the Internet computer network, thereby causing between two thousand and six thousand computers on the network to grind to a halt. Initial estimates of the damage caused by the virus ranged from US$500,000 to US$90-million, though some commentators have suggested that the total damage was more likely in the US$3-million range. Mr. Morris was sentenced to three years probation, fined $10,000, and ordered to perform four hundred hours of community service.

The virus problem is not new. Several years ago, *Time* magazine devoted a cover story to the menace. The widespread publicity given the Morris virus and several other similar incidents more recently has caused even the most tolerant computer professional to ask what can be done about this growing problem, which threatens to be the Achilles' heel of the computer revolution. There are several measures that responsible computer professionals can take to combat viruses. First, programmers employed by software developers or the information-system departments of users must be reminded regularly that by implanting a virus they are committing a criminal offence.

Amendments made to Canada's Criminal Code in the mid-1980s make it illegal for a person to obtain unauthorized access to someone else's computer, or to destroy or alter data, or to obstruct or interfere with the lawful use of data. The last-mentioned crime is clearly committed where a computer virus destroys data. It is perhaps somewhat more problematic whether "benign" viruses would also be covered under the Criminal Code. For example, some viruses do not destroy data or software, but merely convey a message, such as "Merry Christmas," as was the case with a virus that displayed this greeting on countless microcomputer programs on December 25 several years ago. While such a virus seems to be harmless, in fact it still causes users serious anxiety and trouble. While it may not destroy data, it does take up some memory capacity and denies a user, for however short a period of time, access to his or her preferred screen (substituting for it the one with the

unexpected message). Moreover, the existence of even a seemingly benign virus indicates that the program has been infected
with unwanted elements, and hence generally leads users to
expend time and money to eradicate it, inasmuch as they cannot know the nature or extent of the infection. In effect, what a
hacker might have meant to be an innocuous joke turns out to
cause significant damage. Even a benign virus, therefore,
should be caught by the Criminal Code's computer-abuse provisions because it obstructs, interrupts, or interferes with the
lawful use of data.

In addition to making it clear to programmers that implanting viruses can result, upon conviction under the Criminal
Code, in significant fines and imprisonment for up to 10 years,
users should have their staff and outside consultants acknowledge and agree to, in writing, certain "computer protection
rules" in the workplace, such as not loading unauthorized software onto the company's systems. These rules, when coupled
with the technical measures currently available to detect viruses, should help to avoid unintentional infections by viruses.
Organizations can also take certain measures in an effort to
protect themselves from viruses when acquiring software.
(These are discussed in section B.13.) None of these contracting
and legal measures can ensure a virus-free computer environment. They do, however, help foster responsible computing
within the software-development and data-processing commu-
nities, which ultimately is the only effective antidote to the
virus problem.

It is not enough that a company merely have a proprietary
rights protection policy; it must also implement and enforce it.
A policy that is written down, but then left to languish on some
dusty shelf is of no use to the company. Rather, the policy
should be widely distributed, and life should be breathed into it
by a senior officer, or a committee of managers in a larger company, so that its protection policies and procedures become second nature to all staff.

In many respects employee education is the key to a successful
proprietary rights protection policy. Periodic seminars on the
subjects covered by the policy are invaluable, particularly when
they address new issues not adequately covered by the existing
policy. And of course the policy must be enforced. The individual

or the group responsible for the policy should review its implementation to ensure that all relevant employees are aware of and are abiding by the policy; that suitable physical security, document marking, and other measures, are being taken in respect of the company's proprietary information; that third-party software is being used strictly in accordance with relevant licence agreements; and that an inventory is being kept of, and appropriate measures are being taken to preserve and protect, the company's trade secret, patent, copyright, and trade-mark assets.

7. SOURCE CODE ESCROW

As has already been noted, software is most often made available to users in its object code format rather than as source code (for a discussion of this distinction see section A.3 under "Software"). And on more than one occasion previously it has also been mentioned that many software developers are small companies, often consisting of only a few employees, some office furniture, and a large bank debt. These two facts often have the result that the user is left with only the object code version of the software (if the software developer goes bankrupt) and is perhaps unable to obtain maintenance and support for the software. If the software is of particular importance to the user such a state of affairs may be entirely unacceptable, even for a short period of time. Such a risk need not be confined to a bankruptcy situation. The software developer, even a large solvent one, may simply decide to discontinue support of the particular software licensed to the user, again leaving the user in a highly exposed position.

In order to lessen the adverse impact of such a bankruptcy or product abandonment, many users insist that the software developer deposit with a neutral third party, called an escrow agent, a copy of the source code for the program. By an agreement among the user, the supplier, and the escrow agent, the supplier agrees that upon the occurrence of certain events — such as the inability of the supplier to provide the user with software support because of the bankruptcy of the supplier (or any other reason) — the user shall be entitled to receive a copy of the source code from the escrow agent. The escrow agreement serves the security needs of the user by assuring that it has access to the source code if the supplier is unable to service the user, and it meets the key objective of the supplier of keeping the source code out of the possession of the user or any third party until such time as the supplier is in default of its contractual obligations to deliver maintenance and support services. Because they meet these seemingly divergent needs rather effectively, escrow agreements have become a very common form of computer contract.

Many software suppliers have developed their own standard form of escrow agreements. The user should ensure that the following issues are properly dealt with in the agreement before signing it. First, the agreement should include a broad definition of what the supplier must deposit with the escrow agent. Some agreements simply describe the relevant material as the source code for the object code version of the software licensed by the user, and in some cases this may be sufficient. In other situations, however, the user will need documentation and materials other than the source code to maintain or modify the software. For example, in an escrow involving a point-of-sale computer system, which included proprietary hardware and software, the escrowed materials included the technical documentation for the hardware because this, too, would be needed by the user to maintain the particular system in the absence of the supplier. The most comprehensive approach to ensure that adequate materials are put into escrow in the case of software is to require in the agreement that what is to be deposited with the escrow agent is the source code and whatever other materials are required to recreate and maintain the object code version of the software (and hardware, if relevant) licensed by the user.

Software programs are continually being updated and new releases of the same program are constantly superseding earlier ones. Accordingly, the escrow agreement should require the supplier to update regularly the escrowed materials to include any new segments of source code and documents that correspond to the user's most current object code version of the software. Some standard form escrow agreements acknowledge the need for such updating by including a provision that once every calendar year the supplier will put into escrow any additional materials. Such a clause is quite inadequate. If the escrow package is updated in December and a new object code release is delivered in February, the user could go ten months before the corresponding source code and related materials are deposited with the escrow agent. The user would be wise to ensure that the update be put into escrow within a much shorter period of time, say at most fifteen days after the date that the object code version of the new software is delivered to the user. This period should be reasonable to most suppliers, because in order to be able to release the new object code version the supplier would surely have the underlying source code ready for deposit under the escrow agreement.

Users should ensure that the escrow agreement allows them to verify what has been deposited in escrow. The user should have the right to require the supplier, from time to time, in the presence of the escrow agent and the user, to compile the escrowed materials to ensure that what is in escrow accurately reflects the user's current object code version of the software. The verification can take place at the escrow agent's facilities if the agent has the suitable computer equipment, or the escrowed material may be taken off-site under the supervision of the escrow agent to either the supplier's or the user's premises. While such verification procedures will put the user to some expense — invariably the fees of the escrow agent for such activities are borne by the user — it is money well spent.

The selection of the escrow agent can be important. Some suppliers use their law firms as escrow agents; a user should resist such a choice as there is clearly a conflict of interest in such a case. As well, whenever a Canadian user wants the source code of an American program put into escrow it should insist that the escrow be resident in Canada, preferably in the city where the user is located. A good choice of escrow agent in most large Canadian centres is one of the trust companies that specifically offer the service of escrowing source code and related software materials. Taking the source code out of the United States might be a practical way of avoiding the legal and practical difficulties inherent in most American bankruptcy or Chapter 11 proceedings, although it should be noted that an American law was passed in 1988 that gives licensees of technology greater protection in the event that the licensor of the technology goes bankrupt. Under this law, if an American licensor of software (or other intellectual property, except trade-marks) goes bankrupt, the trustee of the bankrupt company can elect to terminate licences for the software. Upon such election, however, a user of the software can in turn elect to have the licence continue, in which case the user would have to continue paying licence fees for the software if any are payable under the licence agreement; but the user would not have to pay support and maintenance fees if these additional services are no longer provided by the bankrupt company. It is therefore a good idea to separate the licence and support fees. As a result of this law, a user who wishes to continue using certain software after the licensor's bankruptcy should promptly take steps to notify the trustee in bankruptcy that it elects to continue the licence; failure to do so could result in the user's losing its right to use the software.

The escrow agreement should set out clearly what events of default on the part of the supplier will entitle the user to obtain the escrowed materials. An obvious event would be the supplier's generally ceasing to maintain and support the software. Another standard triggering event is the bankruptcy of the supplier where such bankruptcy has the effect of preventing the supplier from continuing to provide maintenance services to the user; this is sometimes modified to provide that bankruptcy constitutes default only if within a certain period after the commencement of bankruptcy proceedings another company has not assumed the maintenance obligations of the supplier. This sort of proviso is sometimes used to qualify the first event of default noted as well; often if the supplier ceases to support the software the user must wait, say, thirty days, to see if another company will buy the particular business or division from the supplier. In each such case the user would be wise to have the release of the escrowed materials occur immediately upon bankruptcy or the cessation of business, with the user being obliged to return these materials if the maintenance obligations are in fact resumed in a manner satisfactory to the user. In this way, if the new support capability is not satisfactory to the user, then the user can negotiate improvements at a more relaxed pace and from a superior bargaining position, because in the meantime it would be able to maintain the software itself through use of the escrowed materials.

A user may have a particular need to define additional events that would trigger the release of the escrowed materials. Consider the situation where a supplier, a software development company, has produced a unique custom program for a user. The supplier agrees to provide additional custom programming services at its then prevailing rates, knowing full well that the user will require many enhancements and additions in the future. Sure enough, a year later the user asks for a specific major modification. The supplier responds with an extremely high quote for this project, arguing that it has not been able to interest any other users in the original custom software, and the cost of keeping up to speed several highly trained staff for only one customer is extremely expensive (the supplier originally thought it could amortize future development costs over numerous clients). The user may therefore want to negotiate into the escrow agreement the provision that the escrowed materials will be released if the supplier refuses to provide additional custom development work at standard industry rates, or even better, at certain hourly rates agreed to in advance and subject to increases no greater than the cost of living.

The supplier and the user may disagree as to whether a specific triggering event has occurred. Many standard form escrow agreements provide that if the parties cannot agree then the escrow agent must wait for a court order respecting the disposition of the escrowed materials. As mentioned previously, however, court proceedings can be maddeningly slow and expensive, which may not be of great concern to the supplier but which will very likely worry the user, who may be anxiously awaiting the release of the source code from escrow. Accordingly, the user may wish to consider having any such disputes decided by an arbitrator (for a discussion of resolving disputes through arbitration see section B.22, "Arbitration").

8. SERVICE BUREAU/ OUTSOURCING

A user of computing resources need not purchase or lease a computer system. Instead, it can retain a service bureau to provide various computer services. In such a relationship the user sends data to the service bureau where it is stored and processed; the service bureau then delivers the resulting information to the user either in the form of printed material or, increasingly, in an "on-line" mode, which is received by the user's data terminals. From the user's perspective there are no up-front capital costs, and there is no need to spend money preparing a suitable computer facility and hiring staff to operate it. There are, however, several risks to the user in such a relationship, and the following should be considered in an attempt to reduce such risks.

The user should be careful to set out fully and in the clearest terms precisely what services the service bureau will be performing for the user. The standard form agreements of service bureaus often give an insufficient description of the various services. The contract should enumerate plainly who is going to do what, including what the responsibilities of the user will be. If the data is to be sent by one or more terminals installed at the user's site, who will pay for the telecommunications costs, and who will have to deal with the telecommunications carrier if there is a problem with the link? If the service bureau will be sending the user printed reports containing the results of the processing, how often will they be sent — daily, weekly, or monthly?

The need for specifying with great precision what services will be provided by the service bureau can be illustrated by the following scenario. It is increasingly common that a service bureau will make available to a customer a portion of the processing capacity of the bureau's computer. If, for instance, the bureau's computer is a 12-MIPS (million instructions per second) machine, the customer might be sold 4 MIPS, with two other customers each being sold 4 MIPS as well. It is not enough, however, for the contract to state simply that each customer will have access to one-third of the capacity of the bureau's machine, as this leaves several critical questions unanswered. How will each user's portion of computer capacity be allocated? Does each user get 20 minutes of CPU time per hour, or can the service bureau decide that each customer has exclusive use of the machine for an eight-hour period each day? In fact, it may be that one user is willing to have some of its access limited to weekends, while another user needs all of its computing done during business hours because it uses the machine for on-line customer-related applications. Accordingly, the bureau's agreements with these customers should spell out in detail how each customer's access time on the bureau's machine will be allocated on a day-to-day basis.

It is useful for the user to have a commitment from the service bureau as to the performance levels for the contracted services. That is, if the user has chosen to have on-line access to its data so that it can get immediate answers to certain questions (for clients perhaps), the user should have the service bureau guarantee that the total time between the final query keystroke at the user's terminal and the appearance of the relevant response on the same terminal shall not be more than a certain number of seconds. In addition to a fixed response-time obligation, the user may also request a firm turnaround time for collating, processing, and returning the information submitted by the user. And as noted several times already, a right is only as good as the remedy accompanying it, so the user may want credits against future fees or liquidated damages to kick in if the response or turnaround times are not observed by the supplier; the remedy of terminating the agreement should also be available for serious deficiencies on the part of the service bureau.

With respect to fees, it is essential that the user ensure that the fee schedule to the standard form agreement accurately sets out the moneys intended to flow to the service bureau. While this sounds like a simple exercise, it can be fiendishly difficult, given the many different possible charges and expenses and the user's informational handicap in keeping track of them all. A user could end up paying under a service bureau contract one or more of the following: a fee for installation of an access terminal(s); a fee for connect time; a fee for computer processing time; a fee for data storage; a fee for effecting hardware changes requested by the user; and a fee for early termination. With this many (and other) potential charges, the user should have the agreement provide that beyond the express charges mentioned in the agreement the user shall not be required to pay any further charges unless previously agreed to by the user in writing. A further complication to matters of price is the question of volume discounts which the user will want to explore if its volume of business with the service bureau is substantial. As mentioned above (section B.11 under "Volume Discounts"), the contract provisions and formulas relating to volume discounts must be very carefully drafted so that they accurately reflect the intentions of both parties.

Given that the pricing algorithms in service bureau contracts can be very complicated, disputes over invoices for services rendered by service bureaus are quite common. As a result, many parties to service bureau arrangements provide for arbitration as a dispute-resolution mechanism in the event that the parties cannot themselves settle what is owing under the relevant invoice (for a general discussion of arbitration, see section B.22). Such a provision might work as follows: if the user receives an invoice for $100,000, but believes it should be charged only $50,000, it must pay the $50,000; the question of whether the remaining $50,000 is properly owing is submitted to an arbitrator who has expertise in computers and financial matters (perhaps the arbitrator is a chartered accountant who has computer consulting experience) for a quick decision. In this way, it is hoped that a small misunderstanding can be resolved promptly so that it does not become a major point of contention between the service bureau and its customer.

The user incurs a major risk in a service bureau arrangement in that the user's data, and perhaps the user's licensed software, must be taken from the user's premises to a site outside the direct control of the user. The confidentiality of the user's data and software may be at risk. The service bureau agreement should therefore expressly obligate the service bureau to keep confidential any data and computer programs entrusted to it by the user. If the user is handing over, for example, particularly sensitive third-party customer data, then the user may want to review the bureau's physical security procedures.

Some users are so concerned about preserving the confidentiality of their data that they request the bureau not to take on as a customer any competitor of the user. Such an arrangement will reduce the risk that through inadvertence, or otherwise, the data of the user might end up in the hands of a competitor; this risk would be greater if the two entities were to have their data processed by the same service bureau. An alternative to such a request is to require the bureau to give notice to the user when the bureau is contemplating providing a competitor with services, so that the first user can at least review the adequacy of its and the bureau's security measures at that time with a view to augmenting them if necessary.

The user's service bureau agreement should also provide that any data and software programs submitted by the user shall always remain the property of the user and that the service bureau shall have no rights in this property. This provision should further specify that the service bureau may not impose a lien on such property, or otherwise use it as a bargaining chip in the event of a dispute between the user and the service bureau. For example, if the user is late in paying its bills without any good excuse the service bureau should have the right to suspend services, but not to hold hostage the user's data.

It is often the case that a user's service bureau relationship is intended to be a short, temporary one. The user may need the service bureau's assistance only as an interim measure until the user purchases its own in-house computer system. In such circumstances, the service bureau agreement should contain a provision for its early termination, or should allow the user, unilaterally, to terminate the relationship on relatively short notice. This latter alternative, however, may cause some concern to the service bureau if it must make significant equipment or personnel investments in order to provide the user with specific services in the first place. As a result, early termination privileges typically carry with them hefty termination charges. While such charges are often reasonable, there should be some reflection in the agreement of the concept that if the service bureau promptly replaces the user's business with the business of another customer then the termination charge ought to be reduced accordingly. For example, the term of the agreement might be for two years, with the user having the option to terminate after one year upon payment of six months' charges. If the user exercises the early termination option and the service bureau fills the gap left by the user by signing on a new customer within two months of the early termination, then the initial user ought to be entitled to a refund of about four months' charges or two-thirds of its early termination payment. Better still, the user could structure the early termination payment to be paid in six monthly portions — just as if it had continued using the service bureau — but with each month's payment conditional on delivery of a certificate from the service bureau attesting that the excess capacity left by the user's departure has not been filled by another customer.

Outsourcing

One type of service bureau relationship that has received a great deal of press lately is known as "outsourcing." While some of the activities referred to today as outsourcing differ little from some of the service bureau product offerings (such as facilities management services) that have been around for years, one type of outsourcing is quite new, namely, the practice whereby a company or other organization contracts out all or substantially all of its information-systems requirements to a service bureau for a substantial period of time (say, three to five years or longer). Often as part of such a deal the customer will sell the bureau the customer's data centre, including having the bureau hire all or some of the customer's data-processing staff. While the issues discussed previously in this section dealing with service bureau contracts are also generally applicable to such an outsourcing arrangement, this particular type of arrangement raises several other important issues.

As noted above, confidentiality is an important concern to users of service bureaus. In an outsourcing situation, confidentiality is critical even before the user commences to use the services of the outsourcing vendor. That is, given that the decision to implement an outsourcing solution may eventually eliminate a number of jobs in the data-processing department of the user, the user will want to ensure that all of its discussions with prospective vendors — and even the discussions with its own consultants who may have been retained to assist in reviewing outsourcing alternatives — are kept confidential and are not disclosed to the user's staff. Accordingly, all prospective vendors and consultants should be required to sign nondisclosure agreements to this effect. Moreover, the user should implement a procedure whereby the vendors deal with only designated staff of the user. Indeed, some users assign non-data-processing staff to the early phase of the outsourcing project so that if the outsourcing option is not selected, no data-processing employees even have to know it was considered. Similarly, where the prospective outsourcing vendors need to review documents of the user in order to prepare their proposals, it is useful to have these documents stored, and reviewed by the vendors, at the offices of the user's consultant or legal counsel so that, again, the risk of premature disclosure of the outsourcing option is lessened.

Where a user is considering an outsourcing proposal that entails a sale of its data centre, or some part of it, to the outsourcing vendor (or someone else), a due diligence review must be conducted early on to ascertain whether the user can in fact sell to the vendor the relevant hardware and software. So long as the user owns outright the hardware, selling it to the outsourcing firm should not present a problem. The transfer becomes more complicated if the hardware is leased, in which case it is necessary to ensure that the lease company will allow an assignment of the lease to the vendor (such an assignment provision is discussed in section C.2 under "Lease/Rental"). Even where the user owns the machine, it must be ascertained whether the user's bank or some other lender has a security interest in the machine that must be waived before the sale can proceed because the sale of the equipment will likely be a sale outside of the ordinary course of business.

The biggest potential problem with selling a data centre (as part of an outsourcing deal or otherwise) involves the software utilized by the user. As explained in section B.10, "License of Software," software (whether it is operating system or applications software) is invariably licensed to users subject to a restriction on its transfer. If a user's data centre is being transferred to an outsourcing vendor who will use the facility to process solely the data of that user, then the owner of the software may well consent to a payment-free transfer of the software licence to the outsourcing vendor since this arrangement will not likely represent a loss of future sales to the software owner. However, where the outsourcing vendor wants to process the data of several of its customers on the machine it is purchasing from a single user, then the software owner will probably consent to the transfer of the licence only if additional licence fees are paid to it on account of the additional customers that would be processed by the same software. These additional licence fees may be substantial, and the requirement to pay them may no longer make the outsourcing transaction suitably attractive to the outsourcing vendor (or to the original user if it is being asked to pay more for the outsourcing services as a result of these additional licence fees). As this software licence issue can be a major factor in the viability of an outsourcing proposal involving the sale of a data centre, users contemplating such a venture should review their software portfolio from this perspective as soon as possible so that the accurate cost of the transfer of such software can be conveyed to outsourcing vendors at the outset.

It was noted earlier in this section that a user should have a commitment from the service bureau as to the performance levels for the contracted services. Such performance guarantees are especially critical in an outsourcing arrangement because the user will likely have given up, at least partially but more likely completely, its ability to handle the particular data-processing function that it receives from the outsourcing vendor. Consider the situation where a company retains an outsourcing vendor to provide it with all of its employee-payroll processing. As part of the transaction, the outsourcing vendor hires from the user the payroll clerks and others that previously administered the payroll function at the user's premises. In such a scenario, if the outsourcing vendor provides the user with inadequate service, the user will be hard pressed to correct any temporary deficiencies unless it recreates internally its payroll department — something which it is loathe to do because it would defeat the whole purpose of retaining the services of the outsourcing vendor in the first place. Accordingly, the user in this case would do well to set out with precision what service levels it is looking for from the outsourcing vendor. Service levels might include the following with respect to the employee-payroll-processing service: (1) that the employee-payroll data, once transmitted by the user to the outsourcing vendor (how this activity will be accomplished should be clearly explained in the agreement), will be processed and delivered on magnetic tape (or perhaps electronically) by the vendor to the relevant banks for direct deposit or cheque issuance within a specified number of hours; (2) that the payroll data will be processed to a specific degree of accuracy (i.e. that only a specified number of minimal errors will be tolerated during each pay period); (3) that the cheques containing the required income tax and other benefits-related source deductions will be submitted to the relevant public authorities within the time frames set out by law; and (4) that the employee-payroll data entries will be posted to the user's general ledger within specified time-frames. Each service level would then be backed up by appropriate remedies, typically, that each performance failure results in nonpayment for the service for the month in which the errors occurred, together with a termination right if a specified number of failures occur over a certain period of time.

This particular employee-payroll-processing outsourcing example also raises an issue regarding the limitation-of-liability provision, which inevitably will be included in the outsourcing agreement. As noted in section B.17, a limitation-of-liability clause is not unreasonable, but the amount of the limitation might be. A typical service bureau contract will limit the liability of the vendor to an amount equal to one, or perhaps three, months' worth of fees paid under the agreement. Depending on the amount of monthly fees paid to the vendor in the payroll example, a three-month limitation might be adequate (though six months to a year is probably more reasonable, and one month is probably unreasonable) for most risks under the arrangement. However, the outsourcing vendor will be responsible for calculating the amount of source deductions for employee income tax and related purposes that must be paid by the user, and if the vendor fails to calculate these source deductions properly (particularly if too little is deducted by the user), then the user might incur a significant tax liability, which, depending on the size of the payroll, might quickly surpass the three (to twelve) months' fees stipulated in the limitation-of-liability clause. At the same time, however, the user has no way to verify the appropriateness of the amounts deducted by the vendor, as the user no longer has a payroll department; in effect, the vendor has full control over this aspect of the user's employee payroll. Accordingly, it may be reasonable to have a two-track limitation-of-liability regime in this situation, with a high limit for tax- related claims, and the standard limit for all other types of problems.

9. DISASTER RECOVERY

Over the past few years computer-trade journals have chronicled numerous major emergencies or disasters involving computer installations. The upshot of most of these press reports is that if the user is not adequately prepared for emergencies, such as a fire knocking out its main computer facility, the consequences to the user can be disastrous. One way the user can prepare for such an eventuality is to arrange to have available on short notice temporary computer facilities that can keep the user afloat until the damaged facilities are repaired. In some instances two users arrange to serve as each other's temporary facility, while in other cases users contract for such services with one of a growing number of companies that specialize in providing just such a facility. In either case the user will want to enter into a so-called disaster recovery agreement, which sets out clearly the rights and obligations of each party to this vital relationship. Indeed, the commercial providers of such services typically have a standard form agreement, which the user must ensure adequately reflects its concerns and interests.

The first requirement of such an agreement is to define with some precision the services to be provided by the supplier of the disaster recovery facility. The supplier will usually offer two levels of service: a "cold site," which is merely space in a building in which the user must install its own temporary computer system, and a "hot site," which includes a computer system and often even trained staff to run the equipment. Not surprisingly, the hot site alternative is much more expensive; the key objective from the point of view of the user is to find the cost-effective level of security. In either case, the user must think through comprehensively its disaster recovery needs on an overall basis, and then determine how the disaster recovery facility can best serve these needs. Whatever level of service is chosen, the user should not hesitate to request periodic "tests" of the facility to ensure that what the user expects to be there in the event of the emergency is in fact there. Such verification is, of course, particularly important if the user opts for the hot site recovery package.

The disaster recovery agreement should also be definite about what constitutes a "disaster," that is, what events will permit the user to move into the premises of the disaster recovery facility. The provider of this service will prefer a narrow definition while, not surprisingly, the user will call for a more expansive one in order to keep its options as open as possible. Whatever the two parties agree to, the definition should be expressed in functional terms and geared to the inability of the user's regular computer system to perform certain objective and clearly ascertainable functions.

Given that a single disaster may affect many users (e.g., a major fire that knocks out power and telecommunications services to a whole area of a city will likely affect several computer facilities in the area), the user will want the contract to require that the provider of the disaster recovery service does not have too many clients from any particular geographic area. The disaster recovery firm works somewhat like a bank: if all the bank's customers attempted to withdraw their money simultaneously, the bank simply could not honour all its deposits. Similarly, the hot site facilities of the supplier may be able to accommodate only five or six users at any one time, but the actual customer base of the disaster recovery company may be many times larger than that. This form of computing services insurance policy, therefore, only works as long as all the customers do not suffer a disaster at the same time. To avoid such a situation a user should require an absolute limit on the total number of customers that a supplier may sign up; the user should also insist on limits to the number of customers with computer facilities located in the same office building as the user and within a certain distance (e.g., two kilometres) of the user's facilities. The actual numbers would be based on factors such as the size of the disaster recovery facility and the probability of the occurrence of natural disasters in the geographic area in which the user is located.

Where two users arrange to serve as each other's temporary back-up site, it is important that this relationship be formalized in a written contract. Often the two representatives who spearheaded the arrangement for both organizations merely informally "shake-hands" on the deal, and this can cause serious problems subsequently when one organization actually has need of using the facilities of the other. The written agreement should stipulate clearly when access will be allowed (i.e., is it only outside of the primary business hours of the site that will be used as the back-up facility? etc.), and how much computer time and data storage space will be available for back-up purposes and at what cost. The agreement should also require regular consultation between the parties about excess capacity planning and changes to such plans. Similarly, the agreement should require a party to give lots of advance notice if it plans to change its computing environment, as this will likely render the mutual back-up arrangement unworkable, and the other party will need some time to find a new disaster recovery solution.

10. ELECTRONIC DATA INTERCHANGE

Electronic data interchange (EDI) is the direct computer-to-computer transmission of information in a structured electronic messaging format. Both in Canada and abroad a growing number of businesses and other organizations are using EDI in their commercial and other dealings, given that through EDI more accurate and timely information can be exchanged for less cost than is the case with paper-based documents. In some industries EDI has become virtually indispensable; for example, so-called just-in-time inventory ordering practices in the automotive sector would be impossible without EDI.

The substitution of EDI for paper-based documents (such as traditional purchase orders, invoices, and bills of lading) presents numerous technical, control, and legal challenges. EDI raises many legal questions because in so many respects it differs from the paper-based mode of collecting, storing, presenting, and transmitting information. Paper-based documents are durable and can remain in existence for many years. Alterations to paper documents can be detected quite readily. Documents on paper can be conveniently authenticated by personal signatures or other means. Most importantly, legal systems around the world have had some three hundred years, and in some cases even longer, to develop a comprehensive system of statutory and judge-made rules governing all aspects of the use of paper-based documents in commerce. Familiarity, among other things, breeds reliable legal precedent. Today, business people and their legal advisers have a very good idea of how the law will treat a particular question relating to a paper-based document, such as whether a certain document is admissible in a legal proceeding, because the question will have been addressed, either by a specific provision in a statute or a previous decision of a judge.

The same cannot be said with respect to EDI. While there exist various technical means to help ensure the "durability," "nonalterability," and "authenticity" of information that is collected, stored, presented, and transmitted electronically, legal systems have yet to amend statutory rules sufficiently, or to produce judicial decisions, in order that EDI be accorded the same legal certainty as paper-based documents. Many, many questions remain unanswered. These questions, and the uncertainty caused by them, in most cases will not present an insurmountable hurdle to the implementation of EDI in any particular setting. Managers responsible for EDI, however, should be sensitive to these questions, should come to understand them with the assistance of legal counsel, and should then plan to implement EDI in a manner that reduces, as much as possible, the uncertainty caused by them.

A key mechanism for managing the risks inherent in EDI is the EDI trading partner agreement (TPA). No company or organization should conduct EDI with another entity unless and until the two of them have entered into a suitable TPA. Unfortunately, as noted in a recent study, most EDI activity in the United States is not underpinned by TPAs, and this state of affairs is likely duplicated in other countries, such as Canada, where EDI is becoming ever more popular. This is a mistake. Particularly as the use of EDI increases, such that organizations increasingly use EDI not only for their biggest and best customers but also for smaller and less established customers, it becomes imperative that EDI trading partners implement TPAs.

Technical Issues

The TPA should address a number of technical and operational issues. It should specify the various components of the EDI network that will be implemented between the two parties. This network might consist of each party's computer system linked by regular telephone lines. In many cases, however, one or both parties may use the services of a "value added network" (VAN). A VAN will serve several functions, including collecting and forwarding EDI messages and providing audit and other services. A VAN is particularly valuable in serving as an intermediary between two EDI trading partners with incompatible computer systems. A VAN will invariably make available its services to a customer only after the customer has entered into a "network services" or similar agreement. This agreement is similar to a service bureau agreement, and hence the discussion in section C.8 is relevant to VAN agreements as well.

In addition to specifying the nature of the EDI network, the TPA should set out the date by which each party's equipment must be available in order to send and receive EDI messages. It might also be appropriate, in certain circumstances, to provide for testing of the EDI network to ensure that it operates in accordance with the reasonable expectations of both trading partners. The parties must also stipulate the particular EDI standard that will be used by them. There are several such protocols, the two most common general ones being ANSI-12 and EDIFACT. There are, however, numerous other standards, and indeed there are a number of versions of ANSI-12 and EDI-FACT. It is therefore important to state with precision which one will be used. The TPA should also address how the parties will implement any changes in the chosen standard; at the very least it should provide for a process by which the parties can discuss this important issue periodically.

Contract Law Issues

A key risk with EDI is that it is currently unclear in Canada whether all the contracts concluded by EDI are enforceable, given that legislation exists in most provinces, and in many other jurisdictions, requiring that certain contracts be "in writing." For example, Ontario's Sale of Goods Act provides that a contract for the sale of goods worth $40 or more is not enforceable unless, among other things, "some note or memorandum in writing of the contract is made." Moreover, Ontario's Interpretation Act provides that "writing ... includes words printed, painted, engraved, lithographed, photographed, or represented or reproduced by any other mode in a visible form." In view of these statutory provisions, it is not clear whether EDI messages can be said to constitute "writings." There will not be a resolution to this question until the courts answer it, or until laws are passed that expressly recognize that EDI messages are able to create legally binding commitments. Until one of these solutions comes to pass, the best that EDI trading partners can do is to address the "writing issue" in their TPAs. This is normally done in three ways: (1) the parties acknowledge their mutual intention to create legally binding contracts through specific combinations of EDI messages; (2) the parties agree that each EDI message shall be deemed to constitute a "memorandum in writing" (as required by the relevant statute law); and (3) the parties expressly waive, or give up, any right to argue subsequently in a court of law that such EDI messages do not constitute writings.

Many of the same statutes that require certain agreements to be in writing also stipulate that they be "signed" by the parties to the agreement. The "signature issue," however, is less problematic than the "writing issue" because rather than being defined generally in a statute, in many jurisdictions the term "signature" may be interpreted with flexibility by judges. In this regard, a TPA should provide that each EDI message will incorporate specific codes or other characteristics to permit the receiver to verify that it is an authentic message of the sender. A TPA will also usually provide that each party will have responsibility for controlling the transmission of messages from its machine, and that each party warrants that each such message sent from its machine is duly authorized and binding upon it. These authorization and authentication provisions are then supplemented by a provision, similar to the one related to the "writing issue," whereby the parties agree that each EDI message will be deemed to constitute a signed writing.

EDI also raises the question of "when" a contract comes into existence. Generally speaking, in order to form a contract there must be an offer from one party and an acceptance of that offer by another party. In situations where there is simultaneous conveyance of offer and acceptance in one place, such as in face-to-face negotiations and contract signings, there is rarely an issue regarding when and where the contract was made. Where there are not simultaneous negotiations and communication in one place, the general rule has developed in Canadian law that an offer is not accepted until the acceptance of the offer is communicated to the offerer. About one hundred years ago an exception to this rule was developed by judges for offers and acceptances sent by mail. The so-called post-box rule holds that where an offer is made by the mail, the contract is made immediately at the time the acceptance is posted in the mail (rather than when the acceptance is actually received by the offerer), where use of the mail is reasonable in the circumstances or expressly contemplated by the parties.

It may be asked whether this post-box rule would apply to EDI. It might in the case where an EDI message is sent not directly to the intended EDI trading partner, but rather to a

VAN that holds the message for some period until the intended recipient retrieves it electronically from the VAN service provider. By contrast, the post-box rule would not likely apply to EDI messages that are transmitted directly between trading partners, given that such a relationship approximates more closely instantaneous communication of offer and acceptance.

In this regard it is interesting to note that the courts have not applied the post-box rule to telex communications; rather, for such means of "nearly instantaneous" communication the courts look at a variety of factors to determine when a contract came into existence. Given that this judicial rule for telex communications leaves each court with a fair degree of discretion, and assuming a similar approach would be taken to EDI, again it is recommended that trading partners deal with the issue of when a contractual commitment first arose in their TPA. This can be done by providing in the TPA that an EDI message is deemed to be received only when it is accessible to the recipient at its computer (which machine would be specified in the description of the EDI network discussed above). Many TPAs go on to require that each party acknowledge receipt of an EDI message received by it. Such an acknowledgement, however, does not designate acceptance of the offer in the sender's message. Rather, it is sensible to provide that for contractually binding commitments to arise, certain pre-determined EDI messages must be exchanged. So, for example, if one party sends an electronic purchase order by EDI, the TPA may require that a specific purchase-order acknowledgement (as opposed to a mere functional acknowledgement of receipt of the purchase order) be sent by the recipient of the purchase order. And if such specific acknowledgement is sent, the provision regarding deemed receipt noted above will operate to create a binding contract at the time the specific acknowledgement is received by the computer of the party who sent the purchase order. It is therefore advisable, if the sender is using a VAN and has EDI messages intended for it stored in a mailbox on the VAN's machine, for the sender to check this mailbox periodically, and indeed some TPAs require such checking on a regular basis.

In addition to dealing with the issue of "when" a contract concluded by EDI arises, the TPA should settle the question of "where" such a contract arises. This is an important question because it determines, among other things, which jurisdiction's laws govern the parties' EDI relations. This question may never have to be asked if all the relevant parties are located in the same jurisdiction, such as a single province in Canada. By contrast, consider the following situation. One EDI trading partner is located in France, the other in Ontario; they communicate through the French trading partner's VAN which is located in England, and the Ontario trading partner's VAN, which is located in Ohio. If there is a problem with an EDI transmission that causes damages to one or more of these parties, which of French, Ontario, English, or Ohio law should be applied to the claim? Rather than having to rely on general, and often difficult-to-apply, legal principles to answer such a question, it is preferable for EDI trading partners to stipulate in their TPAs, and in their agreements with VANs, which jurisdiction's law will govern any possible claims. Many TPAs also provide that any disputes will be settled by arbitration, rather than by resorting to the regular court system, for many of the same reasons that commend arbitration to many computer contracting arrangements (see section B.22, "Arbitration"). The particularly dynamic nature of current EDI technology makes EDI disputes especially suitable for arbitration.

In the TPA the trading partners should decide what terms and conditions will govern the underlying transaction effected by EDI. For example, if the TPA is between an automotive company and an auto-parts supplier, the TPA should address what terms will apply to the actual sale of the auto parts from the perspective of product warranties, limitations on liability, etc. In a non-EDI environment these issues are often left to the mercy of the so-called battle of the forms, whereby each side hopes that the terms of its purchase or other document will prevail in the event of a dispute. The EDI environment, however, does not lend itself to fighting a battle of the forms through the transmission of EDI messages, because such messages are not intended for conveying contractual terms such as warranty clauses. What should happen, therefore, is that the parties negotiate a mutually acceptable set of terms and conditions that will apply to the underlying sales or other transactions, which agreement should be appended to the TPA. Some parties, however, try to perpetuate the battle of the forms by attaching to the TPA the contract documents they used prior to EDI, and then stipulating that these various forms will apply as if they were actually being used (but they are not, as the EDI messages are being sent instead!). This results in a very uncertain, unsatisfactory state of affairs. The preferred alternative of settling on mutually acceptable trade terms may require an investment of some time and effort by business people and legal counsel, but it is an investment that tends to pay significant dividends.

Evidence Law Issues

Just as there is some uncertainty whether EDI messages constitute "writings" for purposes of contract law, it is currently unclear whether copies of EDI messages, or the transaction logs kept of such messages, would be admissible as evidence in court or similar proceedings. The rules of evidence law strive to ensure that only reliable evidence is admitted in legal proceedings. With respect to common law jurisdictions, two rules of evidence law are often considered to pose a challenge to the admissibility as evidence of computer-generated records, which would include EDI messages. The first is the "hearsay rule," which stipulates that, whenever possible, evidence should be obtained orally from witnesses, because this form of evidence can be subjected to cross-examination and other forms of truth testing. In the context of written evidence, the hearsay rule, if strictly applied, would require that a document not be admissible unless its author were present in court to attest to its contents. The second rule of evidence is the "best evidence rule," whereby a document is admissible only if it is produced in its original version.

In recognition, however, of the increasing reliability of record-keeping in modern businesses, Parliament and most Canadian provinces have passed statutes governing the law of evidence that allow certain types of "business records" to be admissible as evidence under certain conditions. These statutory rules were not drafted with EDI in mind however, and it may be asked whether copies of EDI messages would be admissible in court and other legal proceedings. No court has yet had occasion to determine whether an EDI message is admissible under such a statute. Courts in Canada have considered, however, whether computer-generated records are admissible under these rules; generally, they have been admitted in circumstances where the computer and the related record-taking and record-keeping procedures have been shown to be trustworthy.

Trading partners in an EDI arrangement should do at least two things to help ensure that their EDI messages are held to be admissible in court and other legal proceedings. First, they should institute appropriate computer security, control, and other measures to create EDI message-making and recording systems that are as trustworthy as possible. This would entail, for example, storing EDI messages on nonalterable media that permit only read and copy, but not write, access. Or it may be sensible to store EDI messages with a VAN under an arrangement that limits access to the material by the personnel of even the EDI trading partner. Further provisions for dealing with security in the TPA itself are discussed below. The second measure to assist in making EDI messages admissible is for the TPA to contain a provision whereby the EDI trading partners agree that the EDI messages stored in a certain way, together with the transaction log recording these messages, shall be admissible in any legal or related proceeding. And, as with the TPA measure related to the "writing issue," the EDI trading partners should agree in the TPA to waive any right to contest the admissibility of any such material.

A similar issue to the evidence law one arises in connection with the record-retention requirements stipulated by numerous statutes in many jurisdictions. For example, Canada's Income Tax Act requires businesses to keep certain books of account and records which, among other things, permit the taxes payable or the taxes or other amounts to be collected by a person or business, to be determined. It is interesting to note that the government department in Canada that administers the tax statute (Revenue Canada) permits companies to keep microfilm copies of books and records of original entry and source documents, provided the microfilming process utilized complies with a certain standard produced by the Canadian General Standards Board and approved by the Standards Council of Canada. It is unclear whether under Canada's Income Tax Act source documents could be kept in an electronic format. For example, Revenue Canada has recently taken the position that images of paper documents stored on optical disks would not satisfy their record-retention rules. Such a process involves transferring a paper-based source document into an electronic format. With EDI, on the other hand, the original message itself is in electronic form and hence the source "document" never is transferred into another medium. In short, it is arguable that EDI messages should be acceptable for record-retention purposes under Canada's income tax law, but currently Revenue Canada is uncomfortable with such a position. Revenue Canada, however, recognizes that its laws, regulations, and policies in this area are causing some uncertainty, and is considering what changes might be useful to eliminate these concerns. Until such time as the legal environment is clarified satisfactorily, users of EDI may wish to approach Revenue Canada or other relevant government departments to discuss their particular EDI circumstances so that they are able to establish electronic recording-keeping measures that will satisfy the applicable public authorities.

Reliability, Security, and Confidentiality

The TPA should contain provisions that address the reliability and security of the EDI network and the confidentiality of the messages transmitted on it. With respect to reliability, the TPA should require the recipient of a garbled message to notify the sender and to request a clarification or corrected version of the message. In a similar vein, some TPAs require a recipient to notify the sender of messages that contain highly unusual terms; for example, if for some time each EDI order was for only 50 units of a particular item, and the recipient received an order for 50,000 units, the recipient would have to verify the original order. The parties could decide what sort of margins of error they could live with before such a duty to notify became effective. The TPA should also address what sorts of disaster recovery measures would be applicable in the event the EDI network becomes disabled.

As for security, most TPAs will merely have a provision requiring both parties to take reasonable measures to prevent unauthorized access to the EDI network. In some cases, however, it may be appropriate to augment the security provisions by stipulating precise steps that each party must take to keep the system free from third-party access. Similarly, in addition to a general confidentiality provision that requires both parties to notify their personnel to keep EDI messages confidential, it may sometimes be desirable to beef-up the confidentiality obligations, particularly where third-party or extremely sensitive information is being conveyed in the EDI messages. Further, the TPA should contain a provision whereby each party is required on a regular basis to retain an independent third party to review and prepare a report on the party's record in adhering to the security and confidentiality requirements of the TPA, which report would be made available to the other party to the TPA.

The EDI Council of Canada has published a model TPA, together with a commentary on the various provisions in it. This is an extremely useful document and it should probably serve as the starting point for the drafting of most TPAs between EDI trading partners. The model TPA, however, does not have all the answers, and in fact it requires prospective users of the form to ask a number of questions. It contains, for example, numerous sections in square brackets, which require particular scrutiny to determine whether they should be used by the trading partners. In short, the parties to an EDI relationship must always modify the model TPA to suit their particular circumstances. It should also be noted that a TPA, however comprehensive it may be, will never be able to dispel completely the legal uncertainty that currently exists in respect of, among other areas, evidence law and records-retention. The only really effective resolution of these issues will come when laws in Canada, and elsewhere, are amended to recognize expressly EDI and other forms of electronic commerce. Accordingly, organizations utilizing EDI should support the law-reform efforts of organizations like the EDI Council of Canada so that a more certain legal environment for EDI can be established as soon as possible. In the meantime, parties considering implementing EDI should review with their legal counsel the particular use to be made of EDI, the legal risks posed by the prospective EDI usage, and the contractual and other methods available to reduce and effectively manage this risk.

11. DOCUMENT IMAGING SYSTEMS

Imaging systems comprise a wide range of computer-based technologies for scanning, storing, and retrieving documents and will become increasingly common in business, government, education, and the professions over the next few years. Ideally, these systems will help organizations manage their document-storage requirements more efficiently and at reduced costs. The task of making sure that imaging systems meet these high expectations will fall, to a great extent, on an organization's data-processing and records-management professionals. These people will also be responsible for tackling the contracting and legal issues raised by imaging systems. To assist in this effort, this section provides a very general discussion of matters that should be addressed by organizations implementing imaging systems: contracting issues, copyright and confidentiality issues, and evidence law and records retention issues.

Contracting Issues

Like any computer-based system, an imaging system that has been carefully selected to meet the needs of the user and that runs without interruption and free of errors is an extremely valuable asset to any organization. There are, however, numerous risks associated with imaging systems, just as with all other kinds of computers. Indeed, as noted in section A.1, for some organizations the computer experience has been a curse, an electronic nightmare of awesome proportions. Even the generally satisfied computer user has occasional doubts about the value of the organization's computer systems, because it is the rare computer system that faithfully and unfailingly performs every task assigned it. There are several contractual steps that a prospective user of an imaging system can take to minimize the risks associated with imaging systems — and other computer systems. The following suggestions highlight several computer contracting issues that are dealt with more thoroughly in Part B of this book. These issues are reiterated here to illustrate how the points addressed in Part B can be applied to a particular type of technology.

There are a number of important contracting issues that should be addressed in each computer contract, including those for imaging systems, but of particular importance are so-called contract control checkpoints which relate to the stages of the acquisition process where computer procurements tend to get derailed. It is therefore particularly important that a supplier's promises and a user's expectations be clearly enumerated in these areas.

Delivery.   The contract for the imaging system should contain a firm date by which the system will be delivered and installed. Having such a firm date is particularly important in those segments of the computer market — and imaging may become just such a segment — where competition among suppliers leads to the announcement of unrealistic product shipping dates. A definite delivery schedule is also very important when the user has a definite date by which it requires the commencement of its imaging operations. Another reason for effectively addressing the delivery issue in the contract may arise from a user's choosing a particularly popular product, which may become back-ordered because demand exceeds supply. One or more of these rationales are usually relevant in the acquisition of an imaging system. Accordingly, in all these cases a firm delivery date for the system should be agreed upon — and backed up by remedies, as noted below.

Acceptance Test.   A user's major contract control checkpoint should be a meaningful acceptance test of the system after it is delivered and installed, but before the user is obliged to call the system its own. This is particularly true in the case of imaging systems, where the technology is often new and complex, and where the vendor will often be supplying an equipment configuration consisting of several sub-components, each produced by different manufacturers, which must all work properly together as a single system. All aspects of the system should be tested, including functionality and performance. For example, it may be that the ability of the imaging system's scanner to faithfully reproduce documents is beyond question, but what about the retrieval response time when a large number of user terminals are hooked up to the system? There will likely be some degradation in response time in this latter scenario. The objective of the acceptance test is to determine whether the supplier's promises on this and other points turn out to be true or not once the system is up and running at the user's site.

To be fair to suppliers an acceptance test should not be based on the user's subjective criteria, such as "the test will be passed if and when the user is satisfied with the system." Such "tests" can be undertaken, but they are not really tests so much as option periods during which the user has the ability to return the system for any reason, no questions asked by the supplier. A more even-handed approach would provide a list of objectively ascertainable performance criteria clearly set out in the acquisition contract, so that both the supplier and the user know what the system must accomplish in order for it to be accepted by the user.

Warranties. Listed below are several supplier warranties that should be considered by a user intending to acquire an imaging system:

- A compatibility warranty. The imaging system will work in conjunction with the other relevant computer systems of the user, and/or certain additional items of hardware and software sourced from other suppliers can be added to the system.

- A capacity warranty. The system as initially configured will be able to handle a certain number of documents without a degradation in the system's performance.

- An expansion warranty. The system will be capable of expansion by the addition of a specified amount of hardware and software to accommodate a certain increase in the number of users, or perhaps to store a certain number of documents, without experiencing a degradation in performance.

These and other warranties should be tested, to the extent possible, during the system's acceptance test, and/or they can be on-going obligations of the supplier that, if proven to be untrue at some point in the future, will give rise to remedies in favour of the user (e.g., that the supplier will supply the additional hardware, software, or services to make good the warranty at no cost to the user).

Remedies. Assuming the user has negotiated a firm delivery date, a meaningful acceptance test, and reassuring warranties, these provisions may not be all that useful unless they are backed up by suitable express remedies also written into the acquisition agreement. The exercise here is to think through some bad (or worst-case) scenarios and to try to provide for practical solutions to these unfortunate situations. For example, if the system is delivered but will not pass its acceptance test, should the supplier be given a second chance? Should the user have the right to get all its money back? What happens when an alternative system becomes necessary because of an initial system's poor performance? Should the user be able to keep the first supplier's system on a no-cost loan basis until the alternative solution is installed? These and other types of contingencies should be addressed by means of express remedies in the acquisition agreement. It should be noted that a staggered payment schedule, where instalment payments are made when certain performance milestones (delivery, acceptance of the system, etc.) are met, is also a very useful contract control device.

Copyright and Confidentiality Issues

The ability of imaging systems to copy, store, and disseminate documents with great ease makes them extremely powerful business aids. These characteristics, however, also raise potentially serious copyright law and confidentiality issues. The Copyright Act gives to the owner of the copyright in a written work the exclusive right to, among other things, make copies of the written work. Thus, when an imaging system scans documents and stores them on optical disks or some other medium, and when users retrieve such documents by making further hard copies of them, copyright infringement tends to occur. Such unauthorized copying usually does not result in legal action because of the nature of the documents being reproduced. Most people who write a business letter to an organization probably do not care that their correspondence is being copied by an imaging system. Some creators of copyrighted materials, however, would take exception to such a practice, and it is in respect of these types of documents that users of imaging systems should be particularly careful.

For example, consider the hypothetical situation where an organization subscribes to an expensive publication that reports on relevant industry and government events. It is perhaps an eight-page document that appears weekly. The organization currently routes the report (without copying it) to the ten top executives at the head office of the firm on a priority basis, then makes the reports available on a secondary routing basis (again without copying them) to another twenty middle managers in the company's four other offices in Canada. This company acquires an imaging system that scans and stores, among other things, the daily correspondence of the firm's managers. Each manager has access to the system by means of a terminal in the manager's office. Someone comes up with the "cost-effective" idea of scanning the weekly reports into the system, thereby allowing all managers across the country to have immediate access to each issue of the publication. Indeed, the managers tend to view each issue on their screens within a day or two of its being scanned into the system, and each manager regularly prints out excerpts of the publication to show to other staff people in the manager's group. Such activity could expose the organization to a legal claim for copyright infringement, particularly where the publisher of the report wished to make an example of the organization so as to deter other would-be illegal copiers. In order to avoid such an embarrassing claim, the organization should seek to negotiate a company-wide distribution arrangement for the report based upon use of the imaging system. While likely resulting in some increase in the subscription fee for the service, such an arrangement would permit the organization to take advantage of its imaging system to distribute the publication internally in a more efficient and timely manner.

In addition to copyright concerns, imaging systems raise confidentiality problems. Consider the hypothetical situation where a business has implemented an imaging system to store all customer correspondence. One benefit of the system is that managers throughout the organization now have quick access to a customer's raw data. The danger inherent in such a system is that unauthorized personnel, perhaps from a competitor of a customer, may more easily than was the case with paper-based records gain access to the customer files. The very features that make the imaging system such a powerful, positive tool raise the real possibility that liability may be visited upon the user if the records of customers make their way into unauthorized hands. Accordingly, serious attention must be given to the security aspects of the imaging system throughout the lifetime of the system. The most advanced security techniques should be implemented when the system is installed, and these should be regularly updated as new security devices become available.

Failure to take such steps, and to properly administer the security devices once they are installed, could prove to be the Achilles' heel of an imaging system installation project.

Admissibility of Documents in Legal Proceedings and Records-Retention Requirements

An important question raised by imaging systems is whether the copies of documents produced by such a system are as admissible as evidence in courts or before regulatory agencies as the original documents. This is a particularly compelling question where the original of the document is destroyed after it is scanned into the system. Where the original is not destroyed, it can conceivably always be retrieved for purposes of a lawsuit. If, however, the original is destroyed, then the possible inadmissibility of the copy could be an extremely negative result of relying solely on the imaging system for the organization's record-keeping purposes. It is currently extremely difficult to predict with any certainty whether a specific copy produced by an imaging system will or will not be admissible in a particular legal proceeding. There are several principles in the law of evidence that will determine this question in respect of any particular copy, including the "hearsay rule" and the "best evidence rule," and given the diversity of judicial opinion in this area to date, absolute predictive certainty is impossible. What users can do, however, is become sensitive to the concerns of the law in this area so that copies of documents produced by their imaging systems stand the best chance possible of being admitted as evidence in legal and related proceedings.

A discussion of this issue must begin by noting the traditional preference of courts to require the production of originals of documents rather than copies, which may be unsatisfactory for a number of reasons. For some time, however, courts have been willing to recognize that copies of records made and relied upon in the course of business or for the efficient operation of business should also be regarded as trustworthy and should also be permitted to be considered as proof of the facts referred to in such documents.

The principle of admitting copies of certain types of business records has even been given statutory recognition in the federal and provincial laws governing evidence. For example, the Canada Evidence Act contains a provision relating to "banking records," which stipulates that a copy of any record kept in any financial institution shall be admitted as evidence if: (1) the book or record was, at the time of the making of the entry, one of the ordinary books or records of the financial institution; (2) the entry was made in the usual and ordinary course of business; (3) the record is in the custody or control of the financial institution; and (4) the copy is a true copy of the record. Another section in the Canada Evidence Act relating to "business records" generally, provides that a copy of a record made in the usual and ordinary course of business is admissible in evidence.

Both of these provisions are subject to certain conditions; for instance, in the case of "business records," the court may require the party intending to rely on a copy of a business record to give evidence as to the circumstances in which the information in the record was written, recorded, stored, or reproduced. This would be done by the court to ascertain the reliability of the record-keeping system that produced the business record.

The Canada Evidence Act also contains a so-called microfilm copy provision, which provides that a print from any photographic film (including a microphotographic film) of a document is admissible in evidence if the photographic film was taken in order to keep a permanent record and if the original was subsequently destroyed by or in the presence of one or more employees of the organization, or was lost, or was delivered to a customer. It should be noted that this provision in the Canada Evidence Act applies only to governments and to certain companies in the private sector (namely, banks, insurance and other financial institutions, and railway, express, telegraph, and telephone companies). The Ontario Evidence Act (and equivalent statutes in most other provinces) has provisions similar to these three found in the Canada Evidence Act, but they often differ to a greater or lesser extent in their particular scope of application. For example, the "microfilm copy" provision of the Ontario Evidence Act has broader application (that is, all corporations and other persons can take advantage of it), but it is also subject to an important qualification not included in its federal counterpart, namely, that if the original of a signed document is destroyed before the expiry of six years from the date when the matter to which it related ceased to be treated as current, the court may refuse to admit it in evidence under the "microfilm copy" provision.

The admissibility of most copies produced by imaging systems may come to be determined by the "business records" provisions of the evidence statutes noted above, except in the case of financial institutions, where the "banking records" provisions will likely be relevant as well. In both cases, managers of imaging systems should ensure the reliability of the whole of the imaging process, in order that the court or regulatory agency feels comfortable in accepting the copy as a true copy of the original. This means that quality-control features should be present at each stage in the imaging system — scanning, verification, storage, searching, retrieval, reading, and copying. Security again plays an important role: the greater the likelihood that an unauthorized person could have access to an alterable optical disk or other medium storing the record, the greater the probability that opposing counsel can argue successfully that the resultant copy should not be admitted as evidence, or that, if it is admitted, it should be given minimal weight. By the same token, a storage device that has only read and copy (but not write) access would be preferable from an admissibility perspective.

What is ideally required in this area is an amendment to the evidence statutes that expressly recognizes the phenomenon of storing images electronically. Such an amendment could provide that a copy produced by an imaging system that complies with a certain national standard would be admissible as evidence. Of course, this in turn requires the establishment of such a national standard for imaging systems. There is such a standard for microfilm, namely, *Microfilm As Documentary Evidence*, produced by the Canadian General Standards Board and approved by the Standards Council of Canada (referenced as CAN2-72.11-'79).

Given the uncertainty in this area, managers of imaging systems should carefully review with legal counsel the rules that might apply to the particular documents proposed to be stored by the manager's imaging system, in order to determine what specific practical steps the organization should take to help ensure that the resultant copies would be admissible as evidence in legal proceedings. While this exercise should be undertaken with every imaging system, it absolutely must be carried out by any organization that intends to destroy originals of documents once they are scanned into the imaging system.

An issue similar to the admissibility question discussed above relates to the records-retention requirements stipulated by many federal and provincial statutes. For example, the Income Tax Act requires businesses to keep certain books of account and records which, among other things, permit the taxes payable, and the taxes or other amounts to be collected by a person (including a business) to be determined. It is interesting to note that Revenue Canada permits companies to keep microfilm copies of books of original entry and source documents, provided the microfilming process utilized complies with the standard set out in *Microfilm as Documentary Evidence* noted above. Revenue Canada takes the position, however, that its current policies do not permit source documents to be stored on an imaging system. For example, Revenue Canada recently indicated to a bank that storing mortgage documents on optical disk would be unacceptable from the perspective of Revenue Canada's records-retention policies. It should be noted, however, that Revenue Canada is looking at the various issues raised by storing records in an electronic format with a view to possibly amending its policies.

With respect to records-retention requirements, again what is required is that the manager of the proposed imaging system carefully review with legal counsel the nature of the documents proposed to be stored on the system in order to determine whether the originals may be destroyed, or whether they must be retained because the imaging system copies are not sufficient for purposes of the relevant records-retention rule. Put more generally, imaging systems present data-processing and records-management professionals with novel contracting and legal issues. It is therefore imperative that people responsible for the acquisition and operation of imaging systems consider these issues, as well as those discussed above, before acquiring an imaging system so that appropriate measures can be taken, and practices established, to lessen the risks associated with imaging systems.

D

Contracting Procedures and Tactics

1. NEGOTIATING THE CONTRACT

By now readers will have acquired an appreciation of the protections that should be included in particular computer agreements. Knowing what to ask for is, of course, not the end of the story. The user or buyer must now negotiate with the supplier in order that the various clauses thought to be important by the user actually appear in a written contract signed by the supplier.

The Request for Proposal

The negotiation process ought to begin early, and ideally it will commence with the user's "request for proposal." That is, for an acquisition of any size the user should initiate contact with suppliers through a document called a request for proposal, or sometimes a "request for quote" or "call for tenders." This request typically sets out in a detailed manner exactly what the user is looking for from a technological perspective by clearly enumerating the user's needs which are to be satisfied by the acquisition of computer resources. For smaller acquisitions the request may be only several pages, while for larger systems it may run to a hundred or more pages. The request should require suppliers interested in bidding on the project to respond in detail and in writing, by means of a thorough proposal, to each issue raised in the request. It is really only in this way that a user can effectively evaluate the various product offerings of several different suppliers because the request for proposal acts as a yardstick by which to measure the various suppliers.

The request for proposal is a perfect place in which to start the process of effective contracting. Unfortunately, many requests deal only with technical and price issues and do not address the sorts of issues discussed in Parts B and C. Such an omission constitutes a failure to take advantage of a golden opportunity. The request ought to include a draft of the computer contract that the user proposes to use for the acquisition. This requires some drafting homework on the user's part, but the investment is well worth it. Short of attaching a whole agreement, the user should at the very least include a summary of the key contracting issues important to the user, such as a specific delivery date and the outline of the user's intended acceptance test, payment schedule, warranty provisions, and remedies. In the case of a software development agreement, for example, the contract summary would also include a description of the staged development and implementation process as well as a statement concerning ownership of the resulting software. This summary of contract issues may be only a few pages long, but its inclusion in the request for proposal is critical. Of course, the more thorough and complete the request for proposal, the better idea suppliers will have as to whether they can do the job, and the better chance the user has of actually choosing a suitable supplier. Unsuitable suppliers are weeded out early in the game.

With the full contract, or at least the contract issues summary, included in the request for proposal, each supplier should be required to respond in detail to the contract clauses or the summary. If the supplier does not agree with the user's preferred clause or position on an issue, the supplier should state its own proposed alternative position. This is an extremely valuable exercise from the user's perspective. It allows the user to gauge effectively what is and is not reasonable to ask of suppliers in a particular situation. It also allows the user to negotiate changes to the suppliers' positions from a position of some strength. How this is done is explained below.

Choosing a Supplier

Assume, for example, that a request for proposal is sent to six suppliers of which five respond with detailed proposals. These proposals are reviewed from a technical and price perspective and the list of five is narrowed to a short list of three viable proposals. After these three proposals are reviewed in detail, one stands out, although the other two are not far behind. At this point many buyers commit the supreme contract negotiating mistake of announcing publicly the "winning" supplier, and only then sitting down with the winner to try to negotiate a better deal.

Such a premature announcement of the successful supplier can be a grave error. The moment a supplier knows it is the winner, the user's power to negotiate changes to price, contract terms, or anything else decreases dramatically. This is not surprising. The competition is over, so why should the supplier bother to bend over backwards for the user at this point? In short, the user must resist the temptation to chose a supplier too soon, as difficult as this may be.

Once the list of credible candidates is narrowed to, say, three, the user should begin a preliminary round of negotiations with all three. For example, on price all three should be asked if the price in the proposal is really their best and final price. Often a simple question like this results in immediate significant price reductions. Of course, much depends on how badly the suppliers want the user's business, but the only way to gauge this effectively is to have the suppliers "compete" with one another. In this regard, it should be noted that under Canada's Competition Act it is a criminal offence for suppliers, in response to a call or request for bids or tenders and without the knowledge of the prospective user or buyer, to submit bids that are arrived at by agreement or arrangement between such suppliers, nor can one supplier agree with another not to respond to a request for bid (thereby allowing the other supplier's bid a much greater chance of success). Such activity, known as "bid rigging," is a very serious violation of the law which is intended to assist buyers in obtaining the best possible terms through the encouragement of inter-supplier competition.

Competition among suppliers should not focus exclusively on the issue of price. Contract terms such as those discussed in Parts B and C are also fair game. For example, the user may want a sixty-day acceptance test period, which has been clearly set out in the request for proposal. Out of five responses, four agree to the sixty-day test but the fifth one, the preferred choice of the user on the grounds of technology and price, offers only a fifteen-day acceptance test. In this case, before announcing a winner the user should make it clear to the preferred (fifth) supplier that the user regards a sixty-day acceptance test period to be a key component of the final contract. The supplier is far more likely to make some sort of concession at this early point in the acquisition process than after it has been awarded the contract.

Of course, the process of trying to get the best deal from a handful of likely suppliers should be carried out with some deftness and delicacy; a crass auction where suppliers are blatantly being played off against each other can alienate the suppliers. The bidding ought to be conducted in a discrete, sophisticated, even-handed manner. For example, a bidder should never be told that a certain concession, say a price drop, will result in that supplier's being chosen if, in fact, after the price drop still further concessions will be sought from the supplier.

Single-Source or Multiple-Source Projects

It is often the case that a user's hardware needs are best met by one supplier while its applications software requirements are best fulfilled by another supplier. In such a situation, the user can enter into two separate contracts, one with each supplier, but care should be taken that the two contracts complement one another in several important respects. For example, ideally, both the hardware and the software supplier, but at least one of them (preferably the larger, more solvent one), should be required to give a warranty in the agreement that their component works in conjunction with the other supplier's in accordance with predetermined standards and specifications (see section B.13 under "Warranty as to Compatibility"). The user should also have the ability, with each supplier, to terminate the respective agreement and return the supplier's component if the warranty proves to be false, even where the problem is caused by the other supplier's component. In short, the user in a multi-supplier procurement arrangement should try to make its obligations under each agreement contingent upon the due performance of all the other suppliers. In any event, when more than one supplier is involved in an acquisition of computing resources, there will inevitably be more responsibility placed on the user to ensure that the various segments of the system come to operate properly together.

Some users prefer to shift this responsibility to one of the suppliers by appointing and contracting with only one supplier, who in turn retains the services of the various other suppliers. Hardware suppliers, or established systems integrators, are usually preferred for this role because they are generally larger and financially more stable than application software developers. Having decided to deal contractually with only the hardware supplier or a systems integrator, the user conveniently avoids some messy problems such as the not uncommon finger-pointing exercise between the hardware and software suppliers over which of them is at fault when the system fails to function as required during the acceptance test. There is, then, additional security to be had in single-source procurements from the user's point of view. Of course, the chosen lead supplier or systems integrator will rarely volunteer to manage the project for free, but, depending on the circumstances and the level of competition prevailing in the market at the time, the premium charged by a hardware supplier or systems integrator to take responsibility for the software developer's activities can be quite reasonable, and the resulting security afforded the user is usually worth the cost.

Letters of Intent

Buyers are often asked by suppliers to sign letters of intent which signify, as their name suggests, the intent of the buyer to purchase a particular system from a supplier. Letters of intent are typically used in situations where the hardware to be installed requires a long manufacturing lead-time and to justify the production of the equipment the supplier needs some assurance of the buyer's intentions but the purchase agreement itself is not yet ready to be signed; usually the supplier requests that a deposit towards the purchase price of the equipment accompany the letter of intent.

Buyers should be wary of letters of intent. The advantages of this device are all on the side of the supplier. Many suppliers find letters of intent to be helpful in committing the user psychologically to the supplier's proposal; however, such a commitment can also be more formal — and legally binding — if the letter of intent is not drafted carefully. It should state clearly that the letter of intent is just that, that it is in no way binding on either party, and that the purchase by the buyer of the supplier's system is conditional upon the entering into of a definitive legal agreement. Further, if a deposit accompanies the letter of intent, the letter should provide that this deposit is to be applied to the purchase price of the equipment if the acquisition proceeds, and that if the acquisition does not proceed for whatever reason, then this deposit is to be returned to the buyer immediately without any penalty, set-off, or withholding whatsoever.

Form of the Computer Contract

Once the supplier agrees to include in the agreement certain contract terms that have been asked for by the buyer, the issue arises how to reduce this agreement to writing. The first question is, should the buyer agree to use the supplier's standard form agreement, albeit with numerous deletions and amendments, or should the buyer insist on its own agreement being used? The individual circumstances will dictate which agreement makes the most sense.

A buyer should always explore the possibility of using the supplier's standard form contract as the basis of the agreement, because this route offers several advantages. First, many suppliers are attached to their particular form of agreement from a psychological perspective, and if a buyer can live with it as the basis of the agreement, this will be much appreciated by the supplier, thus earning the buyer useful negotiating credits. Some Canadian suppliers who are subsidiaries of American companies are under particular pressure from their head offices to use the company's standard form agreement only, and they especially will be appreciative if this request can be accommodated.

Of course using a supplier's standard form contract invariably means that portions of it must be deleted and certain provisions must be added. The deletions can be accomplished simply enough by taking a pen and ruler and crossing out the objectionable clauses, sentences, or phrases, with all such deletions being initialled by both parties. As for additions, one efficient method is to draft an addendum to the standard form which might go on for several pages setting out the parties' agreement on issues such as delivery date, acceptance testing, payment milestones, and warranties. In effect, where the standard form is completely silent on any such matter, the addendum would deal with the whole issue, while if the standard form partially deals with an issue then the addendum would amend the particular clause in the standard form. It is not unusual, for instance, to end up with an amended standard form agreement in which the standard form portion contains the protections required by the supplier, such as warranty disclaimers, limitation of liability provisions, and software licence and related confidentiality issues, while the addendum deals with the issues of importance to the buyer.

Some buyers are hesitant to ask a supplier to change its standard form agreement, whether by deletions or additions. This reluctance, which was referred to in section A.2, is fostered by the myth that standard form contracts cannot be amended. This myth, however, is just that — a myth. There might have been a time years ago when a computer supplier would present its standard form contract and say take it or leave it, but this attitude to marketing is a thing of the past. Given the extremely competitive nature of virtually all segments of the computer industry, a supplier foolhardy enough to deliver such an ultimatum today will likely be left wallowing in its chauvinism. A buyer should never for a minute believe that a standard form agreement is engraved in stone.

The above discussion about how to amend a standard form agreement assumes that the supplier's standard form agreement can be salvaged, without a great deal of work to incorporate necessary changes, to serve as the final contract. If, however, the supplier's standard form is so unreasonably one-sided in favour of the supplier that to amend it would mean it would be almost completely covered with ink, or if the complexity of the acquisition raises a lot of issues not contemplated by the standard form so that a very lengthy addendum is called for, then the parties might as well start from scratch with a new agreement. Even in such a case the person responsible for drafting the agreement should incorporate as much of the standard form as the buyer will accept as, again, this will show a degree of fair-mindedness on the part of the buyer that will be much appreciated by the supplier.

The following practical pointers should be kept in mind when drafting a computer contract. It is helpful if the order of the clauses in the contract reflects the various steps in the actual implementation of the system from a chronological perspective (e.g., delivery should be dealt with before acceptance testing). This sort of order has been followed both in Part B and in the Part E contract checklists and ought to be followed by the person drafting the contract. This will make the contract a more "user friendly" document and allow for a more effective administration of the contract during the actual acquisition process. It is surprising how many standard form agreements do not subscribe to these rules of format, which is a real disadvantage to the buyer because the supplier will invariably be familiar with the (often bizarre) structure and form of presentation of its own agreement.

The key goal in drafting the actual provisions in the contract is clarity. The contract drafter should constantly be asking, "a year from now, will a stranger to this particular buyer-supplier relationship understand my words as to what the parties really intended?" It is in achieving this goal that lawyers can be of great assistance. Putting sometimes difficult concepts and agreements into writing in a clear but concise manner is something the experienced lawyer is particularly good at. In effect, in the computer contract area lawyers should not be looked upon only as advocates helping to ensure that their client's legal rights are protected, though of course this is a key part of their mandate. They also undertake the equally important role of putting into writing, effectively and unambiguously, the business deal arrived at by the parties. An ounce of clarity in the agreement can ward off a ton of misunderstanding later on, especially where both supplier and buyer undergo changes in personnel in their project teams, in which case new staff members may have to rely solely on the original paperwork for their understanding of the agreement.

Negotiating Tips

Negotiating a computer agreement is not unlike negotiating any other commercial arrangement. The most important procedural point to remember is to start early by means of a request for proposal which should include the buyer's essential requirements and then bargaining with all the suppliers for the acceptance of these requirements prior to choosing any single supplier. The importance of preselection negotiations with suppliers cannot be emphasized enough. In addition, even when one supplier is finally chosen, the others on the short list should not be sent too far away. To the extent possible, the buyer should try to "keep honest" the chosen supplier by indicating, usually indirectly but directly as well if need be, that alternatives which do not include the preferred supplier are available to the buyer at all times. Of course this argument becomes weaker as the buyer becomes "locked-in" to a particular supplier's technology, but one of the intentions of an effective computer contract with suitable remedies is to lessen such lock-in by giving the buyer the opportunity to bail out of an acquisition process that has gone sour.

Many wasted hours can be spent on negotiations with the wrong people who must continually run back to the real decision maker for confirmation or direction. Buyers should negotiate only with those representatives of the supplier who have authority to bind the supplier. Buyers should try to avoid the "used-car-salesman" syndrome, where a junior or local representative of the supplier professes that he would very much like to grant the buyer a particular concession, but that if he did head office would fire him (the car salesman pleads that if it were up to him alone the buyer would get the car for $18,000, but the salesman's boss simply will not allow the salesman to sell the car for anything under $20,000). Of course, if the supplier insists on playing this game, so can the buyer.

Another way to expedite the negotiating process is to have outstanding issues reduced to writing. For instance, if the acquisition involves a large system and the buyer has drafted a customized agreement, the draft should be sent to the supplier with the request that the supplier note directly onto the draft any problems or objections and then return the marked-up draft to the buyer. In this way the buyer can see clearly where the disagreements are and can respond to them quickly. If the supplier merely states a bunch of general concerns over the telephone the buyer may never get to the nub of the issues and the ensuing negotiations will take much longer to complete.

Getting comments in writing also helps reduce the potential for so-called contract negotiation backsliding. The intent here is that once a provision has been agreed to there should be no opportunity to reopen that issue for discussion or negotiation. Such backsliding, if it is permitted, is a time-consuming, aggravating exercise. By requesting all comments in writing, the buyer can reduce the chance of backsliding by saying that a certain provision favourable to the buyer wasn't objected to in the supplier's initial response to the buyer's first draft of the contract, that as a result the buyer considered the issue settled, and that to reopen the issue now would be unfair, inasmuch as the buyer may well have compromised on another issue on the basis of the particular provision that the supplier is now trying to remove from the agreement.

Buyers should be aware of the so-called artificial deadline, often used by suppliers to get the paperwork finalized and the contract signed in short order in a manner satisfactory to the supplier. This negotiating tactic typically arises in the following context: the buyer and supplier have been talking price and contract issues for some time, when the supplier announces that its financial year-end is approaching, that the supplier wants to log the sale before the end of this fiscal year, and that if this doesn't happen a new price will be effective for the acquisition commencing at the start of the new year.

There can be, from the supplier's point of view, a seemingly legitimate rationale for this plea: the supplier's (or the individual salesperson's) commission may have a year-end (or quarterly) calculation cutoff and the supplier (or salesman) would dearly love to bump up the current sales numbers in order to get as big a commission as possible. Of course this should be of no concern to the buyer. The buyer should not be hurried into a decision because of financial or any other deadlines of the supplier, and the buyer ought simply to tell the salesperson that a contract will be signed only when it contains all the protections deemed important by the buyer. If a supplier will not accept this, then the buyer may well want to review its choice of a supplier if such an arguably minor matter has the effect of disrupting the buyer-supplier relationship.

A final negotiating point is that all agreements relating to the particular acquisition ought to be signed simultaneously. Many buyers tend initially to concentrate primarily on the hardware purchase and software licence agreements, and only after these are signed do they devote any energy to the relevant maintenance agreement. This is a mistake. Once a buyer has signed a purchase agreement its negotiating leverage on the other agreements declines dramatically. In effect, all the agreements should be treated as one package and signed (or not signed) as a collection of intimately related documents, if the buyer wishes to achieve the best price and general supplier co-operation.

2. ADMINISTERING THE CONTRACT

Assume the buyer has negotiated and signed an effective computer agreement containing, in its favour, all sorts of useful rights and remedies in the event the supplier doesn't live up to its obligations. This is still not the end of the story. The signed contract should not merely be thrown into the back of some dusty filing cabinet and forgotten. Instead, at the very least the key dates and timings in the contract should be noted by the buyer and incorporated into a "bring forward" or reminder system so that if any of these dates are not met, the buyer can quickly begin to exercise its rights under the contract.

On larger acquisition projects this may never be a problem since the parties will continually be working with one another on the various implementation stages and any delays or problems likely will promptly come to the buyer's attention. Where a smaller system is being purchased, however, particularly by a larger organization that may have several acquisitions underway simultaneously, it may be that after the contract signing the next step is the delivery of the equipment some months later. In such a case the delivery date, at least, ought to be noted, and if the equipment is not delivered on that date the buyer immediately should take appropriate action.

A similar issue arises in the case of acceptance tests that run for a specific period, after which, if no problems are brought to the attention of the supplier, the buyer is deemed to have accepted the equipment. As discussed earlier in the section on acceptance testing (B.9), such an "automatic" trigger is often the trade-off required by the supplier in order to agree to an acceptance test in the first place, and it is not an altogether unreasonable request in that it requires the buyer to act with some diligence. Such a provision, however, should force the buyer to institute a tightly organized plan of problem reporting during the acceptance test as well as a predetermined means of notifying the supplier that acceptance has not occurred well before the end of the scheduled acceptance test period, if in fact the system is found deficient. Without such an administrative plan the buyer might find itself having accepted a system it did not really want merely because the relevant acceptance test period had expired without the buyer taking any positive action to refuse acceptance of the system.

The gist of the above discussion is that buyers must exercise their rights promptly when a problem arises in a computer acquisition. Otherwise, they risk forfeiting or greatly diluting their rights. For example, if a system is scheduled to be delivered on 1 April of a particular year, but it is not, and the buyer makes no objection until 1 October, a half a year after the scheduled delivery date, then in any ensuing claim for breach of contract the supplier may be able to base a defence on the buyer's tardiness.

The supplier would argue, essentially, that the system could not have been all that important to the buyer if the buyer took six months to realize that the system was never delivered, and if this is so, then the buyer's claims about significant damages shouldn't be taken seriously.

The need for buyers to exercise contract rights promptly and with care was well illustrated several years ago in a Canadian court case involving a difficult computer acquisition. The buyer was in the business of selling, leasing, and repairing heavy construction equipment and wished to computerize its manual inventory-control, billing, job-costing, accounting, payroll, and other systems. The supplier said it could do this job in six months and, on 1 May 1975, an agreement to this effect was signed between the parties.

Soon after the contract signing, as in many custom software development situations, the supplier realized the job was much bigger than originally anticipated and would take much longer than six months. By December 1975 the parties were actively renegotiating the May 1975 agreement and signed a new contract in April 1976. This second agreement provided, among other things, that the buyer could terminate the agreement if the project were not finished by 31 December 1976. The project was not finished by 31 December 1976, but the buyer chose to continue. Some parts of the required software were delivered during 1977, but by March 1978 the system was still not operational. The buyer wrote a letter in March 1978 requiring the supplier to complete the work by May 1978. Finally, on 31 July 1978 the buyer terminated the agreement and claimed $390,000 in damages. The judge in the case not only refused the buyer's claim, but agreed with the supplier that the buyer had wrongfully terminated the agreement and that the buyer must pay the supplier's resulting damages of $50,000! How could the judge come to this conclusion?

First, there was a clause in the contract that said it could be terminated only on ninety days' notice. The judge said this notice must be very clear, and that the March 1978 letter was not clear enough as it was a mild letter, quite in keeping with the buyer continually letting delivery and project-completion dates slip without making a whole lot of fuss. The second strike against the buyer was that after it had written the March 1978 letter it also requested the supplier to submit a proposal for finishing the project, but the buyer did not make it clear that the termination of the contract would occur regardless of what, if anything, was contained in this plan to finish the project. Therefore, the judge said the supplier was induced into devoting resources to preparing this proposal rather than completing the project during the ninety days after the March 1978 letter.

In short, in this case the buyer had reasonably favourable provisions in the contract, but it did not exercise them in a timely manner nor in a precise enough manner. It would not have been difficult to do either. The judge stated in his decision it would have been enough for the buyer to have written a letter clearly indicating that the ninety-day notice period for termination had begun to run, and that during this time the supplier could propose an alternative plan to finish the project (in addition to just completing it) but that the ninety days would continue to run regardless of the preparation of such a plan, in other words that these negotiations would not have any impact on the ability of the buyer to terminate the agreement.

By not following these procedures the buyer not only failed to recover its damages of $390,000, it ended up having to pay the supplier $50,000. This might seem like an unfair or harsh result, but it illustrates well the need for buyers to administer their computer contracts with great care. Otherwise, important contract rights that were gained through perhaps difficult and trying negotiations could be lost, or worse, even backfire on the buyer if the buyer exercises them improperly, as was the case in the above example. This point again raises the issue of the role of lawyers in drafting, negotiating, and in this case administering computer contracts. A buyer who is confronted with a breach-of-contract situation by a supplier should consult a lawyer early on to confirm the various substantive rights and procedural options open to the buyer so that its rights are preserved as much as possible.

Contract Checklists

Part E contains a contract checklist for each type of computer contract discussed in this book. As well, checklist 13 ("Contracting
Procedures") applies to contracts referred to in checklists 1–7,
10, and 11. These checklists are intended to be handy reference
guides which readers will use regularly. An efficient way to use
a checklist is to review the issues raised in the checklist against
the provisions contained in the particular supplier's standard
form computer contract. In this way the buyer can most readily
identify unacceptable or unreasonable provisions as well as
wholesale omissions of contracting requirements essential to
the buyer. Cross-references to sections in Parts B, C, and D are
given so that the reader can review the discussion given in the
text concerning any of the points mentioned in these checklists.

1. HARDWARE PURCHASE

Contracting Procedures (E.13)

- Review negotiation and administration issues discussed in
  checklist 13.

Description of Hardware and Prices (B.1)

- List all hardware components and related documentation in a
  schedule to the contract.

- List price of each component on a per-unit basis.

- Show all applicable taxes as separate-line items.

- Show all related costs of hardware, including transportation,
  shipping insurance, and installation charges, as separate-line
  items.

Project Management (B.2)

- Designate project co-ordinators and supplier's project team,
  with no transfer of such personnel.

- Review qualifications of supplier's personnel.

- Provide for removal of supplier's personnel at buyer's request.

- Plan a detailed implementation schedule, indicating firm dates for delivery, installation, education and training, and other key project milestones.

Preparation of the Installation Site (B.3)

- Specify whether site preparation is buyer's or supplier's responsibility.

- If supplier's responsibility, specify cost in schedule.

- If buyer's responsibility, specify supplier approval mechanism.

- Set out power and environmental specifications in schedule to contract.

- Keep accurate record of costs.

Delivery Date (B.4)

- The delivery date is a critical contract control checkpoint for buyer.

- Specify delivery date for each item of equipment and related documentation to be acquired by specific calendar date or by duration of time from previous contract milestone. Specify that "time is of the essence."

- Ensure buyer's right to postpone delivery.

- Ensure buyer's right to cancel delivery.

- If phased delivery, secure supplier's acknowledgement that acceptance will not occur until all items have been delivered and installed, and have passed acceptance test.

Transfer of Title; Risk of Loss; Insurance (B.5)

- Identify when title in equipment passes to buyer.

- If title passes at supplier's plant (F.O.B. supplier's facility) then buyer should arrange common carrier and insurance until equipment delivered to buyer.

- If title passes upon payment in full, supplier should be liable for arranging shipping and insurance until equipment delivered to buyer.

- Buyer should arrange for its insurance to cover equipment once delivered.

Installation (B.6)

- Specify whether installation is buyer's or supplier's responsibility.

- If supplier's responsibility, specify cost in schedule.

Conversion of Data (B.7)

- Specify what assistance to be given by supplier, and at what cost.

- Include in contract names of conversion programs suggested by supplier; if such programs prove to be inadequate, supplier pays additional cost.

Education and Training (B.8)

- Provide names and qualifications of trainers.

- Specify amount, timing, and location of training.

- Allow for consultation of buyer in preparation of training program.

- Training methodology: specify whether supplier will train all buyer's people, or train only a few of buyer's people who in turn train all other buyer's people.

- If relevant, provide for in-depth training of technical maintenance staff of buyer.

- Specify how much education and training is free, and cost of additional education and training.

Hardware Test (B.9)

- Distinguish between acceptance test and manufacturer's diagnostic tests for hardware.

- Passage of hardware test should not constitute acceptance of hardware.

Acceptance Test (B.9)

- The acceptance test is a critical contract control checkpoint for buyer.

- No item of hardware will be accepted without first conducting acceptance test.

- Specify period of acceptance test.

- Specify performance criteria (which should be based on readily ascertainable objective criteria) that equipment must meet to pass acceptance test, including documentation, specifications, promises in supplier's proposal and marketing literature, and warranties.

- Specify reliability standard that equipment must meet to pass acceptance test, including recovery times.

- If provision is made for deemed acceptance at end of test period then buyer must institute strict plan for test administration and notification of supplier of any deficiencies.

Price and Payment Schedule (B.11)

• Specify that except for prices and expenses mentioned in agreement buyer is not responsible for additional costs.

• Secure price protection for lengthy delivery period or on future purchases.

• Volume discount formulas must be described accurately.

• Consider joint volume discount arrangements.

• Secure most-favoured-customer pricing protection.

• Payment schedule: instalment payments should consist of progress payments reflecting actual performance milestones.

Taxes (B.12)

• Supplier should pass on to buyer benefit of reductions of customs duties.

• Check whether status of buyer or type of goods exempts buyer from sales taxes.

Warranties (B.13, B.16)

• Warranty period should be distinct from acceptance test period and period during which system is under maintenance.

• Warranty against defects in hardware: specify duration (should commence on acceptance of system) and scope of maintenance services included (should be comparable to paid-for maintenance services).

• Warranty as to new equipment: if not new, notify buyer as to date of manufacture.

• Warranty that supplier either owns the intellectual property rights in the computer system or is authorized to sell/license them.

- Warranty that equipment is the supplier's most advanced technology.

- Warranty as to certification (i.e., approval of Canadian Standards Association (CSA), or Department of Communications for telecommunications equipment).

- Warranty as to compatibility, especially that hardware works in conjunction with specified applications systems, and that resulting system can interface with other specified equipment or software in predetermined manner.

- Warranty as to capacity; statements as to data storage and other capabilities of present system.

- Warranty as to expansion; statements as to costs required to upgrade the equipment to one or more additional configurations.

- Include all other promises made by supplier; all warranties should be based upon readily ascertainable objective criteria.

Warranty Disclaimers (B.14)

- Given existence of disclaimer of implied warranties, it is absolutely essential that all promises of the supplier are included in the contract as express warranties.

Remedies (B.15, B.19)

- Liquidated damages, supply of interim solution, and/or termination of agreement for nondelivery of equipment.

- Liquidated damages, repair of all problems at no cost, and/or termination of agreement for inability of equipment to pass acceptance test.

- Additional remedies: reimbursement of amounts incurred solely to prepare installation site for supplier's particular equipment.

- Express preservation of all other remedies including claim for damages resulting from supplier's or system's inadequate performance.

- Buyer's effective remedy for certain breaches of agreement may not be termination of agreement, but rather some positive form of action by supplier.

Intellectual Property Rights Indemnity (B.16)

- Scope of indemnity should cover patents, copyrights, trade secrets, and all other intellectual property rights.

- Buyer in Canada should be indemnified in regard to Canadian patents and copyrights, or all patents and copyrights, but not just United States patents and copyrights.

- Buyer in Canada should be indemnified in regard to all trade secrets (i.e., there should be no national limitation on trade secrets).

- Scope of indemnity should cover all damages, expenses, and settlement costs, including reasonable legal fees, and not just damages finally awarded by a court.

- Review carefully supplier's ability to terminate agreement upon occurrence of intellectual property infringement claim.

Limitation of Liability (B.17)

- Supplier should be responsible for at least direct damages in an amount equal to purchase price of all equipment.

- There should be no limits on liability for claims regarding intellectual property, unauthorized disclosure of buyer's confidential information, personal injury, or property damage.

- Given limitation of supplier's liability, buyer should ensure it has sufficient back-up and alternative procedures in the event of system malfunction or inoperability.

Excusable Delays (B.18)

- If specific excusable events are listed, delete those reasonably in supplier's control such as inability of supplier to obtain supplies (i.e., supplier should maintain larger parts inventory).

- Supplier should give notice of an excusable event, and must try to work around such event.

- Secure buyer's right to terminate agreement if excusable event continues beyond certain period of time.

Termination (B.19)

- Require written notice of buyer default and that period of time to cure default must precede any termination.

- Only "material" breaches of buyer should give rise to right to terminate agreement.

- Buyer's effective remedy in some cases may not be termination of agreement, but rather some form of positive action by supplier.

Buyer's Confidential Information; Publicity (B.20)

- Require supplier to keep confidential buyer's confidential information.

- Nature of buyer's information may require all supplier's employees who have access to such buyer information to sign nondisclosure agreements with buyer.

- Supplier must obtain buyer's permission to use buyer's name in supplier's marketing literature.

Upgrades and Trade-in Credits (B.21)

- Require supplier's on-going notification of buyer of supplier's new products.

- Trade-in credit will assure market for buyer's used system.

Arbitration (B.22)

- Often an attractive alternative to court system, arbitration is particularly useful where technical problems are at issue.

- Consider arbitration for just a portion of the agreement (e.g., passage of acceptance test or quality of documentation).

- Designate one or more arbitrators or appointing body, place of arbitration, relevant rules, and, if foreign contracting party, language of arbitral proceedings.

Governing Law (B.23)

- Designate law of jurisdiction in which system is to be installed.

- If agreement is to be governed by law of any other jurisdiction, buyer must have contract reviewed by local counsel in that other jurisdiction.

Assignment (B.24)

- Obtain ability to assign agreement to other member of corporate group.

- Consider ability to assign operating system software to purchaser of hardware.

- Ability of supplier to assign agreement or subcontract obligations ought to be subject to buyer's consent.

Notices (B.25)

- Specify deemed receipt of notices to occur within a certain time after delivery or mailing of notice.

Entire Agreement (B.26)

- Given existence of entire agreement clause, ensure that all representations, warranties, or other promises of supplier are included in the agreement.

Amendment (B.27)

- Agreement should be able to be amended only by a written agreement signed by the duly authorized representatives of the parties.

Guarantee of Affiliate (B.28)

- Buyer should consider whether a guarantee of an affiliate of the supplier, or the manufacturer of the equipment, is required.

2. SOFTWARE LICENCE

Contracting Procedures (E.13)

- Review negotiation and administration issues discussed in checklist 13.

Description of Software and Prices (B.1)

- List all software components and related documentation in a schedule to the contract; attach at least detailed functional specifications for customizations.

- List price of each component on a per-unit basis.

- Show all applicable taxes as separate-line items.

- Show all related costs of software, including transportation and installation charges, as separate-line items.

Project Management (B.2)

- Designate project co-ordinators and supplier's project team, with no transfer of such personnel.

- Review qualifications of supplier's personnel.

- Provide for removal of supplier's personnel at user's request.

- Plan a detailed implementation schedule, indicating firm dates for delivery, installation, education and training, and other key project milestones.

Preparation of the Installation Site (B.3)

- Specify whether site preparaton is user's or supplier's responsibility.

- If supplier's responsibility, specify cost in schedule.

- If user's responsibility, specify supplier approval mechanism.

- Set out power and environmental specifications in schedule to contract.

- Keep accurate record of costs.

Delivery Date (B.4)

- The delivery date is a critical contract control checkpoint for user.

- Specify a delivery date for each item of software and related documentation to be licensed by specific calendar date or by duration of time from previous contract milestone. Specify "time is of the essence."

- Ensure user's right to postpone delivery.

- Ensure user's right to cancel delivery.

- If delivery is phased, secure acknowledgement from supplier that acceptance will not occur until all items have been delivered and installed, and have passed acceptance test.

Installation (B.6)

- Specify whether installation is user's or supplier's responsibility.

- If supplier's responsibility, specify cost in schedule.

Conversion of Data (B.7)

- Specify what assistance will be given by supplier, and at what cost.

- Include in contract names of conversion programs suggested by supplier; if such programs prove to be inadequate, supplier pays additional cost.

Education and Training (B.8)

- Provide names and qualifications of trainers.

- Specify amount, timing, and location of training.

- Allow for consultation of user in preparation of training program.

- Training methodology: specify whether supplier will train all user's people, or train only a few of user's people who in turn train all other user's people.

- If relevant, provide for in-depth training of technical maintenance staff of user.

- Specify how much education and training is free, and cost of additional education and training.

Acceptance Test (B.9)

- The acceptance test is a critical contract control checkpoint for user.

- No item of software will be accepted without first conducting an acceptance test.

- Specify period of acceptance test.

- Plan a phased acceptance test if relevant; test each application system, then test all application systems together.

- Specify performance criteria (which should be based on readily ascertainable objective criteria) that software must meet to pass acceptance test, including documentation, specifications, promises in supplier's proposal and marketing literature, and warranties.

- Specify reliability standard that software must meet to pass acceptance test, including recovery times.

- If provision is made for deemed acceptance at end of test period then user must institute strict plan for test administration and notification of supplier of any deficiencies.

Licence of Software (B.10)

- Consider possible modifications of restrictions on use to provide for processing of affiliates' data, site or institution licence, and ability to make modifications.

- Consider possible modifications of restrictions on transfer to permit assignment of licence to affiliates.

- Obtain permission to make back-up copy as exception to restriction on copying.

Price and Payment Schedule (B.11)

- Specify that except for prices and expenses mentioned in agreement user is not responsible for additional costs.

- Secure price protection if lengthy delivery period or on future purchases.

- Volume discount formulas must be described accurately.

- Consider joint volume discount arrangements.

- Secure most-favoured-customer pricing protection.

- Payment schedule: instalment payments should consist of progress payments reflecting actual performance milestones.

Taxes (B.12)

- Check whether status of user or type of goods exempts user from sales taxes.

- If supplier is not resident in Canada, provide for deduction of withholding tax from licence fee and remittance to federal government.

Warranties (B.13, B.16)

- Warranty period should be distinct from acceptance test period and period during which system is under maintenance.

- Warranty against errors in software: specify duration (should commence on acceptance of system) and scope of maintenance services included (should be comparable to paid-for maintenance services).

- Warranty that software is the supplier's most advanced technology.

- Warranty that supplier either owns the intellectual property rights in the software or is authorized to license them.

- Warranty as to compatibility, especially that software works in conjunction with specified hardware, and that resulting system can interface with other specified equipment or software in predetermined manner.

- Warranty as to capacity; statements as to data storage and other capabilities of present system.

- Warranty as to expansion; statements as to costs required to upgrade the software to one or more additional configurations.

- Include all other promises made by supplier; all warranties should be based upon readily ascertainable objective criteria.

Warranty Disclaimers (B.14)

- Given existence of disclaimer of implied warranties, it is absolutely essential that all promises of the supplier are included in the contract as express warranties.

Remedies (B.15, B.19)

- Liquidated damages, supply of interim solution, and/or termination of agreement for nondelivery of software.

- Liquidated damages, correction of all errors at no cost, and/or termination of agreement for inability of software to pass acceptance test.

- Additional remedies: reimbursement of amounts incurred solely to prepare installation site for supplier's particular software.

- Express preservation of all other remedies including claims for damages resulting from supplier's or software's inadequate performance.

- User's effective remedy for certain breaches of agreement may not be termination of agreement, but rather some form of positive action by supplier.

Intellectual Property Rights Indemnity (B.16)

- Scope of indemnity should cover patents, copyrights, trade secrets, and all other intellectual property rights.

- User in Canada should be indemnified in regard to Canadian patents and copyrights, or all patents and copyrights, but not just United States patents and copyrights.

- User in Canada should be indemnified in regard to all trade secrets (i.e., there should be no national limitation on trade secrets).

- Scope of indemnity should cover all damages, expenses, and settlement costs, including reasonable legal fees, and not just damages finally awarded by a court.

- Review carefully supplier's ability to terminate agreement upon occurrence of intellectual property infringement claim.

Limitation of Liability (B.17)

- Supplier should be responsible for at least direct damages in an amount equal to licence fee of all software.

- There should be no limits on liability for claims regarding intellectual property, unauthorized disclosure of user's confidential information, personal injury, or property damage.

- Given limitation of supplier's liability, user should ensure it has sufficient back-up and alternative procedures in the event of system malfunction or inoperability.

Excusable Delays (B.18)

- If specific excusable events are listed, delete those reasonably in supplier's control, such as inability of supplier to obtain supplies (i.e., supplier should maintain larger parts inventory).

- Require supplier to give notice of an excusable event, and to try to work around such event.

- Secure user's right to terminate agreement if excusable event continues beyond certain period of time.

Termination (B.19)

- Require written notice of user default and that period of time to cure default must precede any termination.

- Only "material" breaches of buyer should give rise to right to terminate agreement.

- User's effective remedy in some cases may not be termination of agreement, but rather some form of positive action by supplier.

User's Confidential Information; Publicity (B.20)

- Require supplier to keep confidential user's confidential information.

- Nature of user's information may require all supplier's employees who have access to such user information to sign nondisclosure agreements with user.

- Supplier must obtain user's permission to use user's name in supplier's marketing literature.

Upgrades and Trade-in Credits (B.21)

- Require supplier's on-going notification of user of supplier's new products.

- Trade-in credit will assure market for user's current software.

Arbitration (B.22)

- Often an attractive alternative to court system, particularly where technical problems are at issue.

- Consider arbitration for just a portion of the agreement (e.g., passage of acceptance test or quality of documentation).

- Designate one or more arbitrators or appointing body, place of arbitration, relevant rules, and, if foreign contracting party, language of arbitral proceedings.

Governing Law (B.23)

- Designate law of jurisdiction in which software is to be installed.

- If agreement is to be governed by law of any other jurisdiction, user must have contract reviewed by local counsel in that other jurisdiction.

Assignment (B.24)

- Secure ability to assign agreement to other member of corporate group.

- Consider ability to assign software to purchaser of the hardware.

- Ability of supplier to assign agreement or subcontract obligations ought to be subject to user's consent.

- Secure provision that supplier cannot sell ownership of computer program unless purchaser assumes user's licence and support agreements on same terms.

Notices (B.25)

- Specify deemed receipt of notices to occur within a certain time after delivery or mailing of notice.

Entire Agreement (B.26)

- Given existence of entire agreement clause, ensure that all representations, warranties, or other promises of supplier are included in the agreement.

Amendment (B.27)

- Agreement should be able to be amended only by a written agreement signed by the duly authorized representatives of the parties.

Guarantee of Affiliate (B.28)

- User should consider whether a guarantee of an affiliate of the supplier, or the developer of the software, is required.

3. TURN-KEY SYSTEM (HARD-WARE AND SOFTWARE)

Contracting Procedures (E.13)

- Review negotiation and administration issues discussed in checklist 13.

Description of Hardware, Software, and Prices (B.1, D.1)

- Specify the supplier is providing a complete system.

- List all hardware and software components of system and related documentation in a schedule to the contract; attach at least detailed functional specifications for customizations.

- List price of each component on a per-unit basis.

- Show all applicable taxes as separate-line items.

- Show all related costs of system, including transportation, shipping insurance, and installation charges, as separate-line items.

Project Management (B.2)

- Designate project co-ordinators and supplier's project team, with no transfer of such personnel.

- Review qualifications of supplier's personnel.

- Allow for removal of supplier's personnel at buyer's request.

- Plan a detailed implementation schedule, indicating firm dates for delivery, installation, education and training, and other key project milestones.

Preparation of the Installation Site (B.3)

- Specify whether site preparation is buyer's or supplier's responsibility.

- If supplier's responsibility, specify cost in schedule.

- If buyer's responsibility, specify supplier approval mechanism.

- Set out power and environmental specifications in schedule to contract.

- Keep accurate record of costs.

Delivery Date (B.4)

- The delivery date is a critical contract control checkpoint for buyer.

- Specify a delivery date for each item of the system to be acquired by specific calendar date or by duration of time from previous contract milestone. Specify "time is of the essence."

- Ensure buyer's right to postpone delivery.

- Ensure buyer's right to cancel delivery.

- If delivery is phased, secure acknowledgement from supplier that acceptance will not occur until all items have been delivered and installed, and have passed acceptance test.

Transfer of Title; Risk of Loss; Insurance (B.5)

- Identify when title in equipment passes to buyer.

- If title passes at supplier's plant (F.O.B. supplier's facility) then buyer arranges common carrier and insurance until equipment delivered to buyer.

- If title passes upon payment in full, supplier should be liable for arranging shipping and insurance until equipment delivered to buyer.

- Buyer should arrange for its insurance to cover equipment once delivered.

Installation (B.6)

- Specify whether installation is buyer's or supplier's responsibility.

- If supplier's responsibility, specify cost in schedule.

Conversion of Data (B.7)

- Specify what assistance will be given by supplier, and at what cost.

- Include in contract names of conversion programs suggested by supplier; if such programs prove to be inadequate, supplier pays additional cost.

Education and Training (B.8)

- Provide names and qualifications of trainers.

- Specify amount, timing, and location of training.

- Allow for consultation of buyer in preparation of training program.

- Training methodology: specify whether supplier will train all buyer's people, or train only a few of buyer's people who in turn train all other buyer's people.

- If relevant, provide for in-depth training of technical maintenance staff of buyer.

- Specify how much education and training is free, and cost of additional education and training.

Hardware Test (B.9)

- Distinguish between acceptance test and manufacturer's diagnostic tests for hardware.

- Passage of hardware test should not constitute acceptance of hardware.

System Acceptance Test (B.9)

- The acceptance test is a critical contract control checkpoint for buyer.

- No item of hardware or software will be accepted without first conducting acceptance test for whole system.

- Specify period of system acceptance test.

- Phased acceptance test is probable for software; test each application; then test all software together; then test all of system.

- Specify performance criteria (which should be based on readily ascertainable objective criteria) that system must meet to pass system acceptance test, including documentation, specifications, promises in supplier's proposal and marketing literature, and warranties.

- Specify reliability standard that equipment must meet to pass system acceptance test, including recovery times.

- If provision is made for deemed acceptance at end of test period then buyer must institute strict plan for test administration and notification of supplier of any deficiencies.

Software Licence (B.10)

- Consider possible modifications of restrictions on use to provide for processing of affiliates' data, site or institution licence, and ability to make modifications.

- Consider possible modifications of restrictions on transfer to permit assignment of licence to affiliates.

- Obtain permission to make back-up copy as exception to restriction on copying.

Price and Payment Schedule (B.11)

- Specify that except for prices and expenses mentioned in agreement buyer is not responsible for additional costs.

- Ensure price protection for lengthy delivery period or on future purchases.

- Volume discount formulas must be described accurately.

- Consider joint volume discount arrangements.

- Secure most-favoured-customer pricing protection.

- Payment schedule: instalment payments should consist of progress payments reflecting actual performance milestones.

Taxes (B.12)

- Supplier should pass on to buyer benefit of reductions of customs duties.

- Check whether status of buyer or type of goods exempts buyer from sales taxes.

- If supplier is not resident in Canada, provide for deduction of withholding tax from licence fee portion of contract price and remittance to the federal government.

Warranties (B.13, B.16)

- Warranty period should be distinct from acceptance test period and period during which system is under maintenance.

- Warranty against defects in hardware or errors in software; specify duration (should commence on acceptance of system) and scope of maintenance services included (should be comparable to paid-for maintenance services).

- Warranty as to new equipment; if not new, notify buyer as to date of manufacture.

- Warranty that equipment and software are the supplier's most advanced technology.

- Warranty that supplier either owns the intellectual property rights in the system or is authorized to sell/license them.

- Warranty as to certification of hardware (i.e., approval of Canadian Standards Association (CSA), or Department of Communications for telecommunications equipment).

- Warranty as to compatibility, especially that the system works in conjunction with other specified equipment or software in predetermined manner.

- Warranty as to capacity; statements as to data storage and other capabilities of present system.

- Warranty as to expansion; statements as to costs required to upgrade the system to one or more additional configurations.

- Include all other promises made by supplier; all warranties should be based upon readily ascertainable objective criteria.

Warranty Disclaimers (B.14)

- Given existence of disclaimer of implied warranties, it is absolutely essential that all promises of the supplier are included in the contract as express warranties.

Remedies (B.15, B.19)

- Liquidated damages, supply of interim solution, and/or termination of agreement for nondelivery of system or any component of system.

- Liquidated damages, repair of all problems at no cost, and/or termination of agreement for inability of system to pass system acceptance test.

- Additional remedies: reimbursement of amounts incurred solely to prepare installation site for supplier's particular equipment.

- Express preservation of all other remedies including claim for damages resulting from supplier's or system's inadequate performance.

- Buyer's effective remedy for certain breaches of agreement may not be termination of agreement, but rather some form of positive action by supplier.

Intellectual Property Rights Indemnity (B.16)

- Scope of indemnity should cover patents, copyrights, trade secrets, and all other intellectual property rights.

- Buyer in Canada should be indemnified in regard to Canadian patents and copyrights, or all patents and copyrights, but not just United States patents and copyrights.

- Buyer in Canada should be indemnified in regard to all trade secrets (i.e., there should be no national limitation on trade secrets).

- Scope of indemnity should cover all damages, expenses, and settlement costs, including reasonable legal fees, and not just damages finally awarded by a court.

- Review carefully supplier's ability to terminate agreement upon occurrence of intellectual property infringement claim.

Limitation of Liability (B.17)

- Supplier should be responsible for at least direct damages in an amount equal to contract price of entire system.

- There should be no limits on liability for claims regarding intellectual property, unauthorized disclosure of buyer's confidential information, personal injury, or property damage.

- Given limitation of supplier's liability, buyer should ensure it has sufficient back-up and alternative procedures in the event of system malfunction or inoperability.

Excusable Delays (B.18)

- If specific excusable events are listed, delete those reasonably in supplier's control, such as inability of supplier to obtain supplies (i.e., supplier should maintain larger parts inventory).

- Require supplier to give notice of an excusable event, and to try to work around such event.

- Ensure buyer's right to terminate agreement if excusable event continues beyond certain period of time.

Termination (B.19)

- Require from supplier written notice of buyer default and that period of time to cure default must precede any termination.

- Only "material" breaches of buyer should give rise to right to terminate agreement.

- Buyer's effective remedy may not be termination of agreement, but rather some form of positive action by supplier.

Buyer's Confidential Information; Publicity (B.20)

- Require supplier to keep confidential buyer's confidential information.

- Nature of buyer's information may require all employees of supplier who have access to such buyer information to sign nondisclosure agreements with buyer.

- Supplier must obtain buyer's permission to use buyer's name in supplier's marketing literature.

Upgrades and Trade-in Credits (B.21)

- Require supplier's on-going notification of buyer of supplier's new products.

- Trade-in credit will assure market for buyer's used system.

Arbitration (B.22)

• Often an attractive alternative to court system, particularly where technical problems are at issue.

• Consider arbitration for just a portion of the agreement (e.g., passage of the acceptance test or quality of documentation).

• Designate one or more arbitrators or appointing body, place of arbitration, relevant rules, and, if foreign contracting party, language of arbitral proceedings.

Governing Law (B.23)

• Designate law of jurisdiction in which system is to be installed.

• If agreement is to be governed by law of any other jurisdiction, buyer must have contract reviewed by local counsel in that other jurisdiction.

Assignment (B.24)

• Secure ability to assign agreement to other member of corporate group.

• Consider ability to assign software to purchaser of hardware.

• Ability of supplier to assign agreement or subcontract obligations ought to be subject to buyer's consent.

• Secure provision that supplier cannot sell ownership of computer program unless purchaser assumes user's licence and support agreements on same terms.

Notices (B.25)

• Specify that deemed receipt of notices will occur within a certain time after delivery or mailing of notice.

Entire Agreement (B.26)

- Given existence of entire agreement clause, ensure that all representations, warranties, or other promises of supplier are included in the agreement.

Amendment (B.27)

- Agreement should be able to be amended only by a written agreement signed by the duly authorized representatives of the parties.

Guarantee of Affiliate (B.28)

- Buyer should consider whether a guarantee of an affiliate of the supplier, or the manufacturer of the equipment or developer of the software, is required.

4. LEASE/RENTAL

Contracting Procedures (E.13)

- Review negotiation and administration issues discussed in checklist 13.

Option to Purchase Leased Equipment (C.2)

- An option to purchase must be drafted carefully so as not to result in transaction being characterized as a conditional sale; option price must reflect fair market value at time option exercised.

- Specify clearly when option arises and how it is to be exercised.

Warranties (B.13, C.2)

- Specify that all warranties and obligations of supplier/manufacturer flow through directly to user, and supplier/manufacturer acknowledges this arrangement in writing.

- User must ensure that user or owner negotiates all necessary delivery, acceptance test, warranty, and related remedy provisions (see checklists 1–3).

Termination (B.19)

- Require from finance company written notice of user default and that period of time to cure default must precede any termination.

- Only "material" breaches of user should give rise to right to terminate agreement.

- Termination by finance company for breach by user should not give rise to double recovery (not return of equipment *and* payment of all remaining lease payments).

- Termination of one equipment schedule to the lease should not cause termination of all equipment schedules.

Governing Law (B.23)

- Designate law of jurisdiction in which system is to be installed.

- If agreement is to be governed by law of any other jurisdiction, user must have contract reviewed by local counsel in that other jurisdiction.

Assignment (B.24)

- Secure ability to assign agreement to other member of corporate group or to any financially sound third party.

- Ability of supplier to assign agreement or subcontract obligations ought to be subject to user's consent.

Notices (B.25)

- Specify deemed receipt of notices to occur within a certain time after delivery or mailing of notice.

Entire Agreement (B.26)

- Given existence of entire agreement clause, ensure that all representations, warranties, or other promises of supplier are included in the agreement.

Amendment (B.27)

- Agreement should be able to be amended only by a written agreement signed by the duly authorized representatives of the parties.

5. MAINTENANCE

Contracting Procedures (E.13)

- Review negotiation and administration issues discussed in checklist 13.

Term (C.3)

- Buyer can terminate maintenance services on ninety days' notice.

- Supplier should be committed to providing maintenance for at least probable useful life-span of equipment (i.e., five to ten years.)

Price and Payment Schedule (B.11, C.3)

- Specify that except for prices and expenses mentioned in agreement buyer is not responsible for additional costs.

- Request price protection if term of agreement is lengthy.

- Secure most-favoured-customer pricing protection.

- Don't agree to payments in advance unless supplier is solvent and reliable.

Third-Party Maintainers (C.3)

- Obtain supplier's commitment up front that third-party maintenance company can have access to diagnostic and other technical documents of the supplier.

Description of Services (C.3)

- Specify exactly what services are covered.

- Expand references such as "remedial maintenance" or "preventive maintenance"; obtain functional description of services.

Exclusions from Service (C.3)

- Review carefully the various exclusions.

- Resist ability of supplier to have equipment reconditioned or refurbished at buyer's cost.

Performance Guarantees (C.3)

- Performance guarantees should be based largely on degree of importance of system to buyer.

- If monetary credit scheme is used to guarantee performance, purpose is not to save money, but to build an incentive structure for the supplier.

- Prepare contingency plans if maintenance unavailable for short period.

Limitation of Liability (B.17)

- Supplier should be responsible for at least direct damages in an amount equal to twelve months of maintenance charges.

- There should be no limits on liability for claims regarding unauthorized disclosure of buyer's confidential information, personal injury, or property damage.

- Given limitation of supplier's liability, buyer should ensure that it has sufficient back-up and alternative procedures in the event of an inability to receive maintenance services for a period of time.

Excusable Delays (B.18)

- If specific excusable events are listed, delete those reasonably in supplier's control, such as inability of supplier to obtain supplies (i.e., supplier should maintain larger parts inventory).

- Require supplier to give notice of an excusable event, and to try to work around such event.

- Ensure buyer's right to terminate agreement if excusable event continues beyond certain period of time.

Termination (B.19)

- Require from supplier written notice of buyer default and that period of time to cure default must precede any termination.

- Only "material" breaches of buyer should give rise to right to terminate agreement.

- Buyer's effective remedy may not be termination of agreement, but rather some form of positive action by supplier.

Buyer's Confidential Information; Publicity (B.20)

- Require supplier to keep confidential buyer's confidential information.

- Nature of buyer's information may require all employees of supplier who have access to such buyer information to sign nondisclosure agreements with buyer.

- Supplier must obtain buyer's permission to use buyer's name in supplier's marketing literature.

Arbitration (B.22)

- Often an attractive alternative to court system, particularly where technical problems are at issue.

- Designate one or more arbitrators or appointing body, place of arbitration, relevant rules, and, if foreign contracting party, language of arbitral proceedings.

Governing Law (B.23)

- Designate law of jurisdiction in which system is installed.

- If agreement is to be governed by law of any other jurisdiction, buyer must have contract reviewed by local counsel in that other jurisdiction.

Assignment (B.24)

- Provide for ability to assign agreement together with sale of underlying system to other member of corporate group or to any other party.

- Ability of supplier to assign agreement or subcontract obligations ought to be subject to buyer's consent.

Notices (B.25)

- Specify that deemed receipt of notices will occur within a certain time after delivery or mailing of notice.

Entire Agreement (B.26)

- Given existence of entire agreement clause, ensure that all representations, warranties, or other promises of supplier are included in the agreement.

Amendment (B.27)

- Agreement should be able to be amended only by a written agreement signed by the duly authorized representatives of the parties.

Guarantee of Affiliate (B.28)

- Buyer should consider whether a guarantee of an affiliate of the supplier, or the manufacturer of the equipment, is required.

6. SOFTWARE DEVELOPMENT (AND SOFTWARE LICENCE)

Contracting Procedures (E.13)

- Review negotiation and administration issues discussed in checklist 13.

Check Out Software Developer (C.4)

- Review financial history (including most current financial statements), prospects, and credit rating of software developer.

- Review references and sound out other customers.

Software Specifications: Functional and System Design (C.4)

- Functional specifications and design specifications are critical documents which serve as reference points for the project.

- Attach functional specifications to contract.

- Plan a structured process for user to review and approve specifications and request changes (and for related information exchange process) both before and after acceptance of specifications.

Ownership of Custom Software (C.4, C.7)

- If ownership of software is to rest with supplier, then require on-going maintenance security for user including source code escrow agreement, restriction on marketing of software to user's competitors for a specific period, and reimbursement of development costs upon subsequent permitted licences.

- If ownership is to rest with the user, then require clear statement to this effect as well as waiver of moral rights; employees of supplier must sign copyright assignments and waiver of moral rights in addition to supplier.

Project Management (B.2, C.4)

- Designate project co-ordinators and supplier's project team with no transfer of such personnel.

- Review qualifications of supplier's personnel.

- Allow for removal of supplier's personnel at user's request.

- Plan a detailed implementation schedule indicating firm dates for delivery of each of the several deliverables, installation, education and training, and other key project milestones.

Preparation of the Installation Site (B.3)

- Specify whether site preparation is user's or supplier's responsibility.

- If supplier's responsibility, specify cost in schedule.

- If user's responsibility, specify supplier approval mechanism.

- Set out power and environmental specifications in schedule to contract.

- Keep accurate record of costs.

Delivery Date (B.4, C.4)

- The delivery date (or dates) is a critical contract control checkpoint for the user.

- Specify a delivery date for each specification document and item of software and related documentation to be developed and licensed by specific calendar date or by duration of time from previous contract milestone. Specify "time is of the essence."

- If delivery is phased, secure acknowledgement from supplier that acceptance will not occur until all items have been delivered and installed, and have passed acceptance test.

Installation (B.6)

- Specify whether installation is user's or supplier's responsibility.

- If supplier's responsibility, specify cost in schedule.

Conversion of Data (B.7)

- Specify what assistance will be given by supplier, and at what cost.

- Include in contract names of conversion programs suggested by supplier; if such programs prove to be inadequate, supplier pays additional cost.

Education and Training (B.8)

- Provide names and qualifications of trainers.

- Specify amount, timing, and location of training.

- Allow for consultation of user in preparation of training program.

- Training methodology: specify whether supplier will train all user's people, or train only a few of user's people who in turn train all other user's people.

- If relevant, provide for in depth-training of user's technical maintenance staff.

- Specify how much education and training is free, and cost of additional education and training.

Acceptance Test (B.9)

- The acceptance test is a critical contract control checkpoint for user.

- No item of software should be accepted without first conducting an acceptance test.

- Specify period of acceptance test.

- Plan a phased acceptance test if relevant; test each application system; then test all application systems together.

- Specify performance criteria (which should be based on readily ascertainable objective criteria) that software must meet to pass acceptance test, including documentation, specifications, promises in supplier's proposal, marketing literature, and warranties.

- Specify reliability standard that software must meet to pass acceptance test, including recovery times.

- If provision is made for deemed acceptance at end of test period then user must institute strict plan for test administration and notification of supplier of any deficiencies.

Licence of Software (B.10)

- Consider possible modifications in restrictions on use to provide for processing of affiliates' data, site or institution licence, and ability to make modifications.

- Consider possible modifications in restrictions on transfer to permit assignment of licence to affiliates.

- Obtain permission to make back-up copy as exception to restriction on copying.

Price and Payment Schedule (B.11)

- Specify that except for prices and expenses mentioned in agreement user is not responsible for additional costs.

- Explore joint volume discount arrangements.

- Secure most-favoured-customer pricing protection.

- Payment schedule: instalment payments should consist of progress payments reflecting actual performance milestones.

Taxes (B.12)

- Check whether status of user or type of goods exempts user from sales taxes.

- If supplier is not resident in Canada, provide for deduction of withholding tax from licence fee and remittance to federal government.

Warranties (B.13, B.19)

- Warranty period should be distinct from acceptance test period and period during which system is under maintenance.

- Warranty against errors in software; specify duration (should commence on acceptance of software) and scope of maintenance services included (should be comparable to paid-for maintenance services).

- Warranty that software is the supplier's most advanced technology.

- Warranty that supplier either owns the intellectual property rights in the software (or that the user will own them free and clear of all claims if the user is acquiring ownership of the software) or is authorized to license them.

- Warranty as to compatibility, especially that software works in conjunction with specified hardware, and that resulting system can interface with other specified equipment or software in predetermined manner.

- Warranty as to capacity; statements as to data storage and other capabilities of present software.

- Warranty as to expansion; statements as to costs required to upgrade the software to one or more additional configurations.

- Include all other promises made by supplier; all warranties should be based upon readily ascertainable objective criteria.

Warranty Disclaimers (B.14)

- Given existence of disclaimer of implied warranties, it is absolutely essential that all promises of the supplier are included in the contract as express warranties.

Remedies (B.15, B.19)

- Liquidated damages, supply of interim solution, and/or termination of agreement for nondelivery of software or any other deliverable (e.g., the system design specifications).

- Liquidated damages, repair of all problems at no cost, and/or termination of agreement for inability of software to pass acceptance test.

- Additional remedies: reimbursement of amounts incurred solely to prepare installation site for supplier's particular software.

- Express preservation of all other remedies including claims for damages resulting from supplier's or software's inadequate performance.

- User's effective remedy for certain breaches of agreement may not be termination of agreement, but rather some form of positive action by supplier.

Intellectual Property Rights Indemnity (B.16)

- Scope of indemnity should cover patents, copyrights, trade secrets, and all other intellectual property rights.

- User in Canada should be indemnified in regard to Canadian patents and copyrights, or all patents and copyrights, but not just United States patents and copyrights.

- User in Canada should be indemnified in regard to all trade secrets (i.e., there should be no national limitation on trade secrets).

- Scope of indemnity should cover all damages, expenses, and settlement costs, including reasonable legal fees, and not just damages finally awarded by a court.

- Review carefully supplier's ability to terminate agreement upon occurrence of intellectual property infringement claim.

Limitation of Liability (B.17)

- Supplier should be responsible for at least direct damages in an amount equal to licence and development fee for all software.

- There should be no limits on liability for claims regarding intellectual property, unauthorized disclosure of user's confidential information, personal injury, or property damage.

- Given limitation of supplier's liability, user should ensure it has sufficient back-up and alternative procedures in the event of system malfunction or inoperability.

Excusable Delays (B.18)

- If specific excusable events are listed, delete those reasonably in supplier's control, such as inability of supplier to obtain supplies (i.e., supplier should maintain larger parts inventory).

- Require supplier to give notice of an excusable event, and to try to work around such event.

- Ensure user's right to terminate agreement if excusable event continues beyond certain period of time.

Termination (B.19)

- Require from supplier written notice of user default and that period of time to cure default must precede any termination.

- Only "material" breaches of user should give rise to right to terminate agreement.

- User's effective remedy may not be termination of agreement, but rather some form of positive action by supplier.

User's Confidential Information; Publicity (B.20)

- Require supplier to keep confidential user's confidential information.

- Nature of user's information may require all supplier's employees who have access to such user information to sign nondisclosure agreements with user.

- Supplier must obtain user's permission to publicize user's name in supplier's marketing literature.

Arbitration (B.22)

- Often an attractive alternative to court system, particularly where technical problems are at issue.

- Consider arbitration for just a portion of the agreement (e.g., passage of acceptance test or quality of documentation).

- Designate one or more arbitrators or appointing body, place of arbitration, relevant rules, and, if foreign contracting party, language of arbitral proceedings.

Governing Law (B.23)

- Designate law of jurisdiction in which software is installed.

- If agreement is to be governed by law of any other jurisdiction, user must have contract reviewed by local counsel in that other jurisdiction.

Assignment (B.24)

- Obtain ability to assign agreement to other member of corporate group.

- Consider ability to assign software to the purchaser of the hardware.

- Ability of supplier to assign agreement or subcontract obligations ought to be subject to user's consent.

- If supplier owns software, secure provision that supplier cannot sell ownership of computer program unless purchaser assumes user's licence and support agreements on same terms.

Notices (B.25)

- Specify deemed receipt of notices to occur within a certain time after delivery or mailing of notice.

Entire Agreement (B.26)

- Given existence of entire agreement clause, ensure that all representations, warranties, or other promises of supplier are included in the agreement.

Amendment (B.27)

- Agreement should be able to be amended only by a written agreement signed by the duly authorized representatives of the parties.

Guarantee of Affiliate (B.28)

- User should consider whether a guarantee of an affiliate of the supplier, or the developer of the software, is required.

7. CONSULTING

Nondisclosure of Information; Publicity (B.20, C.5)

- Consultant should not acquire any interest (i.e., ownership, licence, etc.) in information of user or user's clients.

- Consultant should not disclose user's confidential information.

- Consultant should not use or copy user's confidential information except to provide user with consulting services.

- Consultant must obtain user's permission to publicize user's name in consultant's marketing literature.

Noncompetition (C.5)

- A noncompetition clause must be drafted carefully.

- Restrictions on consultant should not be broader than is necessary to protect user's reasonable business interest.

Nonsolicitation of Employees (C.5)

- Absolute prohibition may be unenforceable.

- As an alternative, user pays consultant "finder's fee" if user hires consultant's employee.

Ownership of Work Product (B.10, C.5)

- If user is to own material produced by consultant, it is critical that the consultant agree in writing to assign all ownership in material to user.

- Obtain waiver of consultant's moral rights in work.

Consultant's Employees (C.5)

- Require consultant's employees to sign nondisclosure agreement similar to one signed by consultant.

Project Management (B.2, C.4)

- Designate project co-ordinators and consultant's project team, with no transfer of such personnel.

- Review qualifications of consultant's personnel.

- Allow for removal of consultant's personnel at user's request.

Termination (B.19)

- Require from consultant written notice of user default and that period of time to cure default must precede any termination.

- Only "material" breaches of user should give rise to right to terminate agreement.

- User's effective remedy may not be termination of agreement, but rather some form of positive action by consultant.

Governing Law (B.23)

- Designate law of jurisdiction in which services are to be performed.

- If agreement is to be governed by law of any other jurisdiction, user must have contract reviewed by local counsel in that other jurisdiction.

Assignment (B.24)

- Obtain ability to assign agreement to other member of corporate group.

- Ability of consultant to assign agreement or subcontract obligations ought to be subject to user's consent.

Notices (B.25)

- Specify deemed receipt of notices to occur within a certain time after delivery or mailing of notice.

Entire Agreement (B.26)

- Given existence of entire agreement clause, ensure that all representations, warranties, or other promises of consultant are included in the agreement.

Amendment (B.27)

- Agreement should be able to be amended only by a written agreement signed by the duly authorized representatives of the parties.

Guarantee of Affiliate (B.28)

- User should consider whether a guarantee of an affiliate of the consultant is required.

8. PROPRIETARY RIGHTS PROTECTION — EMPLOYEES

Nondisclosure of Information (B.20, C.5, C.6)

- Employees should not acquire any interest (i.e., ownership, licence, etc.) in information of user or user's clients.

- Require employees not to disclose user's confidential information.

- Require employees not to use or copy user's confidential information except as required for employees to perform their duties for user.

Noncompetition (C.5, C.6)

- A noncompetition clause must be drafted carefully.

- Restrictions on employees should not be broader than is necessary to protect user's reasonable business interest.

Nonsolicitation of User's Customers (C.5, C.6)

- A nonsolicitation clause must be drafted carefully.

- Restrictions on employees should not be broader than is necessary to protect user's reasonable business interests.

Ownership of Work Product (B.10, C.5, C.6)

- Obtain from employees express statement that user is to own all works developed by employees.

- Obtain waiver of employees' moral rights in works.

Time of Signing of Agreement (C.6)

- It is important that employee agreements be signed when employees commence employment with user.

Governing Law (B.23)

- Designate law of jurisdiction in which employee is situated.

- If agreement is to be governed by law of any other jurisdiction, user must have contract reviewed by local counsel in that other jurisdiction.

Notices (B.25)

- Specify deemed receipt of notices to occur within a certain time after delivery or mailing of notice.

Entire Agreement (B.26)

- Given existence of entire agreement clause, ensure that all representations, warranties, or other promises of employee are included in the agreement.

Amendment (B.27)

- Agreement should be able to be amended only by a written agreement signed by the employee and a duly authorized representative of the user.

9. SOURCE CODE ESCROW AGREEMENT

Materials to Be Deposited (C.7)

- Materials deposited with escrow agent, including source code for software, should comprise whatever materials are necessary to produce the product licensed to the user.

- Materials should be updated within fifteen days of user receiving new release of software.

Verification (C.7)

- User should have the right to verify from time to time that the materials in escrow in fact produce the product licensed to the user.

Events Triggering Release from Escrow (C.7)

- In addition to supplier's bankruptcy and supplier's ceasing to support the product licensed to the user, user should consider other possible triggers such as inability of supplier to provide modifications to product at an industry standard cost.

- Events triggering release from escrow should be readily ascertainable.

- Consider submitting to arbitration dispute over whether triggering event has occurred.

Selection of Escrow Agent (C.7)

- Common choice of escrow agent is large trust company; escrow agent should not be someone with possible conflict of interest.

- Escrow agent should be located in same city as user.

Fees (C.7)

- Specify who shall pay fees of escrow agent.

Assignment (B.24)

- Obtain ability to assign agreement to the entity that has been assigned the underlying software licence agreement.

Governing Law (B.23)

- Designate law of jurisdiction in which software is escrowed.

- If agreement is to be governed by law of any other jurisdiction, user must have contract reviewed by local counsel in that other jurisdiction.

Notices (B.25)

- Specify deemed receipt of notices to occur within a certain time after delivery or mailing of notice.

Entire Agreement (B.26)

- Given existence of entire agreement clause, ensure that all representations, warranties, or other promises of the supplier are included in the agreement.

Amendment (B.27)

- Agreement should be able to be amended only by a written agreement signed by the duly authorized representatives of the parties.

10. SERVICE BUREAU/ OUTSOURCING

Contracting Procedures (E.13)

- Review negotiation and administration issues discussed in checklist 13.

Description of Services and Charges (C.8)

- Specify in detail services to be performed and charges to be paid.

- Specify that except for charges and expenses mentioned in agreement user is not responsible for additional costs.

- Volume discount formulas must be described accurately.

Performance Guarantees; Remedies (C.8)

- Provide for performance guarantees for various services, such as specific turnaround times for processing or response times for on-line enquiries.

- Provide for liquidated damages or credits against future fees if performance guarantees are not met.

- Require express preservation of other remedies including claim for damages resulting from supplier's inadequate performance.

Limitation of Liability (B.17)

- Supplier should be responsible for at least direct damages in an amount equal to twelve months of charges. Consider whether higher limit required for certain matters.

- There should be no limits of liability for claims regarding intellectual property, unauthorized disclosure of user's confidential information, personal injury, or property damage.

- Given limitation of supplier's liability, user should ensure it has sufficient back-up and alternative procedures in the event of unavailability of services.

Excusable Delays (B.18)

- If specific excusable events are listed, delete those reasonably in supplier's control, such as inability of supplier to obtain supplies (i.e., supplier should maintain larger parts inventory).

- Require supplier to give notice of an excusable event, and to try to work around such event.

- Obtain user's right to terminate agreement if excusable event continues beyond certain period of time.

Termination (B.19)

- Provide for possible early termination at option of user.

- Require from supplier written notice of user default and that period of time to cure default must precede any termination.

- Only "material" breaches of user should give rise to right to terminate agreement.

- User's effective remedy may not be termination of agreement, but rather some form of positive action by supplier.

- Secure provision that upon termination supplier will assist in transfer of user's data (and software) to alternative supplier.

User's Confidential Information; Publicity (B.20, C.8)

- Require supplier to keep confidential user's confidential information and data.

- Do not allow the supplier to have any lien or other right to hold user's data without user's permission.

- Nature of user's information may require each employee of supplier who has access to such user information to sign nondisclosure agreement with user.

- Supplier must obtain user's permission to publicize user's name in supplier's marketing literature.

Assignment (B.24, C.8)

- If user transferring data processing facilities to vendor of outsourcing services, ascertain whether hardware can be sold, and software assigned, to vendor.

- Secure the ability to assign agreement to other member of corporate group.

- Ability of supplier to assign agreement or subcontract obligations ought to be subject to buyer's consent.

Governing Law (B.23)

- Designate law of jurisdiction in which the user is located.

Notices (B.25)

- Specify that deemed receipt of notices will occur within a certain time after delivery or mailing of notice.

Entire Agreement (B.26)

- Given existence of entire agreement clause, ensure that all representations, warranties, or other promises of supplier are included in the agreement.

Amendment (B.27)

- Agreement should be able to be amended only by a written agreement signed by the duly authorized representatives of the parties.

Guarantee of Affiliate (B.28)

- User should consider whether a guarantee of an affiliate of the supplier is required.

11. DISASTER RECOVERY

Contracting Procedures (E.13)

- Review negotiation and administration issues discussed in checklist 13.

Description of Services and Charges (C.9)

- Specify in detail services to be performed (i.e., "hot site" or "cold site" facility, and what services each entails) and the charges to be paid.

- Specify that except for charges and expenses mentioned in agreement user is not responsible for additional costs.

- Provide for inspection and test by user of supplier's premises.

Definition of Disaster (C.9)

- Specify in detail what constitutes a "disaster" for purposes of permitting user to have access to supplier's facility.

Limitation on Customer Base (C.9)

- Limit total number of customers that supplier may have.

- Limit total number of customers that supplier may have within user's building and within a certain radius of the user.

Assignment (B.24)

- Secure ability to assign agreement to other entity that meets supplier's customer base requirements.

Governing Law (B.23)

- Designate law of jurisdiction in which the customer is located.

Notices (B.25)

- Provide for notices to be given orally in the event of a disaster.

Amendment (B.27)

- Agreement should be able to be amended only by a written agreement signed by the duly authorized representatives of the parties.

Guarantee of Affiliate (B.28)

- User should consider whether a guarantee of an affiliate of the disaster recovery facility is required.

12. ELECTRONIC DATA INTERCHANGE TRADING PARTNER AGREEMENT

Technical Issues (C.10, B.4, B.9)

- Specify components of EDI network, including each party's host computer.

- Specify whether one or both parties will use a value added network (VAN).

- Specify date on which each party's computer equipment will be available to send and receive EDI messages.

- Consider addressing testing procedures.

- Specify EDI standard to be used.

Contract Law Issues (C.10)

- Acknowledge intention to create legally binding contracts through EDI.

- Specify that EDI messages will be deemed to constitute a memorandum in writing signed by its sender.

- Specify that each party waives the right to argue that an EDI message is not a memorandum in writing signed by its sender.

- Provide that specific contracts are formed only when certain EDI messages are sent and received.

- Require regular review by each party of EDI messages received by it.

- Provide that functional acknowledgement of EDI messages does not constitute legal acceptance.

- Negotiate and settle terms and conditions that will apply to the underlying transaction effected by EDI so as to avoid the "battle of the forms."

Evidence Law Issues (C.10)

- Provide for mechanism to store EDI messages and for transaction log to reflect such messages.

- Specify that copies of EDI messages and the related transaction logs will be deemed to be admissible as evidence in legal proceedings.

- Specify that each party waives the right to argue that a copy of an EDI message or the related transaction log is not admissible as evidence in legal proceedings.

- Address any relevant records-retention issues.

Reliability, Security, and Confidentiality (C.10, B.20, C.6, C.9)

- Require that recipient of garbled message notify sender of problem.

- Consider requirement that recipient also notify sender of message containing unusual terms.

- Address disaster recovery procedures in the event of failure of EDI network.

- Provide for parties to take adequate measures to prevent unauthorized access to the EDI network.

- Confidentiality provisions should reflect degree of sensitivity of information being transmitted over the EDI network.

- Provide for third-party review of each party's control, security, and confidentiality procedures.

Limitation of Liability (C.8)

- Consider whether any limitations on liability, such as exclusion of consequential damages, are relevant.

Excusable Delays (B.18)

- Require each party to give notice of an excusable event.

Arbitration (B.22)

- Consider whether arbitration is appropriate as dispute resolution mechanism; it generally should be.

Governing Law (C.10, B.23)

- Designate jurisdiction of one of the trading partners, particularly when parties and VANs are located in different jurisdictions.

Notices (B.25)

- Specify deemed receipt of notices to occur within a certain time after delivery or mailing of notice.

Amendment (B.27)

- Agreement should be able to be amended only by a written agreement signed by the duly authorized representatives of the parties.

13. CONTRACTING PROCEDURES

Request for Proposal (D.1)

• A request for proposal should be used for all acquisitions of any size.

• The request should contain a summary of contracting issues important to buyers, or better still a draft agreement, in addition to technical requirements.

Check Out Supplier (C.4)

• Review financial history (including most current financial statements), prospects, and credit rating of supplier.

• Review references and sound out other customers.

Choosing a Supplier (D.1)

• Don't announce a "winner" too soon.

• Encourage competitive tendering among suppliers.

Turn-Key or Multiple-Source Contract (D.1)

• Weigh benefits (and costs) of having one supplier or a systems integrator agree to be responsible for the whole system.

• If several suppliers are used, agreements should cross-reference one another for purposes of acceptance testing.

Letters of Intent (D.1)

• Letter of intent should state clearly that it is not legally binding, and that any accompanying deposit will be refunded if no definitive agreement is signed.

Form of Agreement (D.1)

- Buyers should be prepared to use supplier's standard form agreement, provided that suitable amendments are made to it so that issues important to buyer but which are not dealt with in standard form agreement are addressed in an addendum to the contract.

- All standard form agreements can be amended.

- If standard form agreement is too one-sided in favour of supplier, then user should start with new agreement.

- Contract clauses should be set out in agreement in chronological order (i.e., in the order that such issues will arise in the actual project implementation).

Negotiating Tips (D.1)

- Negotiate only with those representatives of supplier who have authority to bind supplier.

- Get comments on agreement in writing to reduce potential for later contract negotiation backsliding.

- Resist supplier's artificial deadlines; the buyer should not be hurried into signing a contract.

- All agreements relating to a certain acquisition should be signed simultaneously.

Administering the Contract (D.2)

- Monitor closely key dates in the contract and exercise remedies promptly if supplier does not meet any performance deadlines.

- Monitor closely deemed acceptance provision which results in a system being accepted if the buyer does not notify the supplier about any deficiency.

- Comply with all relevant contractual provisions if terminating agreement for nonperformance or poor performance by supplier.

NOTES

These end-notes list the titles of books, articles, and other materials referenced in the body of the text. Each end-note begins with the page number and a brief excerpt of the text where the item is referenced.

Introduction

page iv   "...the subject of several books published both in Canada and abroad." For general discussions of the subject of computer law, see J. Fraser Mann, *Computer Technology and the Law in Canada,* Carswell, 1987; Barry B. Sookman, *Sookman Computer Law,* Carswell, 1989; George S. Takach (with others), *The Software Business: Funding, Protecting and Marketing Software,* McGraw-Hill Ryerson, 1992; Michael D. Scott, *Computer Law,* Wiley Law Publications, 1984; and J. A. Keustermans and I. M. Arckens, *International Computer Law,* Matthew Bender, 1988.

Part A: The Need for Effective Computer Contracts

page 2   "...a recent press report indicated that a software error was responsible for the failure of a Patriot missile launcher..." "Glitch Let Scud Beat Patriot," *Computerworld,* 27 May 1991.

page 3   "...microchips and on-board computers in automobiles..." see Ted Laturnus, "So Long, Grease Monkey," *Report on Business Magazine,* March 1989.

"...there have been cases of established businesses forced into bankruptcy..." See, for example, Accusystems Inc. v. Honeywell Information Systems Inc., 580 F. Supp. 474 (S.D.N.Y. 1984); Triangle Underwriters, Inc. v. Honeywell, Inc., 604 F.2d 737 (2d Cir. 1979).

page 5   "One such press report appeared recently in *Computerworld.*" "$80 MIS Disaster," *Computerworld,* 1 February 1988.

"Consider one such tale of woe that involved a Vancouver-based company several years ago."

Listo Products Ltd. v. Phillips Electronics Ltd. British Columbia Supreme Court (unreported) 2 December 1983.

page 10 "All too many histories like this one litter the Canadian computer landscape." For other examples of Canadian computer acquisition disasters, see Burroughs Business Machines Ltd. v. FeedRite Mills (1962) Ltd. (1973), 42 D.L.R. (3d) 303 (Manitoba C.A.); M. L. Baxter Equipment Limited v. Geac Computer Corporation (1982), 133 D.L.R. (3d) 72 (Ontario H.C.); Citibank Leasing Canada Limited v. Action Fasteners Ltd. (New Brunswick Q.B.) 1 October 1986 (unreported); Group West Systems Ltd. v. Werner's Refrigeration Co. (1988), 85 A.R. 82 (Alberta Q.B.); Imperial Brass Ltd. v. Jacob Electric Systems Ltd. (Ont. H.C.) December 14, 1989 (unreported); and Jonas & Erickson Software v. Fitz-Wright Company Ltd. (B.C.S.C.) 5 October 1990 (unreported).

page 11 "Disasters Get Bigger As Tech Goes Higher," *Globe and Mail*, 12 November 1990; "Fundamental Breach in Computer Contract," *Canadian Commercial Law Guide*, 27 November 1990; "Recall Issued for Smoking Printer," *Toronto Computes*, April 1989; "Busy Airline Systems Blank Out Screens," *Computerworld*, 24 July 1989; "TSE Paralyzed at Critical Time: Trading Slowed as Computer Malfunction Coincides with Baker's Press Conference,"*Globe and Mail*, 10 January 1991; "With Complexity, a Threat of Chaos," *Computerworld*, 5 November 1990; "Flaw Found in 486 Chip," *Toronto Computes*, December 1989.

"...excerpt from an advertisement..." Ad appeared in *Computerworld*, 24 June 1991.

page 20 "The following short description of computer technology is by no means an attempt to give such technical knowledge." For a good general discussion of computer technology, see Marilyn Bohl, *Information Processing*, 4th edition, Science Research Associates, Inc., 1984.

Part B: General Contract Provisions

page 38   "...the degree to which the terminology in the computer sector can be misleading or confusing is attested in the following passage from an American judge's court decision in 1970..." Honeywell Inc. v. Lithonia Lighting Inc., 317 F. Supp 406 (N.D. Ga. 1970).

page 50   "...*Time* magazine ran an article on [vapourware and brochureware]..." *Time*, 3 February 1986.

page 51   "...*Computerworld* documented fourteen cases of vapourware..." *Computerworld*, 4 April 1988.

"...a major computer supplier's profit during a particular quarter was lower than expected..." *Globe and Mail*, 18 March 1989.

"...a computer manufacturer was fined $275,000..." United States v. Commodore Business Machines, Inc. (February 27, 1990) 2 CCH Computer Cases 46,281.

page 63   "...the presumption in Canadian law relating to the sale of goods..." See, for example, Ontario's Sale of Goods Act, R.S.O. 1990, c. S.1.

page 66   "...a recent story in the press told of silicon semi-conductor chips..." *Computerworld*, 24 October 1988.

page 80   "...the amendments to Canada's Copyright Act..." Copyright Act, R.S.C. 1985, c. C-42.

page 81   "...there was a report a few years ago of a company ..." Business Recovery Systems Inc. v. Rochester Midland Corp., reported in *Computer Industry Litigation Reporter* (CILR), 28 March 1988.

page 82   "...other large software developers (such as Ashton-Tate)..." Ashton-Tate Co. v. Volt Delta, reported in *CILR*, 12 May 1986.

"In the last few years Lotus has brought..." Lotus cases: Lotus Development Corp. v. Rixon Inc., reported in *CILR*, 27 February 1984; Lotus Development Corp. v. Health Group Inc., reported in *CILR*, 13 August 1984; and Lotus Development Corp. v. Mueller Co., reported in *CILR*, 14 January 1985.

"The following example illustrates how the SPA operates." Lotus Development Corp, et al. v. Davy McKee Corp, (1991) 2 CCH Computer Cases 46,432.

page 84 "...a software developer was unable to get full compensation..." Dickerman Associates, Inc. v. Tiverton Bottled Gas Co., reported in *CILR*, 12 January 1987.

page 92 "Canada's Competition Act requires..." Competition Act, R.S.C. 1985, c. C-34, Section 50.

page 98 "...the Ontario government's policy..." Ontario Ministry of Revenue, Information Bulletin No. 2-85, November 1985.

page 116 "A Hawaiian telephone company..." Hawaiian Telephones Co. v. Microform Data Systems, Inc. (9th Cir. 1987) (unreported).

page 118 "A patent is a legal right..." Patent Act, R.S.C. 1985, c. P-4.

"Several recent court cases in the United States..." Whelan v. Jaslow 797 F.2d 1222 (3rd Cir. 1986); Pearl Systems Inc. v. Competition Electronics, reported in *CILR*, 8 August 1988.

"...it is arguable that one Canadian judge..." Gemologists International Inc. v. Gem Scan International Inc. (1986) 7 C.I.P.R. 225 (Ont. H.C.).

"Some commentators have argued..." See, for example, Robert Kost, Whelan v. Jaslow, "Back to the Rough Ground," 5 *Computer Law Reporter* 145 (1986).

page 120 "...in the United States and some other countries..." Semiconductor Chip Protection Act of 1984, Chapter 9 of Title 17 of the United States Code.

"...(and likely soon in Canada)..." On 28 June 1990 royal assent was given in Canada to the Integrated Circuit Topography Act, S.C. 1990, C.37, but as of 1 March 1992 this statute was not yet in force.

page 135 "...the United Nations Convention on Contracts for the International Sale of Goods..." This Convention, which has been incorporated into Canadian law, sets out a broad set of rules governing the formation of contracts for the sale of goods and the obligations of buyers and sellers. See the International Sale of Goods Contracts Convention Act (Canada), S.C. 1991, c.13; International Sale of Goods Act (Ontario), R.S.O. 1990, c.I.10.

"Canada, together with its NATO allies, Japan and Australia, has implemented a regulatory system of export controls..." Canada's rules on export control are set out in The Export and Imports Permits Act (R.S.C. 1985, c.E-17) and related regulations.

Part C: Additional Contract Provisions

page 165 "A recent court decision..." Diversified Graphics, Ltd. v. Ernst & Whinney, (9th Cir. 1989) reported in *CILR*, 27 March 1989.

page 170 "(The Canadian artist Michael Snow..." Snow v. Eaton Centre Ltd. (1982) 70 CPR (2d) 105 (Ont. H.C.).

page 177 "In a highly publicized case recently..." See jury instructions in the Morris case in CCH Guide to Computer Law 60,113.

"Several years ago, *Time* magazine..." *Time*, 28 September 1988.

"Amendments made to Canada's Criminal Code..." Criminal Code, R.S.C. 1985, c.-46, sections 301.2 and 387.

page 181 "...an American law was passed in 1988..." Intellectual Property Bankruptcy Protection Act of 1988, Public Law, 100-56.

Part D: Contracting Procedures and Tactics

page 195 "...as noted in a recent study..." "The Commercial Use of Electronic Data Interchange — A Report," American Bar Association, (1990) 45 Bus. Law. 1645.

page 196 "...Ontario's Sale of Goods Act..." Sale of Goods Act (Ontario), R.S.O. 1990, c. S.1.

"...Ontario's Interpretation Act..." Interpretation Act (Ontario), R.S.O. 1990, c. I.11.

page 200 "...Parliament and most Canadian Provinces have passed statutes governing the law of evidence..." Canada Evidence Act, R.S.C. 1985, c. C-5; Evidence Act (Ontario), R.S.O. 1990, c. E.23.

"Courts in Canada have considered..." See R. v. Bell and Bruce (1982), 35 O.R. (2d) 164.

page 201 "...Canada's Income Tax Act..." Income Tax Act; R.S.C. 1952, C.148, as amended. For Revenue Canada's document retention policy, see Revenue Canada Information Circular No. 78-1OR2, 14 July 1989.

page 225 "...a Canadian court case involving a difficult computer acquisition." M. L. Baxter Equipment Ltd. v. Geac Canada Ltd. (1982), 133 D.L.R. (3d) 72 (Ontario H.C.).

INDEX